Analyzing & Translating

New Testament Discourse

Analyzing & Translating

New Testament Discourse

DAVID J. CLARK

Fontes Press

Analyzing and Translating New Testament Discourse

Copyright © 2019 by David J. Clark

ISBN-13 (paperback): 978-1-948048-15-6

All rights reserved. No part of this publication may be reproduced, stored in a retrieval system, or transmitted in any form or by any means—electronic, mechanical, photocopy, recording, or any other—except for brief quotations in printed reviews, without the prior permission of the publisher.

Fontes Press
DALLAS, TX

www.fontespress.com

To Glenys, my dear wife of 56 years, without whose love and support I would not have been able to do all the work with translators that led to these articles being written.

CONTENTS

	List of Figures	xi
	Abbreviations	xiii
	Preface	xv
1	Our Father in Heaven	1
2	After Three Days	7
3	Discourse Structure in Matthew's Gospel (with Jan de Waard)	13
4	Vocative Displacement in the Gospels: Lexico-Syntactic and Sociolinguistic Influences	113
5	The Sermon on the Plain: Structure and Theme in Luke 6.20–49	127
6	Vocative Displacement in Acts and Revelation	135
7	Discourse Structure in Titus	149
8	Discourse Structure in Jude	177
9	A Discourse Marker in the Synoptic Gospels: ἀμὴν λέγω ὑμῖν/σοι	195
10	Discourse Structure in 3 John	211
11	Vocatives in the Epistles	221
12	Structural Similarities in 1 and 2 Thessalonians: Comparative Discourse Anatomy	239
13	Discourse Structure in Ephesians, with Some Implications for Translators	253
14	A Discourse Marker in John: ἀμὴν ἀμὴν λέγω ὑμῖν/σοι	271
	Acknowledgements	279

LIST OF FIGURES

Figure 1.1	Synoptic Parallel Expressions of Kingdom of Heaven/God	3
Figure 1.2	Heavenly Father as Euphemism for God in Matthew	4
Figure 1.3	Equivalence of "My Father in Heaven" and "God" in the Synoptics	5
Figure 2.1	Comparison of Three Day Formulas in the Synoptics	7
Figure 4.1	Interrelations of Categories of Displaced Vocatives	119
Figure 8.1	The Macrostructure of Jude	178
Figure 8.2	Four Analyses of the Structure of Jude	179
Figure 8.3	Detailed Display of Jude's Structure	185
Figure 9.1	Comparison with Mark and Luke	202
Figure 9.2	All Occurrences of ἀμὴν λέγω ὑμῖν in the Synoptics	208
Figure 10.1	Two Options for 3 John 12	213
Figure 11.1	Number of Vocatives in the Epistles	223
Figure 12.1	Comparison of 1 and 2 Thessalonians	241
Figure 12.2	Parallels from Chart 1 Simplified	244
Figure 12.3	Parallels in the Second Sections of 1 and 2 Thessalonians	245
Figure 12.4	Essay Analysis Compared with Translator's Handbook	251

ABBREVIATIONS

ABD	D. N. Freedman, ed., *Anchor Yale Bible Dictionary*
BDAG	W. F. Bauer, W. Danker, W. F. Arndt, and F. W. Gingrich, *Greek-English Lexicon of the New Testament and Other Early Christian Literature*
BDF	F. Blass, A. Debrunner, and R. W. Funk, *A Greek Grammar of the New Testament and Other Early Christian Literature*
BFBS	Η ΚΑΙΝΗ ΔΙΑΘΗΚΗ, *Second Edition.* London: The British and Foreign Bible Society 1958.
BT	*The Bible Translator*
CBQ	*Catholic Biblical Quarterly*
ICC	International Critical Commentary
JBL	*Journal of Biblical Literature*
L-N	J. P. Louw and E. A. Nida, eds., *Greek-English Lexicon of the New Testament Based on Semantic Domains*
LSJ	H. G. Liddell, R. Scott, and H. S. Jones, eds., *A Greek-English Lexicon*
NA^{27}	Nestle-Aland: Novum Testamentum Graece, 27th edition (Deutsche Bibelgesellschaft)
NCB	New Century Bible
Robertson	A. T. Robertson, *A Greek Grammar of the Greek New Testament in the Light of Historical Research*
Souter	Souter, Alexander, *Novum Testamentum Graece, Editio Altera.* Oxford: Clarendon Press 1947.
UBS^3	United Bible Societies: Greek New Testament, 3th edition
UBS^4	United Bible Societies: Greek New Testament, 4th edition

PREFACE

The essays in this collection were written over a period of 25 years, but what they have in common is the conviction that a clear understanding of an ancient Biblical text is dependent on a grasp of its structure. The texts as we have received them, whatever sources they may have used, were put into the form in which we see them today by some author or editor for whom their structure was purposeful and meaningful. So if we are to cross the historical and cultural barriers that separate us from those writers, and come to a fuller grasp of their intentions, we need to start by analysing their textual structures on their own terms before we bring to bear the academic presuppositions of our own era.

This is especially the case if the Biblical text is being studied with a view to translating it into another language, particularly if the translation is a first for that language. Dependence solely on versions in English or any other major language can be confusing because they differ significantly in their division of the Biblical text into sections, paragraphs and even sentences. Such divisions may frequently seem to be impressionistic rather than based on serious linguistic analysis. The subject matter of these essays often arose from some question or problem encountered in my work with Bible translators as a Translation Consultant, so they had a practical as well as a theoretical purpose.

Given the time span of these essays, they may contain some perspectives that now seem dated, but it is to be hoped that they will nevertheless help readers to come to a fuller understanding of what the Biblical texts originally intended to convey. It hardly needs saying that the essays are not inspired, and readers who study the Greek texts for themselves may see things that eluded me. If so, then there is always scope for them to write further articles to expand our knowledge of God's message to the world.

1

OUR FATHER IN HEAVEN

Father in heaven is a favourite expression in the gospel of Matthew. It occurs in slightly different forms twenty times in this gospel, but only once each in Mark (11.25) and Luke (11.13) and not at all in John.

The differences in the form of expression in Matthew are minor ones. The form most familiar to Christians is the form *Our Father in heaven*, because this is the form used in Mt 6.9, the Lord's Prayer. In fact, this is the only time that the possessive pronoun *our* occurs in this phrase. The possessive pronoun is *your* (*plural*) in ten places in UBS³ (Mt 5.16, 45, 48; 6.1, 14, 26, 32; 7.11; 18.14; 23.9) and *my* in nine places (Mt 7.21; 10.32, 33; 12.50; 15.13; 16.17; 18.10, 19, 35). Eight times the article occurs before the word *heaven* in Greek (Mt 5.16; 6.1, 9; 7.11, 21; 10.32, 33; 16.17) and five times it does not (Mt 5.45; 12.50; 18.10, 14, 19). Seven times the noun phrase *in heaven* is replaced by the adjective *heavenly* (Mt 5.48; 6.14, 26, 32; 15.13; 18.35; 23.9). All the possible combinations of *my* and *your* with *in heaven, in the heaven* and *heavenly* occur at least twice.

Taking all this into account it seems fair to assume that these variations are related to the contexts where they occur, and do not represent any significant difference in the basic meaning of the expression. So the task that faces the translator is in principle the same in all twenty places where the phrase occurs.

Father

There is usually no difficulty at all in choosing a term for *Father*. All societies and languages have a term for a natural or biological father, even though in some cases, the term can also be used in an extended sense to include other male relatives, especially the father's brothers. Sometimes, however, there is a problem with the social meaning (rather than with the natural meaning) of the term for *father*.

In Jewish society, it was the job of the father to supply love, care, provision and discipline for the children, and this is the basis of the comparison between God and an earthly father. But in certain other societies, some or all of these tasks would normally be performed by some other male relative, such as the grandfather or the mother's eldest brother. Accordingly, some translators have considered using expressions that would mean *Our Grandfather in heaven* or *Our Uncle in heaven*. However, such terms would distort the Jewish setting of scripture, and I know of no case where the translator finally decided to use anything other than the term for biological father.

Heaven

There is more commonly a problem in finding a term for heaven. In Hebrew and Greek, as well as in several modern European languages, the word used for *heaven* is the same as the word for *sky*, or is at least clearly related to it. English is somewhat unusual in having quite different words.

In many places where *heaven* occurs in scripture, a term whose basic meaning is *sky* will fit quite well. But in the expression we are considering here, *Our Father in heaven*, it may mislead the reader if a term for *sky* is used. In some languages, if we speak of *our Father in the sky*, the expression gives the meaning that God is "up there," and it follows from this that he cannot be "down here" at the same time. So if Christians learn to pray to *Our Father in the sky*, they are in effect removing God from the world of their everyday life and experience. The term *Father* should carry the message that God is near and important to his people. But the phrase *in the sky* may, so to speak, blot out this message with another false message that God is distant and irrelevant. If this happens, Christians can become more concerned with simply repeating the words of the Lord's Prayer than with enjoying a living relationship with the Lord.

The translator therefore needs to ask himself what is the underlying meaning of the words *in heaven* or *heavenly* in this context. It is important to find a satisfactory answer, because this expression is used in the Lord's Prayer, and will become familiar to many people who cannot or will not read the

Scriptures for themselves. It may therefore play a part in determining their whole response to the gospel. If the words used have the effect of pushing God into the distance, they are unlikely to encourage people to respond positively to the Christian gospel as a whole.

Matthew's Use of Heaven

Let us look at the places in Matthew and in the other gospels where *heaven* occurs. When we do this, we notice first that only Matthew uses the phrase *kingdom of heaven*, and he uses it about thirty times. Matthew also uses the phrase *kingdom of God* five times (UBS[3] Mt 6.33; 12.28; 19.24; 21.31, 43), but this phrase is much more common in Mark where it comes about fifteen times, and in Luke, where it comes over thirty times. The interesting point is that often Mark and/or Luke use *kingdom of God* in a passage which is exactly parallel to one where Matthew uses *kingdom of heaven*. The following are among the best examples (quotations are from the RSV):

Matthew	Mark	Luke
5.3 Blessed are the poor in spirit, for theirs is the *kingdom of heaven*.		6.20 Blessed are you poor, for yours is *the kingdom of God*.
11.11 Truly, I say to you, among those born of women there has risen no one greater than John the Baptist; yet he who is least in *the kingdom of heaven* is greater than he.		7.28 I tell you, among those born of women none is greater than John; yet he who is least in *the kingdom of God* is greater than he.
13.11 And he answered them, "To you it has been given to know the secrets of *the kingdom of heaven*, but to them it has not been given."	4.11 And he said to them, "To you has been given the secret of *the kingdom of God*, but for those outside everything is in parables..."	8.10 ... he said, "To you it has been given to know the secrets of *the kingdom of God*; but for others they are in parables..."
19.14 Jesus said, "Let the children come to me, and do not hinder them; for to such belongs *the kingdom of heaven*."	10.14 But when Jesus saw it... he said to them, "Let the children come to me, do not hinder them; for to such belongs *the kingdom of God*."	18.16 But Jesus called them to him, saying, "Let the children come to me and do not hinder them; for to such belongs *the kingdom of God*."

19.23 And Jesus said to his disciples, "Truly I say to you, it will be hard for a rich man to enter *the kingdom of heaven.*"	10.23 And Jesus looked around and said to his disciples, "How hard it will be for those who have riches to enter *the kingdom of God!*"	18.24 Jesus looking at him said, "How hard it is for those who have riches to enter *the kingdom of God!*"

Figure 1.1: Synoptic Parallel Expressions of Kingdom of Heaven/God

Passages like these have led scholars to conclude that *kingdom of heaven* and *kingdom of God* have exactly the same meaning, but that Matthew usually followed the Jewish custom of avoiding direct mention of God. Instead he would often use the word *heaven*, which stood for *God* in a figure of speech called a euphemism.

This custom is found occasionally in the other gospels also, and sometimes even in places where Matthew does not follow it. For instance in Mark 14.62, the high priest asks Jesus "Are you the Christ, *the Son of the Blessed?*" In the parallel passage, Matthew 27.63, the plain meaning is stated with no euphemism "Tell us if you are the Christ, *the Son of God.*" In Luke 15.18 and 21 (which have no parallel in Matthew or Mark) the words of the Prodigal Son are given as "Father, I have sinned against *heaven* and before you." Here *heaven* is clearly a euphemism for *God*.

We have now shown that the use of the word *heaven* was frequently a way of avoiding mention of God directly, and that its occurrence was particularly common in Matthew's gospel. Is there any evidence to suggest that "*heaven*" or "*heavenly*" may be a way of avoiding mention of God in the expression *Father in heaven/heavenly Father*? I believe there is.

The phrase *your heavenly Father* occurs in both Mt 6.26 and 6.32. These verses are paralleled in Luke 12.24 and 12.30 and the wording is as follows (RSV):

Matthew	Luke
6.26 Look at the birds of the air; they neither sow nor reap nor gather into barns, and yet *your heavenly Father* feeds them.	12.24 Consider the ravens: they neither sow nor reap, they have neither storehouse nor barn, and yet *God* feeds them.
6.32 For the Gentiles seek all these things; and *your heavenly Father* knows that you need them all.	12.30 For all the nations of the world seek these things; and *your Father* knows that you need them.

Figure 1.2: Heavenly Father as Euphemism for God in Matthew

In the first instance, Luke has *God* where Matthew has *your heavenly Father* and in the second Luke has *your Father*. This suggests that Luke's expressions *your Father* and *God* can both be regarded as equivalent in meaning to Matthew's *your heavenly Father*.

In another passage, there are interesting parallels between Matthew, Mark and Luke, as follows (RSV):

Matthew	Mark	Luke
12.50 For whoever does the will of *my Father in heaven* is my brother, and sister, and mother.	3.35 Whoever does the will of *God* is my brother, and sister, and mother.	8.21 My mother and my brothers are those who hear the word of *God* and do it.

Figure 1.3: Equivalence of "My Father in Heaven" and "God" in the Synoptics

This suggests that the expressions *my Father in heaven* and *God* are also equivalent in meaning.

We could go on to ask whether the words *God* and *Father* are ever used together in the gospels, in expressions like *God your Father*, or *my Father God*.

It is rather a surprise to find that no such expressions occur in Matthew, Mark, or Luke. The nearest approach to such a phrase is in Jn 6.27 *God the Father*. The use of *God* and *Father* together is of course very common in the NT letters. Every one of the letters that bear Paul's name mentions *God our Father* or *God the Father* in the opening greeting, and from these frequent occurrences, such phrases have come into common use in the speech and prayers of Christians all over the world.

Conclusion

So far, then, we see three facts: (1) Only Matthew uses the distinctive expressions *heavenly Father and Father in heaven*. (2) Jewish custom often avoided direct mention of God by the use of euphemisms such as *heaven*. Parallel passages in Mark and Luke suggest that *heaven/heavenly* in Matthew's distinctive expressions may be such a euphemism. (3) Matthew, Mark and Luke never use *God* and *Father* together in a single phrase.

Taking all these points into consideration, we suggest that it would be quite legitimate to translate *Father in heaven* and *heavenly Father* in Matthew by *my/our/your Father God* or *God my/our/your/the Father*. Such a procedure will avoid the problems of a literal translation of *heaven/heavenly* which we discussed earlier. It will also retain a special expression distinctive of Matthew. This expression will add no new element of meaning to scripture, since it is already common in the letters of Paul.

The expression which would then be distinctive of Matthew would certainly be different in form from the Greek, but its underlying meaning would be substantially the same. It would be clearer, because it would avoid a euphemism, and it would also be unlikely to mislead the reader as a literal translation might. It may therefore be proposed that where *Father in heaven* or *heavenly Father* is a translation problem, translators should consider an expression equivalent to Father God as a possible solution.

2

AFTER THREE DAYS

With what expressions does the NT speak of the time interval between the death of Jesus and his resurrection? How should translators handle these expressions so as to be both consistent and clear? These are questions which have arisen in field consultation, and the present article will attempt to deal briefly with them, and with their implications for other passages. All Greek references are to UBS³. English versions checked include KJV, RSV, JB, NEB, NAB, J. B. Phillips, NIV, and TEV (third and fourth editions).

The two most common Greek phrases used to describe the timing of the resurrection are τῇ τρίτῃ ἡμέρᾳ and μετὰ τρεῖς ἡμέρας, which can be literally glossed as *on the third day* and *after three days* respectively. The following table sets out the occurrences of these two phrases in parallel passages in the synoptic gospels.

Mt 16.21	=	Mk 8.31	=	Lk 9.22
τῇ τρίτῃ ἡμέρᾳ		μετὰ τρεῖς ἡμέρας		τῇ τρίτῃ ἡμέρᾳ
Mt 17.23	=	Mk 9.31	=	
τῇ τρίτῃ ἡμέρᾳ		μετὰ τρεῖς ἡμέρας		
Mt 20.19	=	Mk 10.34	=	Lk 18.33
τῇ τρίτῃ ἡμέρᾳ		μετὰ τρεῖς ἡμέρας		τῇ ἡμέρᾳ τῇ τρίτῃ

Figure 2.1: Comparison of Three Day Formulas in the Synoptics

This comparison strongly suggests that Matthew and Luke saw the expression τῇ τρίτῃ ἡμέρᾳ (and its variant τῇ ἡμέρᾳ τῇ τρίτῃ, cf. Hos 6.2 LXX) as conveying essentially the same meaning as Mark's μετὰ τρεῖς ἡμέρας (cf. Gen 42.17, 18 LXX). This view seems to be generally agreed among commentators.[1]

Further evidence for a basic identity of meaning between these two phrases can be derived from a study of Mt 27.63, 64. In v. 63, the Jewish leaders say that Jesus had claimed that he would be raised μετὰ τρεῖς ἡμέρας. In fact, only the expression τῇ τρίτῃ ἡμέρᾳ has occurred in Matthew up to this point (Mt 16.21; 17.23; 20.19), which strongly hints that the two phrases were seen as synonymous. Additional confirmation to this view is given in v. 64, where the Jewish leaders request that the tomb should be guarded ἕως τῆς τρίτης ἡμέρας. Unless this expression referred to as space of time identical with, or at least as great as, that referred to by μετὰ τρεῖς ἡμέρας in the previous verse, then the guard would not extend over the whole of the critical period, and the entire paragraph would thus lose its point.

In short, the view that the two expressions μετὰ τρεῖς ἡμέρας and τῇ τρίτῃ ἡμέρᾳ carry the same meaning is very widely held among commentators, and appears to be thoroughly well founded.

It is therefore nothing less than astonishing that this view seems to be totally ignored by translators of all major versions in English, except for the fourth edition of TEV. In the synoptic passages already referred to, the major modern English versions (except TEV4) all render τῇ τρίτῃ ἡμέρᾳ by "on the third day" and μετὰ τρεῖς ἡμέρας by "after three days" or by some variant such as "three days later" or "three days afterwards" which is not significantly different in meaning. The KJV has "on the third day" in Mk 9.31 and 10.34, but this is based on weaker manuscript evidence rather than superior translation principles.

These translations thus entirely overlook the awkward fact that "after three days/three days later" does not mean the same thing in English as "on the third day." It seems clear that if the two Greek expressions carry the same meaning, they should be translated in English in such a way as to bring this out. One would therefore expect that either "on the third day" or "after three

---

[1] See, for instance, on Matthew, W. C. Allen, *The Gospel according to St. Matthew*, ICC (T&T Clark, 1907), 180; A. H. McNeile, *The Gospel according to St. Matthew* (Macmillan, 1915) 244–245; Floyd V. Filson, *The Gospel according to St. Matthew* (A&C Black, 1960), 188, 299; on Mark, see Vincent Taylor, *The Gospel according to St. Mark* (Macmillan, 1952), 378; Robert G. Bratcher and Eugene A. Nida, *A Translator's Handbook on the Gospel of Mark* (Brill, 1961), 263; on Luke, see A. R. C. Leaney, *The Gospel according to St. Luke* (A&C Black 1958), 165; E. E. Ellis, *The Gospel according to Luke*, NCB (Oliphants, 1966), 218. If there is any difference in meaning, it is merely that Mark's μετὰ τρεῖς ἡμέρας is a little "less exact" (Filson, *Matthew*, 188).

days/three days later" would be used consistently in all the relevant synoptic passages. Which one would be preferable? With Friday, the day of the crucifixion, as the starting point, the English "after three days/three days later" could refer only to Monday. It was quite evidently not the intention of the gospel writers to indicate that the resurrection took place on a Monday, for they all specify that it was on the first day of the week, i.e. Sunday (Mt 28.1; Mk 16.2; Lk 24.1; Jn 20:1). With the Friday starting point, the English "on the third day" refers naturally to Sunday, and one would therefore expect this to be the general expression used in translations.

The fourth edition of TEV has at least sensed that there is a problem here, and has responded to it by using a single expression in all the relevant passages referring to the resurrection. Inexplicably, it has selected "three days later," which implies that the resurrection took place on a Monday, and thus carries the wrong meaning even in those texts where a literal translation of τῇ τρίτῃ ἡμέρᾳ would give the correct meaning. If it is felt that an expression of the form "x days later" or "after x days" is desirable, the only value of x that would convey the right meaning in English is two. However, although it would be acceptable in terms of translation principles to put "two days later/after two days" for μετὰ τρεῖς ἡμέρας, it is extremely unlikely that this rendering would commend itself to churches or individual bible readers. The use of the numeral three/third in connection with the resurrection has become so deeply embedded in Christian tradition that any attempt to change it would be sure to provoke a hostile reaction.

Thus the conclusion seems inevitable that in all the texts discussed so far, the most accurate and clear English rendering would be "on the third day."

What about other passages in the NT where the expressions τῇ τρίτῃ ἡμέρᾳ and μετὰ τρεῖς ἡμέρας occur, both in relation to the resurrection and in connection with other events? Τῇ τρίτῃ ἡμέρᾳ (Lk 24.7, 46; Acts 10.40), its alternative form τῇ ἡμέρᾳ τῇ τρίτῃ (1 Cor 15.4), and its shorter form τῇ τρίτῃ (Lk 13.22; Acts 27.19) are generally translated "on the third day," and this does not give rise to any problems. There is more interest in the texts which have μετὰ τρεῖς ἡμέρας (Acts 25.1) or its equivalent μετὰ ἡμέρας τρεῖς (Lk 2.46; Acts 28.17). There is no reason to suppose that in these texts, the variation in word order conveys a difference in meaning, or that the phrase in either order carries a meaning different from its meaning in Mt 27.63; Mk 8.31; 9.31; 10.34. In Acts 25.1, 28.17, the cohesion of the narrative is not affected by the period of time involved, but in Lk 2.46, it seems rather unlikely that the evangelist intended to say that Jesus' parents spent three full days searching Jerusalem for him. At least some translators have been aware of this, and both NAB and TEV have translated μετὰ ἡμέρας τρεῖς as "on the third day" here. Commentators seem to agree with this, and it certainly fits the context better.[2] One can only speculate as to why neither NAB nor TEV has applied this solution to Mt 27.63; Mk 8.31; 9.31; 10.34, where it would make a significant improvement in the clarity and consistency of the translation.

In Acts 25.1; 28.17, the length of time covered by μετὰ τρεῖς ἡμέρας/μετὰ ἡμέρας τρεῖς is not crucial to the flow of the narrative, but in the absence of any evidence to the contrary, it is reasonable to suppose that "on the third day" would be the most appropriate rendering in these passages also. Since there is no traditional emotional attachment to these verses on the part of Bible users, "two days later/after two days" might be an acceptable solution here (cf. Luke 9.28 where ὡσεὶ ἡμέραι ὀκτώ, literally about eight days, is translated about a week in TEV).

There are a few other places where expressions involving the phrase "three days" occur in the gospels in reference to the resurrection, either directly or by implication. In Mt 27.40 and its parallel Mk 15.29, as well as in Jn 2.19, 20, the phrase ἐν τρισὶν ἡμέραις occurs. It is uniformly rendered as "in three days" in major English versions, and no problems arise from this. In Mt 26.61 and its parallel Mk 14.58, the expression is διὰ τριῶν ἡμερῶν. All major English versions translate both passages with "in three days," except TEV which has "three days later" in Mt 26.61 and "after three days" in Mk 14.58. As argued earlier, these expressions are misleading, and would be better replaced by "in three days," or "within three days" as the KJV has in Mk 14.58.

In Mt 12.40, there is the quotation from Jonah 1.17 LXX which includes the words τρεῖς ἡμέρας καὶ τρεῖς νύκτας. All major English versions translate as "three days and three nights." The difficulty in relating this text to other statements about the resurrection is not a translation problem, and thus is not dealt with here.

There remains only Mt 15.32 and its parallel Mk 8.2, where ἡμέραι τρεῖς occurs in a context that contains no reference to the resurrection. All major English versions translate "by three days" or "for three days," and this sets up no problems in the cohesion of the narrative. However, if the usual inclusive method of counting days was in use here, probably two days would be a more accurate modern English equivalent.

---

[2] E.g., Alfred Plummer, *The Gospel according to St. Luke*, ICC (T&T Clark, 1896), 76; Ellis, *Luke*, 86.

To sum up, then, this article proposes that the phrase "on the third day" is the most appropriate equivalent in English, not only for τῇ τρίτῃ ἡμέρᾳ/τῇ ἡμέρᾳ τῇ τρίτῃ in Mt 16.21; 17.23; 20.19; Lk 9.22; 18.33; 24.7, 46; Acts 10.40; 1 Cor 15.4 but also for μετὰ τρεῖς ἡμέρας/μετὰ ἡμέρας τρεῖς in Mt 27.63; Mk 8.31; 9.31; 10.34; Lk 2.46; Acts 25.1; 28.17. But it should be noted that even if this argument holds good for English, it will not necessarily hold good for translations into other languages. However, it is reasonable to suppose that it may apply in some other languages, and translators should certainly consider it before making decisions. They should especially beware of an unthinking adherence to TEV in the relevant passages, since in this matter TEV is the least satisfactory of all the major English versions.

3

DISCOURSE STRUCTURE IN MATTHEW'S GOSPEL

WITH JAN DE WAARD

1. Introduction

1.1. General

Human language is patterned activity. Within the discipline of linguistics, scholars have until relatively recently concentrated on the patterns occurring in the phonological, morphological and syntactic levels of language. Attention was focused on the structure of stretches of speech or writing that were one sentence or less in length. Within the last few years, however, greater interest has been shown in the patterning of larger stretches of language.[1]

This article is an attempt to analyse a substantial piece of writing, namely the gospel of Matthew, and to see from a linguistic perspective what its com-

---

[1] See for instance Joseph E. Grimes, *The Thread of Discourse* (Mouton, 1975); M. A. K. Halliday and Ruqaiya Hasan, *Cohesion in English* (Longman, 1976); Robert E. Longacre, *Discourse, Paragraph and Sentence Structure in Selected Philippine Languages* (Summer Institute of Linguistics, 1968); idem., *Hierarchy and Universality of Discourse Constituents in New Guinea Languages* (Georgetown University, 1972).

ponent parts are. Though this study is to some extent impressionistic and intuitive, it is not thereby automatically invalidated. Impressions and intuitions are not unmotivated, and even if it is not possible to pin down immediately all the stimuli that cause them, a careful record of what they are is a first step in the direction of greater understanding. It is hoped therefore that the record will be of interest both to linguists working on discourse analysis and also to biblical scholars in illuminating part of their field from a different angle.

A major concern of the authors is with the translation of Scripture into other languages. It is often necessary for them to put themselves in the place of people reading the gospel for the first time, bringing to it little or nothing in the way of Christian background. But however little people in this category may bring to the reading of Matthew by way of theological presuppositions, they must of necessity bring certain linguistic presuppositions.

These would include at least: 1) that the gospel was put purposefully into the form in which it now stands, and 2) that it is a coherent whole. The naïve reader does not start by asking questions about sources, oral traditions, redactions and so on. He normally assumes a text to be a coherent whole unless and until he finds that within his particular frame of reference and at his level of interpretation, it is not. He takes the gospel as a unit, and reads and understands it in its own terms. An approach of this kind, lacking the sophistication of a modern academic background, must have characterized many of the original readers of the gospel, and it is surely worth while to see what can emerge by trying in a measure to simulate it.

In this study, therefore, we shall attempt to understand what the gospel says as a literary unit in itself. It is not only comprehensible as a literary whole, but also, at some level, as an *independent* whole. Despite its clear relationships with other pieces of writing, most notably the gospels of Mark and Luke, it does not make direct cross-reference to them. The probable use of Mark as a source by Matthew does not mean that the reader must have Mark available before he can understand Matthew. For Matthew often was originally (and still is today) read and understood by people who did not have access to Mark or to Luke. In any case, a writer or editor cannot assume that readers will make extensive comparisons of his work with other similar ones even if this option is open to them. In another direction, Matthew has a close relationship with the OT, but this again does not alter its status as an independent unit in literary terms.

To take an approach of this kind is not to deny the usefulness of other approaches. Textual, source, form and redaction criticism all have their roles to play, and all have shed light in their different ways. A discourse analysis approach is not a substitute for other approaches, and is not to be taken as an attempt to answer the same questions from another direction. Rather it is to be taken as an attempt to ask different questions, of which the primary one is "How does Matthew as a piece of writing cohere as a whole?" The answers suggested will at some points no doubt reinforce the answers given to the questions asked in other approaches. At other points they may weaken or even contradict them. Hopefully, the ultimate result will be a deepened understanding of the gospel.

In light of these considerations, the works of biblical scholars were deliberately avoided in the initial stage of this investigation, which was the work of Clark. This must not be construed as an act of contempt, but rather as a desire to try a linguistic approach without being influenced in advance by conclusions arrived at by other routes. At a later stage, an attempt was made to redress the balance by a comparison and contrast of the discourse analysis results with the results of other approaches. This attempt was the work of de Waard and is recorded largely in the footnotes.

This study is in no way concerned with the historicity of the various incidents in the gospels. Such questions are not discussed at all. However, in keeping with the attempt to simulate the approach of the naïve reader, the analytical comment is written as though each incident is taken as historical. This is not a devious means of prejudging the issue of historicity, but rather a short-hand way of avoiding it, in order to concentrate on other matters. Greek quotations are from UBS³.

1.2. Terminology

The labels for the analytical units proposed in this study are largely taken from drama. But before these terms are applied, the gospel is divided into 'blocks,' which separate the 'narrative' from the 'discourse.'[2] The discourse blocks (roughly chs. 5–7, 10, 13, 18, 23–25) are each analysed as their content demands, and no regular scheme of internal labelling is applied to them. The dramatic terms of Act, Scene and Episode are applied primarily to the narra-

---

[2] In this context, the word 'discourse' is used in the relatively non-technical sense familiar in Matthaean studies. It is not to be confused with the relatively technical usage within the discipline of linguistics in such expressions as 'discourse analysis,' 'discourse structure,' etc.

tive material. These terms are hierarchically related: a Scene consists of two or more Episodes, and an Act of two or more Scenes. In addition to these Scenes, an Act contains also one or more of the five discourse blocks, though these stand outside the Scene structure.

In considering the semantic structure of the gospel, it is much less easy to set up a hierarchy of terms. We might suggest such terms as Plot, Theme, Motif and Topic (in roughly descending order) but at present not enough is known about the semantic structure of discourse to ensure that these terms are used in a rigorous way. In this paper the terms Theme and Motif are used quite frequently, but there is no clear-cut relationship established between them. In a biblical text, this is probably an area of analysis where final decisions should be in the hands of biblical scholars.

1.3. Establishment of Narrative and Discourse Blocks

The division of the gospel into narrative and discourse sections is traditional. It is accepted and used as a basic structural feature here because each of the five discourse blocks ends with the formula καὶ ἐγένετο ὅτε ἐτέλεσεν ὁ Ἰησοῦς (7.28; 11.1; 13.53; 19.1; 26.1). Though there are many places in the narrative sections where there are quite long pieces of direct speech from the mouth of Jesus, it is in these five places, and only these, that the above closing formula is used. It seems fair, therefore, to take it that Matthew intended to imply that these five passages, and these alone, are in some sense units in the overall structure of the gospel in a way in which other pieces of direct speech are not.[3] Hereafter, the blocks are referred to as N blocks or D blocks.

---

[3] See B. W. Bacon, "The 'Five Books' of Matthew against the Jews," *The Expositor* 8th Series 15 (1918): 56–66 and especially his *Studies in Matthew* (Henry Holt & Co., 1930). See also G. D. Kilpatrick, *The Origins of the Gospel according to St. Matthew* (Clarendon Press, 1946) and Krister Stendahl, *The School of St. Matthew* (C. W. K. Gleerup, 1954), especially p. 24ff. For Bacon, the fivefold structure of the gospel pointed to a homiletic milieu and for Kilpatrick to a liturgical one, since it was considered as the Christian counter part to the Torah which was read in the synagogues. On the other hand, for Stendahl the pattern which guided Matthew in systematizing his material was that of a handbook. However, the discussions of this particular issue are not pertinent to our study, since we are not primarily interested in the *Sitz im Leben* of the different units. Bacon and also J. A. Findlay ("The Book of Testimonies and the Structure of the First Gospel," *The Expositor* 8th Series 20 [1920]: 388–400) go so far as to make a detailed division of the gospel into five consistent books (each book consisting of narrative and discourse) with five distinct headings, but it is clearly impossible to make such a detailed division. Stendahl is certainly right in stating that the "disposition which Matthew accounts for is primarily that of the discourses" (*Matthew*, 27).

All the remaining sections of the gospel apart from the 5 D blocks ending with the same formula, are regarded as N blocks, even though they may contain substantial sections of dialogue. The N blocks form the framework into which the D blocks are embedded, since the latter are neither independent nor self-explanatory, and need the surrounding narrative to supply their context. However, the D blocks are easier to identify first, since they are, so to speak, the marked units.

Giving only the chapter numbers for simplicity's sake, the blocks are identified as follows.

	N	D	N	D	N	D	N	D	N	D	N
chs.	1-4	5-7	8-9	10	11-12	13	14-17	18	19-22	23-25	26-28

1.4. The Establishment of Three 'Acts'

Thus far, the divisions are the same as traditional ones and are not very illuminating. But in the course of reading through the gospel, a clear link becomes apparent between 4.23 and 9.35. In the former place the content of Jesus' ministry is announced as διδάσκων ἐν ταῖς συναγωγαῖς αὐτῶν καὶ κηρύσσων τὸ εὐαγγέλιον τῆς βασιλείας καὶ θεραπεύων πᾶσαν νόσον καὶ πᾶσαν μαλακίαν, and this is exemplified in chapters 5–9. At the end of ch 9, in v. 35, identical wording is used as a summary of the preceding chapters, and is thus taken to be a formal closure of the section. From this lead, it becomes apparent that 4.23 and 9.35 are both located in short transition paragraphs pivotal to the development of the gospel as a whole. 4.23–25 provide the link between Jesus' preparation for his ministry and its detailed description; 9.35–38 summarizes progress thus far, and opens the way for the wider possibilities chronicled in subsequent chapters.

So there seems reasonable ground for positing a major structural division around the end of ch. 9. Chapters 1–9 are approximately one third of the total length of the gospel, and therefore it also seems reasonable to anticipate a 3-part structure in the whole work. No "formulaic" evidence was found for making another break, but there does seem reason to suggest a major break at the end of ch. 18. The reason for this is semantic rather than formal. In 19.1, there is a decisive change of location. Apart from the brief excursion to Phoenicia in ch. 15, the record from 4.12 on is largely set in Galilee. The mention of leaving Galilee in 19.1 initiates the events leading to the climax of the record, and it therefore seems an appropriate point for a crucial structural break. Formally it is unobtrusive, but this can be taken as a product of Matthew's literary craftsmanship. In a symphony or concerto, one movement sometimes leads into another without the music actually stopping, so may there not be something analogous in literature?[4]

What is the effect of breaking the gospel into three 'acts,' as suggested? (Act 1, chs. 1–9, Act 2, chs. 10–18, Act 3 chs. 19–28). The narrative and discourse blocks then fall out as follows. (Again, only chapter numbers are given; the detailed breaking points will be discussed at the appropriate places in the text.)

Act 1	Narrative	chs.	1–4
	Discourse	chs.	5–7
	Narrative	chs.	8–9
Act 2	Discourse	ch.	10
	Narrative	chs.	11–12
	Discourse	ch.	13
	Narrative	chs.	14–17
	Discourse	ch.	18

---

[4] Jean Radermakers in his recent work *Au fil de l'évangile selon saint Matthieu*, 2 vols. (Institut d'Etudes Théologiques, 1972) follows the method of the *Redaktionsgeschichte*. In his second volume he also seems to think of some form of three part structure on account of the twice occurring formula ἀπὸ τότε ἤρξατο ὁ Ἰησοῦς (4:17 and 16:21) which according to him demarcates major sections of the gospel. However, the fivefold formula has priority for him, though—quite distinct from Baconian interpretation—he regards this formula as a link between preceding discourse and following material according to the scheme word/action. Radermakers divides the gospel into twelve stages (1–2, 3–4, 5–7, 8–9, 10, 11–12, 13, 14–17, 18, 19–23, 24–25, 26–28) or six binary groups of discourse-narrative. For a criticism of such a division see especially A. Vanhoye's review in *Biblica* 55 (1974), 292–293.

On the other hand, J. D. Kingsbury in "The Structure of Matthew's Gospel and His Concept of Salvation-History" (*CBQ* 35 [1973], 451–474) claims that the formula ἀπὸ τότε ἤρξατο ὁ Ἰησοῦς is pivotal to the broad outline of the whole of the gospel thereby following the earlier views of E. Lohmeyer (*Das Evangelium des Matthäus*, 2nd ed. [Vandenhoeck & Ruprecht, 1958], 1, 64 and 264), N. B. Stonehouse (*The Witness of Matthew and Mark to Christ* [Presbyterian Guardian, 1944], 129–131) and E. Krentz ("The Extent of Matthew's Prologue," *JBL* 83 (1964): 409–414). His whole article is a development and defence of the threefold pattern resulting from the acceptance of this formula as distinctive. However, the treatment of ἀπὸ τότε ἤρξατο ὁ Ἰησοῦς as a 'formula' is very questionable. A phrase should occur at least three and preferably more times before it can be called a 'formula.' The argument that a phrase occurring twice is intended to be of greater structural significance than one occurring five times is intrinsically weak, and requires overwhelming evidence in support.

Discourse Structure in Matthew's Gospel

Act 3	Narrative	chs.	19–22
	Discourse	chs.	23–25
	Narrative	chs.	26–28

Within Act 1 and Act 3 there is a 'key' pattern as it may be called, of blocks:

$$N \mid D \mid N$$

Within Act 2 there is a more elaborate version of the same pattern:

$$D \mid N \mid D \mid N \mid D$$

In the three acts as a whole there is the key pattern again on a larger scale, with Acts 1 and 3 being of identical internal structure, and Act 2 a variation of the same structure:

$$\text{Act 1} \mid \text{Act 2} \mid \text{Act 3}$$

Notice also the balance in the distribution of the discourse blocks. Acts 1 and 3 both contain a single long block of discourse, each 3 chapters long. Act 2 also contains a comparable amount of discourse, but here it is split into three single chapter blocks. In Acts 1 and 3, the narrative blocks form the sandwich, with the discourse blocks as the filling. In Act 2, the discourse blocks form a double sandwich with the narrative blocks as the filling.

These patterns are too symmetrical and too aesthetically pleasing to be either accidental or imaginary. It must be emphasized that heuristically the division into acts was not made in order to obtain the block pattern. The acts were hypothesized for the reasons given, and only afterwards did the block pattern emerge. No other division would yield such a satisfactory pattern.

2. Act 1

Act 1 has already been established as consisting of chs. 1–9 of the gospel. It consists of 2 N blocks and a D block, arranged in the key pattern.

NEW TESTAMENT DISCOURSE

```
N │ D │ N
```

The first N block is chs. 1–4, the D block chs. 5–7, and the second N block, chs. 8–9. These will now be analysed in order.

2.1. Formal Division of the First N Block

The first N block breaks up fairly readily. The genealogy of 1.1–17 stands apart from the rest of the section, and perhaps ought not to be included. It seems to be just as much a prologue to the whole gospel as is Jn 1.1–18. The birth narrative and associated events (1.18–2.23) constitute the next section (labelled Scene 1), while 3.1–4.25 form a further discrete section concerning the preparation for Jesus' ministry (labelled Scene 2).

2.1.1. The Prologue

Verses 1–17 are clearly a discrete unit, marked as they are by a title (v. 1), a highly repetitive internal structure, and a closing summary (v. 17). Thus already one key pattern is apparent, with the main content balanced by brief introduction and closure.

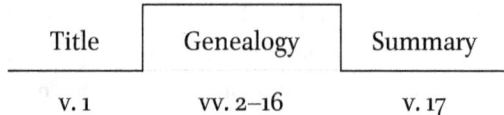

Verse 1 introduces the key figures of Jesus, David and Abraham, and v. 17 balances these by mentioning the same figures in reverse order. The mention of the Babylonian captivity in v. 17 is an additional feature, but it does not upset the basic rhythm. Verses 2–16 are broken up into 3 sections, vv. 2–6a (Abraham to David), vv. 6b–11 (David to the captivity) and vv. 12–16 (the captivity to Jesus).

The first section is the most complex, for as well as the standard formula "x δὲ ἐγέννησεν τὸν y" it contains several additional pieces of information. For present purposes, we are interested in the distribution rather than the content of this extra information. Of the 13 pairs of names in this section, it is pairs 3, 4, 10 and 11 that have extra information appended. Is it too far-fetched to see another key pattern, with the pairs of names numbered as follows?

DISCOURSE STRUCTURE IN MATTHEW'S GOSPEL

```
pairs  1  2 | 3  4 | 5  6  7  8  9 | 10  11 | 12  13
```

The pattern is a key with a double notch, and is symmetrical in terms of the distance of the notches from the beginning, middle and end of the list. The remaining piece of additional information, namely that David was the king (v. 6a), is taken as closing this first section of the genealogy. Thus it has its structural place on a higher level or rank than the additional information in pairs 3, 4, 10 and 11.

The second section is more straightforward, with 14 pairs of names, with which only the first and last have any added information. This will give a simple key pattern.

```
pairs    1 | 2–13 | 14
```

In the 14th pair, καὶ τοὺς ἀδελφοὺς αὐτοῦ is taken to balance ἐκ τῆς τοῦ Οὐρίου (v. 6b) and ἐπὶ τῆς μετοικεσίας Βαβυλῶνος to close this section, as the mention of David's kingship closed the first.

The third section is almost the same as the second with 13 pairs of names, of which the first pair has an added piece of chronological information, and the last pair has divergent content to explain why the standard formula is not used to link Joseph and Jesus.

The pattern structure of the prologue, then, emerges as key patterns of varying complexity on two levels:

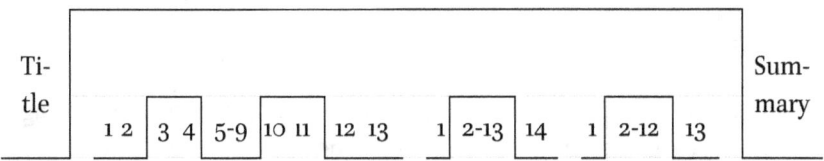

2.1.2. Scene 1

This scene is fairly clearly marked off from what precedes and follows. 1.18 opens with a clear announcement of the content of the section, and 2.23 ends with a reference to the OT, which is in this gospel a common way of clinching a point.[5] And ch. 3 opens with a totally new topic, which dissoci-

---

[5] This is especially true of the so-called "formula quotations" peculiar to Matthew. With

ates it from what precedes in terms of content.

The scene is itself divided into three episodes (1.18–25, 2.1–12 and 2.13–23). Each of these is initiated with a genitive absolute construction, which throughout the gospel is very common as a formal marker of transition to a new section.[6] This formal feature ties in well with the content, as each episode is a semantic whole, and reasonably complete in itself. The third episode is further subdivided into three sections, the flight into Egpyt (2.13–15), the murder of the children (2.16–18), and the return from Egypt (2.19–23). The first and third of these begin with a genitive absolute, and are verbally closely parallel. The second begins with τότε, another frequent transition marker. All three close with an OT formula quotation peculiar to Matthew.

Formally, then, this scene exhibits what can be called a chain pattern – the sort of pattern which typically links chronologically related incidents. It can be represented as follows (with a further key pattern involved in episode 3).

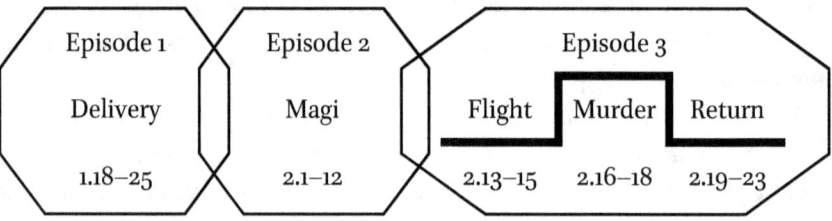

The handling of participants in this section will be dealt with in Appendix A.

2.1.3. Scene 2

This scene starts with a distinct new topic, introduced by a rather vague temporal marker (3.1) and concludes with the important transitional paragraph 4.23–25. It is probably best taken as composed of three episodes,

---

regard to these quotations in the nativity story, Stendahl rightly maintains that the "whole context seems to be constructed with the quotation as its nucleus—and as its germ from the point of view of growth" (*Matthew*, 204).

[6] Compare also Rudolph Bultmann, *Die Geschichte der synoptischen Tradition* (Vandenhoeck & Ruprecht, 1970), 376: "Auch ohne solche Formeln erreicht Mt eine engere Verknüpfung der Einzelgeschichten, sodass ein zeitlicher und örtlicher Zusammenhang entsteht. So gebraucht er haüfig den schon bei Mk gelegentlich vorkommenden absoluten Genitiv ...."

though it could be alternatively analysed as four. The first deals with the activities and preaching of John the Baptist, and closes with the end of the direct quote of John's words (3.1–12). In 3.13 Jesus re-enters the account, following another τότε, and his life is at once linked with that of John. This episode is taken to go as far as 4.11, and the baptism and temptation are taken as two sides of the divine authentication of Jesus' work. This is because there is only a weak transition (another τότε) at 4.1, and there is no real change of focus. It is Jesus who is the main subject of the whole passage. However, it would also be possible to analyse this section as consisting of two separate episodes.[7]

The third episode (4.12–25) gives the beginning of Jesus' ministry. It opens both with a link reference back to the (now completed) work for John, and a setting in terms of place. There is no good reason for a break between vv. 16 and 17, or 17 and 18. The calling (and obedience) of the four fishermen is an example of a response, in this case positive, to Jesus and his message. 4.23–25 summarises the content and effects of Jesus' early ministry, and is very important both structurally and semantically. Structurally on the small scale it rounds off the brief account of this third episode of Scene 2. Structurally on the large scale it gives the framework on which the rest of Act 1 hangs. The lynch pin is v. 23, and its connection already noted with 9.35, καὶ περιῆγεν...διδάσκων ἐν ταῖς συναγωγαῖς αὐτῶν καὶ κηρύσσων τὸ εὐαγγέλιον τῆς βασιλείας καὶ θεραπεύων πᾶσαν νόσον καὶ πᾶσαν μαλακίαν. Here semantically is the manifesto of Jesus' movement, and here formally is the two-fold outline of chs. 5–9, διδάσκων and θεραπεύων. In chs. 5–7 (the D block) we are given an extended example of the διδάσκων (taken up in 5.2 and 7.28, 29); and in chs. 8 and 9 various examples of θεραπεύων (8.2, 3, 7, 8, 13, 16; 9.21, 22, 25, 30, 33), though other themes are also present in this section. 9.35 repeats much of 4.23 and is a closing summary of what chs. 5–9 have covered.

Perhaps justification should be given for taking as a two-fold ministry what looks at first sight (and has often been taken as) a three-fold one. If διδάσκων...καὶ κηρύσσων...καὶ θεραπεύων are taken as three coordinate elements, the evident content of the succeeding chapters must be played down.

---

[7] In the analysis of the sources, 4.1–11 has rightly been isolated as containing Palestinian material—at least formally—in all probability used by both Matthew and Luke. Marcan influence can only be detected in vv. 1 and 2 and especially in v. 11b (see Bultmann, *Geschichte*, 271–275). However, on the level of discourse analysis, the arguments from source analysis are not necessarily decisive. It should be noted that vv. 1–11 contain three temptations and that the gospel shows a preference for arranging incidents or sayings into numerical groups. The threefold pattern of incidents and sayings is much more frequent than the fivefold and sevenfold patterns. For a complete list see Allen, *Matthew*, lxv.

The θεραπεύων aspect clearly stands apart, but there is no clear evidence for a dichotomy between διδάσκων and κηρύσσων. So 4.23 is construed to mean that κηρύσσων τὸ εὐαγγέλιον τῆς βασιλείας is the *content* of διδάσκων ἐν ταῖς συναγωγαῖς αὐτῶν, not a parallel activity. In other words the construction is a hendiadys. This fits the succeeding chapters much better, and is paralleled by the construction in 4.17, where the καὶ λέγειν· Μετανοεῖτε cannot be taken as anything but the content of κηρύσσειν.[8]

To sum up, then, Scene 2 also shows a chain pattern.

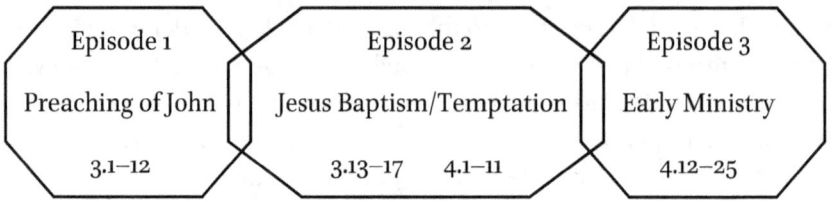

2.1.4. Summary of First N Block

This block contains a prologue whose relations are mainly with the gospel as a whole, linking it to its cultural and historical context; and two scenes which ring up the curtain on the overall drama. Each scene contains three episodes linked to each other in a chain pattern. One episode in each scene shows signs of further internal structure.

2.2. Formal Division of the D Block

In chs. 5–7 we enter upon a very different form of literature. In "rhetorical" terms, it would appear to fall in the category of exposition. In structural terms, it is marked by a high frequency of asyndeton, and a high number of

---

[8] Gerhard Friedrich states: "Ob Mt. 4,23 u 9,35 ἐν ταῖς συναγωγαῖς auch zu κηρύσσειν gehört, oder ob das κηρύσσειν u θεραπεύειν bei der Reise durch Galiläe erfolgte, ist unwichtig zu entscheiden" (s.v. κηρύσσω in Gerhard Kittel, *Theologisches Wörterbuch zum Neuen Testament* [Kohlhammer, 1950], 3:703n33). However, in this particular connection such a decision cannot be said to be without importance. Anyway, it seems hardly possible to speak of a dichotomy between the events of διδάσκων and κηρύσσων. The different verbs may imply a difference of setting, διδάσκων taking place in the synagogues and κηρύσσων everywhere, as well as a difference of receptors (pious Jews versus everybody) as Friedrich points out (ibid., 713), but, on the other hand, Acts 9.20 makes clear that κηρύσσειν also takes place in the synagogues and texts like Mark 3.14–15 and Mark 6.30 show that both verbs can be used as synonyms.

imperative sentences, i.e. many of its sentences would belong to a different sentence class from most of the sentences in the N blocks.

This analysis sees the Sermon on the Mount as an exordium, a series of seven principles, each accompanied by illustrations and/or applications, and a peroration.

The exordium consists of the so-called Beatitudes (5.1–10) and the peroration of 7.24–27. The rest of the Sermon (5.11–7.23) supplies the seven principles and their supporting material. Thus again a key pattern can be seen, with brief opening and closing sections balancing each other on either side of the main body of the discourse.

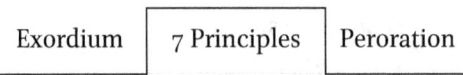

The exordium and peroration only are in the third person – the seven principles and their illustrations are all in the second person. This is a formal reason for calling 5.1–10 and 7.24–27 different units from the rest of the sermon.[9]

2.2.1. The Exordium

The introductory words of 5.1–2 give the setting, and the word ἐδίδασκεν (v. 2) gives the clue that what follows exemplifies the διδάσκων aspect of Jesus' ministry stated in 4.23.

The eight beatitudes immediately follow.[10] They are totally asyndetic, and have a balanced internal structure, all having the form of μακάριοι οἱ... ὅτι αὐτῶν/αὐτοί. The second clause of the first and last beatitudes (vv. 3 and 10) is identical, and all the intervening ones are different.[11] In the second halves of

---

[9] Though Bultmann (*Geschichte*, 376) considers the text of Lk 6:20–21 as generally more original than the text of Mt 5:3–9, he takes it that Luke changed the originally 3rd person in Matthew into the 2nd one. He rightly argues that beatitudes are normally formulated in the 3rd person. Also Bultmann uses this formal reason as one of his arguments for separating Mt 5:11ff. as a different unit.

[10] There has been considerable dispute about the number of the beatitudes. Since Bacon and Wellhausen (*Das Evangelium Matthaei* [Georg Andreas Reimer Verlag, 1904]) they have been reckoned as seven by regarding v. 5 as a marginal gloss. Also according to Bultmann (*Geschichte*, 115) v. 5 is secondary and v. 10 stems from Matthew who wants to complete the seven beatitudes.

[11] For a more detailed analysis of the discourse structure of the beatitudes, see Howard A.

the six central beatitudes (vv. 4–9) there is a balance of active and passive verbal forms. The passive (avoiding the mention of God) predominates but the active occurs in the second and fifth places, thus giving a pattern of inverted parallelism, as follows:

v. 3	αὐτῶν	Present
v. 4	αὐτοί	Future Passive
v. 5	αὐτοί	Future Active
v. 6	αὐτοί	Future Passive
v. 7	αὐτοί	Future Passive
v. 8	αὐτοί	Future Active
v. 9	αὐτοί	Future Passive
v. 10	αὐτῶν	Present

2.2.2. The Seven Principles

These were arrived at basically by reading through the text and separating the plain statements from the illustrative ones. The assumption was that extended figurative passages were likely to have a different purpose from literal passages.

The First Principle. This is contained in 5.11–12. It is usually tacked rather awkwardly on to the end of the beatitudes, presumably because of its semantic link with v. 10. This departs from the rhythm of the beatitudes, neglects the shift from third to second person at v. 11, and affords no obvious connection with the verses that follow (vv. 13–16). In this treatment a paragraph break is made after v. 10 and vv. 11–16 are treated as a unit.[12] Verse 11 enunciates a principle for which v. 12 gives a reason, and vv. 13–16 give two illustrations of the circumstances in which the principle operates (or three, if the city on the hill is taken as a separate one).[13] The principle is that persecution ἕνεκεν ἐμοῦ brings blessing. Persecution of this type arises because a follower of Jesus stands out against his background, often opposing its values and assumptions (like the prophets, v. 12). Salt and light also stand in contrast to

---

Hatton and David J. Clark, "From the Harp to the Sitar," *BT* 26, no. 1 (1975): 132–138.

[12] Compare also Bultmann, *Geschichte*, 100: "die Anreden ὑμεῖς ἐστε κτλ. V 13 und 14 sind Bildungen des Mt, um die Worte dem Zusammenhang der Jüngerrede einzugliedern."

[13] This option faithfully reflects the results of source analysis according to which the statement about the city on the hill has been taken from a different tradition and inserted here. However, the meaning of the utterance has now been conditioned by its context.

their surroundings – salt has no other purpose than to change the taste of what it goes with, and light has no possibility of coexisting with darkness, but must dispel it. Thus the follower of Jesus is to stand out, and risk persecution for doing so, though paradoxically (v. 16) by so doing he may make some people give glory to God.

Thus this passage can be said to expand the paradox of v. 10, which summed up the beatitudes by contrasting blessing from God with persecution from men.

The Second Principle. Having in the first principle established a contrast with the background, Jesus next goes on to establish a connection. Far from being antinomians, he and his followers have a high regard for the Law. His second principle clarifies his relationship with that foundation stone of the society in which he ministered. The Law will not be abolished, but given a fullness it never had before (v. 17). Such righteousness as it could confer would be quite inadequate for the followers of Jesus (v. 20; cf. Phil 3.9). Thus the principle is laid down in v. 17 and expanded in vv. 18–20.

The rest of ch. 5 is taken up with specific examples of how the Law is to be "fulfilled." These six illustrations make this by far the longest section of the whole sermon, and presumably thereby indicate the importance attached by Matthew to this aspect of the gospel.

The six examples, as has often been noted, are all introduced with a similar formula (vv. 21, 27, 31, 33, 38 and 43) of which the basis is Ἠκούσατε ὅτι ἐρρέθη, followed by the contrastive ἐγὼ δὲ λέγω ὑμῖν (vv. 22, 28, 32, 34, 39 and 44). In v. 31 the formula has only an apocopated form Ἐρρέθη δέ, and this, together with the relatedness of the topics (adultery and divorce) could be taken as a ground for linking this section with the previous one and reducing the number of illustrations from six to five. Matthew evidently likes odd numbers (3s, 5s and 7s) but should not be forced into displaying them where he may not have intended to!

Each of the examples of the new attitude to the Law is backed up by practical applications, though these will not be examined in great detail. Suffice it to say that the general effect is to internalise obedience to the Law.

This section ends in a brief summary which gives its teaching and challenge in a nutshell (5.48). Of the seven principles, the second, fourth, and sixth have these short summaries, which in each case are introduced by οὖν (5.48; 6.31–34; 7.12).

The Third Principle. This section runs from 6.1 through 6.18, and turns from the Law to religious practices. The principle is laid down in v. 1 that religious activity is to be directed towards God, not towards other men. This is then applied in the three areas of almsgiving (6.2–4), prayer (6.5–15) and fasting (6.16–18). Each area is introduced by a ὅταν clause, with a negative apodosis. The first and third have μὴ with a subjunctive (6.2, 16) and the second οὐκ with a future indicative (6.5). In each area, the behaviour expected of Jesus' followers is introduced with "but you" (6.3, 6, 17). Each application closes with a reference back to the principle itself, and a mention of the Father (6.4, 15, 18). The three applications are thus highly parallel in their internal structure. The biggest difference, as might be expected in a group of three, is in the middle one; this is the passage on prayer, which is considerably longer than the other two, and contains the "pattern prayer" of vv. 9–13 with its own clear internal structure. It consists of two balanced sets of three requests each (vv. 9c–10b and 11–13). In the first set are three third person aorist imperatives (ἁγιασθήτω, ἐλθέτω, γενηθήτω) and in the second, three second person aorist imperatives (δός, ἄφες, ῥῦσαι). The first three show an internal key pattern, the first and third having a passive verb form and a neuter noun subject, and the second an active verb form and a feminine noun subject. The qualifying phrase in v. 10c, ὡς ἐν οὐρανῷ καὶ ἐπὶ γῆς, probably goes with all three verbs, not just the last. It can be taken as balancing the invocation of v. 9b, so that this first strophe has a key pattern.

The second set has longer requests, but again an internal key pattern structure. In the first and third (vv. 11 and 13) the imperative comes near the end of the clause, with the qualifying material before the main verb. In the second (v. 12) the imperative comes at the beginning, with the qualifying material at the end. In all three there is the first person pronoun in both halves of the request (just as there was a second person pronoun in each request in the first set). In the first and third the pronoun comes once in each half, and in the second one, twice in each half.

The completeness of the structural pattern without the doxology might be seen as further evidence in support of its omission.

The Fourth Principle. This section, 6.19–34, deals with possessions in general, and especially money. Worldly wealth is contrasted with heavenly, and the latter extolled (6.19–20). These two verses have a parallel and antithetical structure, each with an imperative main clause and two descriptive subordinate clauses. Verse 19 has a negative main verb and positive subordinates and v. 20 a positive main verb and negative subordinates. This is so clear even on a casual reading that no diagram is called for. Verse 21 rounds off the principle with a reason which is also in a careful, epigrammatic, symmetrical form.

The rest of ch. 6 enlarges on this principle, and it is helpful here to distinguish illustrations (vv. 22–24) from applications (vv. 25–34).

The illustrations are in highly figurative language, and are usually presented as separate paragraphs. This makes the "light of the body" seem like an irrelevant intrusion, and breaks the clear train of thought linking vv. 19–21 with vv. 24ff. It will reduce the awkwardness if vv. 22–23 are linked with v. 24 as a double illustration of vv. 19–21. Internally vv. 22–23 show a 'diamond' pattern, with an opening general statement, a closing deduction, and in between an examination of the results of contradictory possibilities.

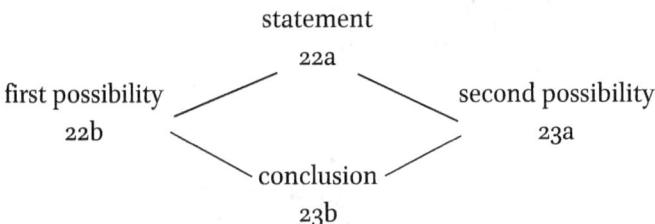

To make sense of the content in its context of talking about money, ἁπλοῦς and πονηρός are best taken as 'generous' and 'envious' respectively (cf. 20.15).[14] This yields a sort of word play in Greek which cannot be fully carried over into English because it would involve a (to us) incongruous mixture of metaphors. The two hypotheses of vv. 22b–23a might be rendered "If your outlook is generous, your whole life will be bright, but if your outlook is envious, your whole life will be gloomy."

---

[14] Allen (*Matthew, ad loc*) rightly observes that in Jewish idiom "a good eye" is a metaphor for liberality, "an evil eye" for niggardliness. Compare Deut 15:9; Prov 22:9 and 23:6; Ecclus 14:10: ὀφθαλμὸς πονερὸς (= Hebrew עַיִן רַע see Israel Levi, *The Hebrew Text of the Book of Ecclesiasticus* (Brill, 1951) φθονερὸς ἐπ ἄρτῳ / καὶ ἐλλιπὴς ἐπὶ τῆς τραπέζης αὐτοῦ (NEB: A miser grudges bread / and keeps an empty table); Pirqe Aboth 5.19 (for text and commentary see Charles Taylor, *Sayings of the Jewish Fathers* [Philo Press, 1970], 90–91): "There are four characters in almsgivers. He who is willing to give, but not that others should give, his eye is evil towards the things of others: that others should give, and he should not give, his eye is evil towards his, own .... As to the first character, he is clearly unwilling that others should share with him the credit of liberality." See also O. Bauernfeind: "Handelt es sich aber um sittliche Begriffe, dann ist ἁπλοῦς mit *lauter* zu übersetzen im Sinne einer opferbereiten Lauterkeit. Dafür spräche ... die Möglichkeit ὀφθαλμὸς ἁπλοῦς als einen spezifischen Gegensatz zu ὀφθαλμὸς πονηρός (="missgünstiges Auge") zu verstehen" (s.v. ἁπλοῦς in Kittel, *Theologisches Wörterbuch* 1:385). See further P. Fiebig, "Das Wort Jesu vom Auge," *Theologische Studien und Kritiken* 89 (1916): 499–507; C. Edlund, *Das Auge der Einfalt* (Ejnar Munksgaard, 1952).

Verse 24 can almost be seen as an explanation of vv. 22–23 in less cryptic language, in case the point has not got through. It has a similar internal structure to that of vv. 22–23, a general statement, a closing deduction, and in between, an examination of alternative possibilities. In this case the closing deduction is very clear both in its content and in its link with the principle expressed in vv. 19–21. For modern readers standing outside the cultural context in which the gospel was written, it also diminishes the opacity of the previous illustration. All three verses, 22–24, are saying that an obsession with money blights the life of the victim, and prevents him from serving God.

Verses 25 on are linked to what precedes in a type of converse causality. A craze for things precludes a full relationship with God: likewise, a trust in God precludes an anxiety over even the most basic physical needs of life—food and clothes. Anxiety over food is discussed in vv. 26–27 and over clothes in vv. 28–30.

This passage gives applications of the principle laid down in 6.19–21.[15] It opens with the basic application (v. 25a and b), for which a reason is given in interrogative form (v. 25c). (The way in which this is followed up with a two-

---

[15] The analysis may be set out as follows:

Base (v. 25) μὴ μεριμνᾶτε   (a) τῇ ψυχῇ ὑμῶν
                                  τί φάγητε
                           (b) μηδὲ τῷ σώματι ὑμῶν
                                  τί ἐνδύσησθε
Reason   (a) οὐχὶ ἡ ψυχὴ πλεῖόν ἐστι τῆς τροφῆς
            (b) καὶ τὸ σῶμα τοῦ ἐνδύματος
Illustration (a)
  Analogy (v. 26)   ἐμβλέψατε εἰς τὰ πετεινὰ τοῦ οὐρανοῦ
                      ὅτι οὐ σπείρουσιν οὐδὲ θερίζουσιν οὐδὲ συνάγουσιν εἰς
                      ἀποθήκας, καὶ ὁ πατὴρ ὑμῶν ὁ οὐράνιος τρέφει αὐτά·
  Application   οὐχ ὑμεῖς μᾶλλον διαφέρετε αὐτῶν;
  Conclusion (v. 27) τίς δὲ ἐξ ὑμῶν μεριμνῶν δύναται
                      προσθεῖναι ἐπὶ τὴν ἡλικίαν αὐτοῦ πῆχυν ἕνα;
Link (v. 28) καὶ περὶ ἐνδύματος τί μεριμνᾶτε;
Illustration (b)
  Analogy   καταμάθετε τὰ κρίνα τοῦ ἀγροῦ
                    πῶς οὐ ξαίνουσιν οὐδὲ νήθουσιν οὐδὲ κοπιῶσιν
                    (v. 29) λέγω δὲ ὑμῖν ὅτι οὐδὲ Σολομὼν ἐν πάσῃ
                    τῇ δόξῃ αὐτοῦ περιεβάλετο ὡς ἓν τούτων.
  Application (v. 30) εἰ δὲ τὸν χόρτον τοῦ ἀγροῦ σήμερον
                    ὄντα καὶ αὔριον εἰς κλίβανον βαλλόμενον ὁ θεὸς
                    οὕτως ἀμφιέννυσιν, οὐ πολλῷ μᾶλλον ὑμᾶς,
  Conclusion   ὀλιγόπιστοι;

fold illustration suggests the omission of ἢ τί πίητε as an analogical intrusion from v. 21.)

The twin needs of food and clothing are shown from analogies in nature to be areas where God's providence is to be expected. Each analogy is set up with a command and (especially if the reading of ℵ* f¹ 892 is followed) three parallel negative descriptions. The point is made that God supplies the natural needs, and the application of both analogies is made by *a fortiori* reasoning. In the first case, there is a further statement labelled a conclusion, and which in the second case seems to be balanced by the ὀλιγόπιστοι as a sort of challenge (cf. 8.26). The remaining clause (v. 28a) is a link from the base in v. 25 to the opening of the second analogy. The whole principle is then resumed in the summary which follows (vv. 31–34).

This is introduced by οὖν (cf. 5.48, 7.12). It is longer and more complex than the summaries of principles two or six, and indeed v. 34, with its own οὖν is almost a summary of the summary. Perhaps the added complexity is related to the fact that this is the central of the seven principles, and therefore an appropriate place for unique elaboration.

The Fifth Principle. The principle is laid down in 7.1, and its reason added in 7.2. The short section enlarging on this contains one expanded and rather humorous illustration, followed by the related double word-picture in the famous chiasmus of v. 6. Some texts, by having v. 6 start a new paragraph, imply that it stands apart from vv. 1–5. If the whole paragraph is viewed as one more example of a key pattern, perhaps a relationship may become clearer. If vv. 1 and 2 give the principle and vv. 3–5 the illustration, v. 6 gives a rider or qualification, so that the principle will not be misapplied.[16]

---

[16] The *mashal* v. 6 has, of course, rightly been isolated by source analysis and has been compared with Mandaean (see M. Lidzbarski, *Ginza* [Göttingen, 1925], Rechter Teil 7, p. 218, 30: "The words of the wise to the fool are as pearls for a swine") and Parthian parallels (see G. Widengren, *Iranisch-semitische Kulturbegegnung in parthischer Zeit* [Opladen, 1960], 36). Also an Aramaic approach has been made to this saying which is peculiar to Matthew (see especially Matthew Black, *An Aramaic Approach to the Gospels and Acts* [Clarendon Press, 1971], 200–201). It has been argued that, formally this verse forms part of a group of three prohibitions: μὴ θησαυρίζετε (6.19); μὴ κρίνετε (7.11) and μὴ δῶτε (7.6). It has also been said that this saying has no particular connection with the preceding and that it simply may have stood here in the Logia (so Allen, *Matthew, ad loc*). Though this may be true on the level of source analysis, discourse analysis may be able to provide a more satisfactory answer with regard to the semantic relationships.

Principle	Illustration	Rider
vv. 1–2	vv. 3–5	v. 6

The principle is "Don't be hypercritical" and the rider is "But don't fail to be discriminating." It would be hard to find a more concise exposition of how to handle everyday interpersonal relationships!

The Sixth Principle. This section is structurally similar to the previous one—the principle briefly stated 7.7 (cf. 7.1), justified 7.8 (cf. 7.2), illustrated 7.9–11a (cf. 7.3–5) and concluded 7.11b (cf. 7.6). It is an *a fortiori* argument—if even sinful human beings give good things to their children, how much greater is God's willingness to do the same for those who ask him.

Verse 12, a summary with οὖν (cf. 5.48, 6.31–34), extends the principle as seen in the illustration from the limited realm of family relationships to the general realm of communal life, and again the point is clinched with a reference to the OT. To reflect God's attitudes towards us in our attitudes towards others is indeed the pith of the Law and the Prophets. Thus this summary, like those following principles two and four, broadens the scope of the teaching in the preceding section. The consideration of the Law leads to the demand for total imitation of God's character (5.48); the consideration of legitimate human needs leads to the demand for total trust in God's providence (6.34); and the consideration of God's generosity leads to the demand for a total reflection of his attitudes (7.12).

The Seventh Principle. After six principles dealing, in general, with the ethics of the kingdom, the seventh principle speaks of entry into the kingdom. Perhaps significantly in the light of 13.10–17, this is the only one of the seven principles to be expressed wholly in figurative language. The principle itself is given very tersely in v. 13a, while vv. 13b and 14 show constrastive parallelism in their double-barreled expansion of the principle. The reading ὅτι in v. 14 would make the parallelism even closer, but even reading τί it is still very close.

Verses 15–23 show the principle of entry to the kingdom at work on two levels. Verses 15–20 describe would-be leaders who have failed to enter the narrow gate and are therefore false; and vv. 21–23 describe would-be followers who have failed to enter the narrow gate, and are therefore false. These are typical of the many who travel the broad and easy road, and are identified primarily by their deeds (vv. 20, 21).

In the first application (vv. 15–20), the false prophets are given one brief pictorial characterisation (v. 15), then the metaphor is abruptly changed for the rest of the paragraph. The means of identification is stated in v. 16a, two specific cases are given in v. 16b, and the two-sided generalisation arising from this follows in v. 17 and v. 18. A consequence is asserted in v. 19, and the means of identification repeated in v. 20.[17] There is thus quite a complex recursive pattern, with formal and semantic elements closely interwoven. This section may be displayed as a pattern of inverted parallelism.

Means	v. 16a
Specific cases	v. 16b
Double generalisation	vv. 17–18
Consequence	v. 19
Means	v. 20

It is interesting to see that at least one modern translation (TEV) seems to have reacted to the text in this same way, in that it has dropped the metaphor in the outer layer (vv. 16a and 20) but retained it in the inner layers (vv. 16b–19).

The second application (vv. 21–23) is structurally very different, and is the only piece of the whole sermon which has dialogue form (5.22 and 7.4 are not dialogue, because although there is direct speech, there is only one participant). Is not the extra vividness introduced by this change particularly effective here in the mounting climax of the sermon? The final principle is dealing with the $64 thousand question of entry to the kingdom. The first application has considered would-be leaders. Not all aspire to leadership, but here in the final thrust, the scope is widened to take in all who would follow. And the personal nature of the challenge is surely heightened by putting it in the form of a face to face confrontation with the Son. So much for the use of dialogue form at this point. Internally, the structure is simple, a generic statement in v. 21, with a single example of its application, through a single utterance-response pair. The triple claim of the false followers is dismissed by the single refutation and sentence of the Son.[18]

---

[17] Compare Bultmann, *Geschichte,* 99: V 16a (ist) eine Übergangsbildung, die den Zusammenhang mit "... V 15 herstellt. V 16b ist überliefertes Logion, aber V 17 ist eine pedantische Neubildung, der bei Lk nichts entspricht, und die den in Q vorhandenen Zusammenhang zwischen V 16b und V 18 stört."

[18] It is interesting to consider the possibility of a link between the first seven beatitudes and the seven principles. The 'poor in Spirit' of 5.3 may be seen as those who, lacking great

2.2.3. *The Peroration*

The last few verses of the sermon give the final, overall summary, again introduced by οὖν (cf. 5.48; 6.31–34; 7.12). Their relevance to the sermon as a whole is evidenced by their very general mention of μου τοὺς λόγους τούτους (vv. 24, 26). And in their position as a final challenge, they invite a response

---

personal pride, are willing to rely on Jesus, and if necessary, be ill-treated for doing so. In this very situation they experience the rewards (v. 12) of the kingdom of heaven (v. 3). In the second beatitude, if the mourners are those who mourn over their own sins, it is not inappropriate to link them with the new attitude to the Law shown in the second principle. This new attitude can leave no-one in doubt about the state of his own heart. In the third pair, the 'meek' of the beatitude are those who are not concerned with human evaluation of them, and who will receive "what God has promised" (5.5, TEV), i.e., the rewards spoken of in 6.4, 6 and 18. The fourth beatitude (5.6) which speaks of hungering and thirsting for righteousness, forms a contrastive parallel with the fourth principle, where anxiety for food and drink is repudiated. It is those whose dependence on God is strong enough to be comparable with their dependence on physical nourishment who find full and true satisfaction. The 'merciful' of the fifth beatitude link readily with those in the fifth principle who are not over-critical of others. They will find the mercy of God because they show mercy to their fellows. The subjects of the sixth beatitude are those whose hearts are pure. These will ask the right things from God, and of the good things he wants to give, what better than the unimpaired vision (5.8) of himself? The seventh beatitude links with the seventh principle in that it speaks of those whom God will acknowledge as his true sons. Those who 'make peace' between their fellows are surely following the example of Christ (cf. Col 1.20, the only other NT occurrence of this root), and thus walking in the narrow way, and being identified by their fruit. This leaves the eighth beatitude as a summary of the first seven, a statement of what happens to people who come in the first seven categories (note the passive participle δεδιωγμένοι). It is also a semantic link with the first of the principles that immediately follows.

We might diagram the links thus:

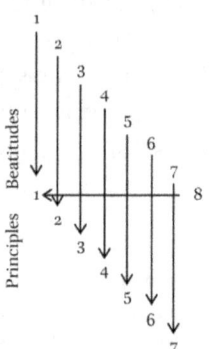

It is important to note that the total analysis of the Sermon does not depend upon the acceptance or rejection of this suggestion of links between the beatitudes and the principles.

from *all* who hear. The theme of response is one which assumes increasing centrality as the gospel proceeds. The two-fold possibility of obeying or disobeying Jesus is shown in the two-fold simile of housebuilding. The two halves are very closely matched in structure, for apart from the punch lines, and lexical changes and negative/positive changes necessary to the sense, the only other difference is between the relative clauses in v. 24 and the participial clauses in v. 26. In typical parabolic fashion, the challenge is given only through the simile, and is not elaborated. Thus the sermon ends.

The introductory words of 5.1–2 are balanced by the narrative comment of 7.28–29, which contains the D-block closing formula, and a note on reaction to Jesus' words. The recurrence of διδάσκων (v. 29) is another glimpse back to 4.23. But whereas in 4.24–25, the reaction to Jesus' activities is rather neutral, here it is recorded as the more positive one of amazement, because of his authoritative pronouncements.

2.2.4. Summary of the D Block

The D Block consists then of an exordium, a main section of seven principles, and a peroration. The exordium consists of eight beatitudes, the eighth of which serves topically as a link between the exordium and the beginning of the main section. Within the main section, there is a symmetry of arrangement in that principles two, four and six have appended a summary (S) introduced by οὖν.

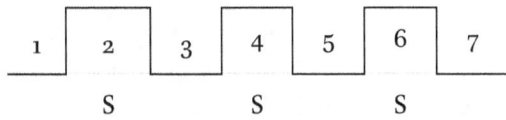

Each Statement of a principle is reinforced by various illustrations and/or applications. With one major exception, these too are of symmetrical distribution.

1	2	3	4	5	6	7
2 Ill			2 Ill.	3 Ill.	2 Ill.	
	6 App.	3 App.	2 App.			2 App.

Apart from the six applications of principle 2, the numbers of illustrations/applications are balanced around the fulcrum of the fourth principle.

There is a second type of balance in that the fourth principle is the only one to be followed both by illustrations and applications. It is preceded by one illustrated principle and two applied principles, and followed by two illustrated principles and one applied principle.

2.3. Formal Division of the 2nd N Block

On the ground of the sense connections of the various incidents recorded in this block (8.1–9.38), it seems most appropriate to divide it into four scenes, which will be labelled in continuing sequence from the end of ch 4. The main (but not exclusive) emphasis of this block is on healing, as we would expect from the programme outlined in 4.23. Scene 3 includes 8.1–17, an account of three healing miracles. Scene 4, 8.18–34, links three episodes at first sight disparate, but actually related in terms of the reactions to Jesus that they record. Scene 5 (9.1–17) links another three episodes apparently unrelated but actually linked in terms of the teaching for which Jesus uses them as a launching-pad. Scene 6 (9.18–34) contains three more healing miracles, and 9.35–38 is a transition paragraph which is an epilogue to Act 1, recapitulating the programme laid down in 4.23, and pointing towards the widening ministry of Act 2. Although each scene holds three episodes, this was not contrived for convenience, but rather, arose from the sense links.

2.3.1. Scene 3

This scene is marked off from the D block by a change of location (8.1) and concluded by a clinching OT formula quotation peculiar to Matthew (8.17). The three episodes involve the healing of a leper (8.1–4), the healing of the centurion's servant (8.5–13), and the healing of Peter's mother-in-law and others (8.14–17). The first two episodes begin with a genitive absolute, and the third with a nominative participle. The key pattern is again apparent in various ways. There are short initial and final episodes, enclosing a longer middle one. In the first and third episodes, Jesus deals with Jews, and the episodes are appropriately closed by a reference to the OT (8.4, 17). In the second episode, Jesus deals with a Gentile, and there is no closing reference to the OT. In this episode there are two utterance-response pairs between Jesus and the centurion 8.6–9, 13, but they are interrupted by an "aside" from Jesus to the crowd, drawing a lesson from the centurion's words. This lesson holds up a Gentile as an example of faith to the Jews, and includes reference to the OT. This interruption of the dialogue flow for didactic purposes anticipates the recording of incidents purely for their didactic value in Scene 5. In this scene, however, the absence of teaching in the first and third episodes, and its incidental introduction in the second, show that in this scene the emphasis is on resuming the theme of healing announced in 4.23, and thus establishing Jesus' role as a healer, and concomitant fulfilment of Messianic prophecy.[19]

2.3.2. Scene 4

This scene is both marked off externally from others by changes of location, and bound together internally by the same means. In 8.18 Jesus orders a change to escape from the crowds, and in 8.34 the Gadarenes request him to leave, which he does in 9.1. Internally, the first episode (8.18–22) takes place between the time of the decision to move (8.18) and its execution (8.23). The second episode takes place on the journey, and the third immediately following its conclusion (8.28).

This scene introduces a new theme, in that each of its episodes focuses on people's response to Jesus. This is an appropriate point to introduce such a change, for his reputation as teacher (chs. 5–7) and healer (8.1–17) has now been firmly established. In the first episode people say "We want to follow" and in the last "We don't want to follow." In between, those who are following ask "What kind of man is this?" There is thus a sort of progression from a positive reaction to a neutral reaction to a negative reaction. The neutral, interrogative reaction of the second episode is the climax of that episode, and left as it is as an unanswered question, it invites reader participation. Probably any literature which tries to carry a message uses the technique of the unanswered question (or more precisely, the implicitly answered question) to stimulate reader involvement.

There seems to be much less obvious internal structure in these three ep-

---

[19] We might note in passing the variety of verbs used of the healing process, as they seem to have both a hierarchical domain structure and limitations imposed by syntagmatic constraints. θεραπεύω seems to be the most generic term and is used in the general contexts of 4.23 and 9.35. In the specific incidents, certain verbs seem to be colligated with certain diseases. Leprosy requires καθαρίζω (8.2, 3), spirits require ἐκβάλλω (8.16). Paralysis (8.6) seems to require θεραπεύω though in keeping with its generic nature, this verb is also used with the vague πάντας τοὺς κακῶς ἔχοντας in 8.16. Where the emphasis is on the restoration rather than the disease, the passive of ἰάομαι is used (8.8, 13, cf. also 10.8).

isodes, though there is something of a chain sequence in the lengthy narrative episode 3. Finally, it may be noted that each episode is introduced by a participial clause, only the last being a genitive absolute. The significance of this case as against others in participial constructions seems to be one of focus.[20] (See Appendix B.)

2.3.3. Scene 5

The three episodes of this scene are linked in that they are recorded not so much for their intrinsic value as for the reaction they provoked, and the resultant teaching given by Jesus. The whole of this scene (and the next) is set somewhat vaguely in "his own city" (9.1), presumably Capernaum, but the exact locations are not prominent. The second episode opens with a participial clause (9.9) and closes with an OT reference (9.13).[21] The third episode opens with τότε, and is separated from the beginning of Scene 6 by the genitive absolute with which that scene starts (9.18). This is a structural break: semantically, the end of Scene 5 and the beginning of Scene 6 are closely linked in their time sequence.

In episode 1, Jesus is shown as deliberately provoking a confrontation with the scribes by his claim to forgive sins (9.2). The healing of the paralysed man is almost incidental, and serves merely to substantiate Jesus' claim, and face the scribes with the need to change their view.

In the second episode, the teaching arises out of the situation more readily. Matthew's calling and response simply provide the setting for the meal with the tax collectors and sinners. Jesus' association with such people is used as an object lesson about God, and about the purpose of Jesus' ministry.

In the third episode, there is a question from John's disciples, which is the springboard for the teaching in the three-fold metaphor of the wedding party, the new cloth and the new wine.

---

[20] Already Bultmann (*Geschichte*, 376) noted the importance of the participle clause: "Ebenso oft (as the genitive absolute) steht das *Participium coniunctum* das durch Bezugnahme auf das Vorige die Verbindung herstellt ... Gelegentlich enstaht aus einer solchen Bildung eine kleine Szene; so 8,18, wo Mt von dem summarischen Bericht der Krankenheilungen 8,16f zu den Apophthegmen von der Nachfolge durch den Satz überleitet: ἰδὼν δὲ ὁ Ἰησοῦς...." However, the difficult and important questions of focus have never been dealt with before.

[21] This quotation from Hos 6.6 also is peculiar to Matthew, but it lacks the introductory formula of fulfilment.

2.3.4. Scene 6

As remarked already, the beginning of Scene 6 is temporally closely linked with the end of Scene 5, but is structurally set off by its initial genitive absolute. The scene has three episodes, the first and third initiated by a genitive absolute (9.18, 32) and the second by a participial clause in the dative (9.27). Each episode involves further instances of healing. The remaining verses (9.35–38) serve as a sort of epilogue to round off this particular N Block, and indeed the whole of Act 1.

The first episode (9.18–26) is perhaps the archetypal example of a key pattern, imposed in this case probably not for the sake of artistic design, but as a reflection of the actual events. The synoptic writers all agree that the woman with the haemorrage touched Jesus between the time of the official's request and Jesus' arrival at the man's house. It seems right to treat this section as a composite episode with its own further internal structure, rather than as two separate episodes. The focus is upon the healing but the result of the raising of the official's daughter was, not surprisingly, a further increase of Jesus' reputation.

In the second episode, it is important to note the reactions of the blind men; they both express faith in Jesus and address him as 'Son of David.' This recognition is the object of the strong ἐνεβριμήθη in v. 30. In the third episode, the actual healing is rapidly dismissed (9.33a) in order to concentrate on the result.

This is conveyed effectively in a two-fold reaction which is a fitting climax to Act 1, and at the same time a shadow of things to come. From the crowds came the wondering acknowledgement that such events were utterly unprecedented (9.33). But from the religious leaders came the willful blindness of attributing these miracles to powers demonic rather than divine.

The closing paragraph 9.35–38 joins together again the twin avenues opened up in 4.23 and explored in chs. 5–7 and 8–9 (9.35). In the closing verses (9.36–38) the sight of the helpless crowds is the stimulus to the prayer for more workers to gather them into God's kingdom. In this thought lies the link with the opening section of Act 2, in which the disciples are sent out to share in and enlarge the reach of Jesus' ministry.

2.3.5. Summary of 2nd N Block

This block contains four scenes, each with three episodes. They may be viewed as follows:

Scene 3	3 plain healing miracles (8.1–17)
Scene 4	3 instances of reaction to Jesus (8.18–34)
Scene 5	3 causes of opposition to Jesus (9.1–17)
Scene 6	1 healing, 1 reaction, 1 opposition (9.18–34)

and could be diagrammed thus:

Scene 3	Scene 4	Scene 5	Scene 6		
3 Eps. of healing	3 Eps. of reaction	3 Eps. of opposition	1 Ep. healing	1 Ep. reaction	1 Ep. opposition

This arrangement shows the thematic unity of the whole block, and reveals Scene 6 as thematically focal. The healing miracle it contains is in fact a raising from death, the only one in this gospel, and a fitting pinnacle to the healings in Scene 3. The 'reaction' is the blind men's recognition of Jesus as 'Son of David,' a theme suppressed by Jesus here, but accepted at the end of his ministry in 20.29–21.17. The 'opposition' is the ultimate blasphemy of attributing Jesus' power to a demonic source, a theme developed in Act 2. Thus the picture suggested here makes the analysis of chs. 8 and 9 both internally coherent, and externally relevant to the total development of the gospel.

2.4. Summary of Act 1

At this point it may be helpful to summarise what we have found in Act 1 in diagram form. In each scene, the episodes are linked, usually somewhat loosely, in a chain pattern, which for simplicity is omitted from the diagram. Arrows indicate a link of sense and ⊓ indicates a key pattern linking the units embraced, or the constituent parts of an episode if written below its number. ⇧ indicates that an episode has two parts. The summary in diagram form is found on the following page.

Summary of Act 1

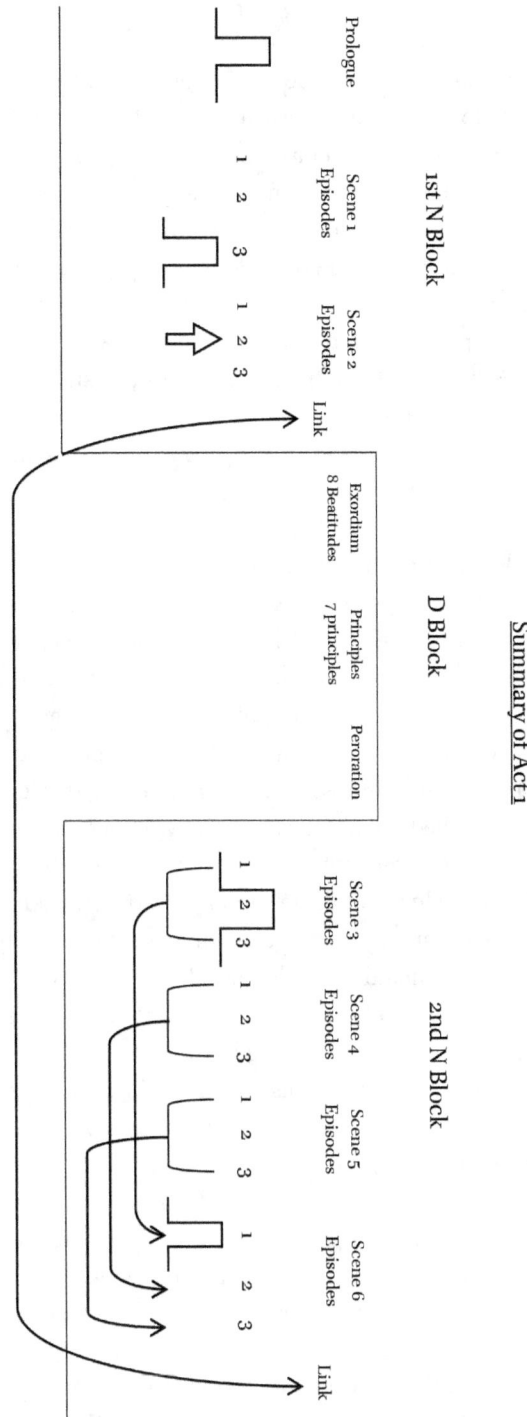

3. Act 2

Act 2 is taken as embracing chs. 10–18. It contains three separate D Blocks enclosing two N Blocks, in the pattern ⌋D⌊N⌋D⌊N⌋D⌊. The three D Blocks (using only chapter numbers for simplicity) are chs. 10, 13, and 18. In terms of the blocks, then, the double key pattern has already been noted.

Now it is worthy of comment that Matthew alone of the evangelists makes any significant use of repetition. Mark and John apparently do not use repetition at all, and Luke has only a couple of occurrences, whereas in Matthew topics are repeated, often with very similar wording, in a number of important places. This can be noticed most readily in such occurrences as ch. 5 and ch. 23 with their formulaic repetitions, and in the closing formula used to end each of the five D Blocks. But it occurs also in a number of places where it seems to be structurally significant, e.g., 4.23 = 9.35; 9.34 = 12.24 (cf. also 10.25); 12.38, 39 = 16.1, 4; 9.27–31 = 20.29–34.[22]

The particular themes of interest in Act 2 are those of John the Baptist, and of the demand for a sign. The first demand for a sign is in 12.38, and initiates a lengthy response from Jesus. This interchange is seen as the climax of a series of clashes in ch. 12, and as a suitable break as the end of a scene. The demand is repeated at the beginning of ch. 16, and is again refused. Yet almost all the narrative material between these two points consists of signs, signs more dramatic and impressive than the healing miracles of chs. 8 and 9. They include the feeding of the 5,000, the walking on the water, and the feeding of the 4,000. The repeated demands can, then, be viewed as semantic parentheses, or an inclusio, and the material between them taken as some kind of unit in itself. This argument gains force from the fact that Matthew is the only gospel which includes the demand for a sign twice. The very repetition suggests structural significance in the development of the story.

John the Baptist is mentioned at the beginning of ch. 11, and at the beginning of ch. 14. In the first instance, his question from prison leads Jesus into a lengthy discussion of the role and significance of John, and in the second instance, John's death is reported. Both of these occurrences are at the beginning of the units suggested above, and this is at least congruent with the use of John's ministry as an opening theme in Act 1, Scene 2. John is also mentioned in ch. 17, following the transfiguration, where he is identified with the Elijah of the eschatological interpretation of the scribes. This is not by

---

[22] There are also echoes here and there which seem to be less important, such as 5.29, 30 = 18.8, 9; 7.16–20 = 12.33; 9.13 = 12.7; 10.22 = 24.9, 13; 10.38, 39 = 16.24, 25.

any standards at the beginning of a new scene. Rather it is near the end of an N Block before the D Block of ch. 18. Of this, more later.

If this hypothetical division of the N Blocks is accepted, the units will be as follows: 11.2–12.45; 14.1–15.38; 16.1–17.?. On this scheme, the second N Block, which is a lot longer than the first, breaks almost exactly in half, so we can bear in mind the possibility of regarding the N Blocks as effectively three rather than two (cf. the uncertainty over the number of episodes in Act 1, Scene 2).

Now it will be noticed that a small amount of material remains unallocated – 12.46–50; 13.53–58; and a rather fuzzy-edged area at the end of ch. 17. References to the exact extent of the D Blocks have up to this point been somewhat loose, and have been only to chapter numbers: in Act 2, this means chs. 10, 13 and 18. As was noted in section 1.3 the N Blocks have some kind of priority over the D Blocks, since the latter are not self-explanatory, and must be embedded in some kind of narrative framework to give them an explicative context. We must now examine the extent of the embedding of the D Blocks. In Act 1 this question was passed over, since the sole D Block presented no real problems in this direction. The immediate setting is very brief (5.1–2; 7.28–29), but it is able to be so because a broader setting has already been established in 4.23–25. This was recapitulated in 9.35–38, and the latter passage, which includes the prayer for harvest workers, can be seen as the broader setting for the D Block of ch. 10.[23] Following this prayer, Jesus selects his workers (10.1–4) and thus these strictly speaking narrative verses form the immediate setting in which the mission charge is embedded (10.5–42). 11.1 is the closing setting. Thus although the actual monologue runs only from 10.5–42, the total D Block is best regarded as 10.1–11.1 (just as in Act 1, the D Block is 5.1–7.29, though the monologue is only 5.3–7.27).

This may seem to be labouring a point which is obvious, but it must be clearly made in order to apply it to the odd sections of Act 2 that are as yet unaccounted for. The D Block of ch. 13 differs from the previous D Blocks in that in addition to the immediate setting material of 13.1–3a, 53, it also contains *internal* setting material (13.10–11a, 24a, 31a, 34–37a, 51b–52a). It is here

---

[23] Indeed, it would be quite possible to regard the paragraphs 4.23–25 and 9.35–38 as part of the extended setting of the first and second D Blocks. Syntactically, such an analysis might even be preferable, but in this paper, the importance of the verbatim repetition of 4.23 in 9.35 for the thematic development of Act 1 as a whole has been the overriding consideration, and these two paragraphs have been allocated to the 'embedding' N Blocks rather than to the 'embedded' D Blocks.

viewed as differing also in containing wider setting material, namely 12.46–50 and 13.53–58. In both of these incidents, members of the immediate nuclear family of Jesus are featured. In the first, Jesus uses their presence to show how spiritual relationships transcend physical ones. In the second, the people of Nazareth use their presence as an excuse for recognizing nothing beyond Jesus' natural relationships. These two incidents, then, form a complementary and appropriate setting for the D Block whose main elements concern the growth of the kingdom of heaven, i.e., the manner in which human relationships can be changed and transcended.

The D Block in ch. 18, in addition to the immediate setting material of vv. 1–3a and 19.1–2, also has an internal setting piece in 18.21–22a. The last incident of the previous chapter, 17.24–27 is also here regarded as part of the D Block setting. If attached to what precedes, it forms a strange anticlimax after the transfiguration, the healing of the demoniac boy, and the second passion prediction. Furthermore it contains two important topical links with the opening verses of ch. 18. The σκανδαλίσωμεν of 17.27 is resumed six times in 18.6–9, and also Jesus' words about kings and their sons (17.25–26) lead very naturally into the disciples' question of 18.1 which is otherwise abrupt and unmotivated. We may also note both the close temporal link of 18.1 with what preceded, and the repetition of the particle ἄρα in 17.26 and 18.1.[24]

A certain amount of support for the foregoing suggestions may be gained from the pattern of the resultant pieces. We may now divide the whole act into three reasonably well balanced and reasonably homogeneous units. Each unit consists of a D Block plus an N Block or half-block. Giving the precise verse divisions, the three units are as follows:

D Block (10.1–11.1) + N Block (11.2–12.45)
D Block (12.46–13.58) + 1/2 N Block (14.1–15.39)
1/2 N Block (16.1–17.23) + D Block (17.24–19.2)

In diagram form (abbreviated), this is
D + N | D+ 1/2 N | 1/2 N + D

---

[24] ἄρα is used three times in this act: in Mt 12.28; 17.26; 18.1. In the first text, it occurs in synoptic parallel with Lk 11.20. But in the case of 17.26 synoptic parallels are lacking since 17.24–27 is peculiar to Matthew, whereas in the Marcan and Lucan parallels to 18.1 ἄρα is not used at all. For the suspense marker ἄρα see especially Kenneth Willis Clark, "The Meaning of ἄρα," in *Festschrift to Honor F. Wilbur Gingrich, Lexicographer, Scholar, Teacher, and Committed Christian Layman*, eds. Eugene Howard Barth and Ronald Edwin Cocroft (Brill, 1972), 70–85.

To obtain a key pattern of the type familiar from Act 1, the unit with the deviant order of elements ought to be the middle one. However we have already noted that *semantically*, the demand for a sign, coming at the end of the N in the first unit, and at the beginning of the 1/2 N in the third unit, encloses the whole of the second unit in 'thematic brackets.'

The N section of the first unit and the 1/2 N section of the second unit both begin with reference to John the Baptist, while the third reference to John comes almost at the end of the 1/2 N section in the third unit. That is to say that the unit with the reversed sequence of elements also displays a reversed position of its reference to John.

3.1. Formal Division of the First D Block

It has already been noted that the exact extent of the D Block is 10.1–11.1, and that 10.1–4 and 11.1 comprise the setting for the actual monologue of 10.5–42. The opening setting gives Jesus' choice of 12 disciples, and is a kind of answer to his suggested prayer of 9.38 for more workers. The 12 are given a share in Jesus' ἐξουσία (v. 1), and in the occurrence of this word, there is perhaps a backward glance to the closing setting of the previous D Block in 7.29. Verses 10.2–4 give the names of the 12, and it is interesting to observe the occurrence of such a list at precisely this point, where it is the equivalent of the genealogy at the beginning of Act 1.

The actual monologue of 10.5–42 can be divided into four sections three of which have the phrase ἀμὴν λέγω ὑμῖν in their final sentence. The sections then consist of vv. 5–15, 16–23, 24–33 and 34–42. The third of these is the one which lacks the ἀμὴν λέγω ὑμῖν, and also cuts across the usual paragraph breaks.

The first section is concerned with the practical aspects of the mission. The disciples are told where to go (vv. 5–6), what to say and do (vv. 7–8), what preparations to make (vv. 9–10), and how to interact with their hearers and/or hosts (vv. 11–14). The final verse sums up the fate of those who reject the messengers and their message (v. 15) and receives emphasis from the formula ἀμὴν λέγω ὑμῖν to which attention has already been drawn.

The second section deals with the psychological aspects of the mission. Despite Jesus' warning in v. 15, many people will reject the message, and this paragraph forewarns and forearms the disciples. Verse 16 speaks of the attitudes required from them for the mission. The hostile treatment they will receive is made clear (vv. 17–18), as is the help they can expect from God (vv.

19–20). Despite the divisive effects of the message, the disciples will require a resilient endurance (vv. 21–23). They can carry on in the assurance that the task will not become impossible before some cryptic eschatological intervention. Again the final assurance gains added emphasis from the ἀμὴν λέγω ὑμῖν formula.

There is no compelling reason for linking vv. 24–25 with the preceding verses, whereas the οὖν at the beginning of v. 26 suggest that they are to be closely linked with vv. 26–31. In the same manner the οὖν in v. 32 serves to give a closer link between vv. 24–31 and 32–33 than some editions of the Greek text allow.

If the second section gives the disciples the emotional equipment to face the rejection of the message, the third section gives them the intellectual equipment for reconciling this rejection with the content of the message – ἤγγικεν ἡ βασιλεία τῶν οὐρανῶν (v. 7). Not that a full rationalization is given, but vv. 24–25 point to the rejection of the king himself as the key to the understanding of the rejection of the kingdom. The reference to Beelzebul in v. 25 harks back to 9.34, and looks on to 12.24. (The occurrence of this motif here is perhaps intended to show how deeply this insult had affected Jesus. It gives strength to the view that 9.34 is a fitting climax to the first Act.) If Jesus himself (the διδάσκαλος, κύριος and οἰκοδεσπότης vv. 24–25) could endure such rejection, then *a fortiori*, the disciples can expect nothing better. Like Jesus they should fear God rather than men (v. 28) for he knows all and will eventually set everything in its right perspective (v. 26). In light of this, those who trust Jesus publicly can be confident of a final public vindication, while those who do not trust him can expect only a final public rejection (vv. 32–33). This division makes the section vv. 24–33 into a more coherently argued unit than other paragraph breaks would. If the use in this D Block of the ἀμὴν λέγω ὑμῖν formula as a paragraph closure indicator is valid, the question may be raised why it does not occur in v. 33. The answer suggested is that it would give too strong a semantic clash with the ἀρνήσομαι κἀγὼ which is already present.[25]

---

[25] The threefold (!) formula has a synoptic parallel only in the occurrence at 10.42 (Mk 9.41). The two other instances are peculiar to Matthew who shows a strong preference for the use of the introductory ἀμήν in the sayings of Jesus: thirty occurrences in Matthew over against thirteen in Mark and only six in Luke (see Heinrich Schlier, s.v. ἀμήν in *Theologisches Wörterbuch zum Neuen Testament*, ed. Kittel, 1:341). Though the suggestion made in the case of 10.33 can be taken into consideration, it is, of course, true that the saying had a particular form in the Logia source (compare Lk 12.9) which may have made this kind of change undesirable.

The final section (vv. 34–42) speaks of the spiritual demands of the mission upon its proponents (v. 34). It will provoke painful decisions about priorities in both the closest personal relationships (vv. 35–37) and in the individual experience (v. 38). Yet the right decisions will validate themselves contrary to all natural expectations (v. 39). The closing verses (vv. 40–42) are something like an epilogue summarizing the results of the mission. Despite the opposition mentioned earlier, there will be those who receive and in their reception will find present blessing (v. 40) and future reward (v. 42). The certainty of this outcome is again emphasized with the formula ἀμὴν λέγω ὑμῖν.

A certain amount of parallelism can be observed between section 1 and section 2, and between section 3 and section 4. Perhaps this will be seen most easily if set out in parallel columns.

vv.	Section 1	Section 2	vv.
5–6	Imperatives Animal Analogy πρόβατα	Imperatives Animal analogies πρόβατα λύκοι, ὄφεις, περιστεραί	16–17a
7–8	Content of the mission	Reaction to the mission	17b–18
9–10	Absence of physical anxiety	Absence of emotional anxiety	19–20
11–14	Reactions to the messenger	Reactions to the messenger	21–22
15	Eschatological implications	Eschatological implications	23
	Section 3	**Section 4**	
24–25	Analogies from human relationships	Analogies from human relationships	34–36
26–31	Whom to fear	Whom to love	37–39
32–33	Eschatological implications	Eschatological implications	40–42

Some of these labels are perhaps a bit vague, but the fact that they can be given at all lends a certain amount of *a posteriori* support to the original division into these sections. It is also interesting to observe the prominence of eschatological considerations at the end of each of the four sections. This is unlikely to be accidental.

3.2. Formal Division of the First N Block (Scene 1)

Each N or 1/2 N block in Act 2 can be said to constitute a scene. Small divisions can be made, though they tend not to be so clear cut as in Act 1. This is because the focus of attention is often more on the discussion arising out of an incident than on the incident itself. The label 'episode' is therefore sometimes less appropriate than it was in Act 1, but is retained to avoid multiplying terminology.

Scene 1 is coterminous with the first N Block of Act 2 and runs from 11.2–12.45. It may be divided into five episodes, after the third of which there occurs a brief editorial comment which we label an interlude. Other divisions are possible and are discussed as they arise.

Episode 1 is the longest and most complex, and is taken to embrace 11.2–30, i.e., the whole of ch. 11 apart from the first verse. A brief historical incident leads into a lengthy monologue from Jesus which can be further divided. The incident is the question from the imprisoned John via his disciples as to whether Jesus is ὁ ἐρχόμενος. Perhaps the reference to Messiahship was made in such a veiled way for political reasons.[26] Anyway, the conditions he found himself in seem to have removed the certainty John showed in 3.14–15 about Jesus' true identity. Jesus' reply to the messengers is couched in prophetic language reminiscent of Isaiah, and they depart, apparently satisfied with an answer as veiled as the question (v. 7a).

Then begins the monologue. In light of the various pieces of setting material, it can be divided into three parts, with successively decreasing connection with John (11.7b–19; 11.21–24; 11.25b–30). The first part is spoken to the crowds (v. 7a) and the second has no audience specified, though the crowds could still be in view. The third part, overfamiliar for its spiritual content, is a curious mixture of prayer to God and invitation to people,[27] though whether

---

[26] The phrase ὁ ἐρχόμενος may allude to Ps 118.26 (see the quotation of this text in Mt 21.9) or perhaps to the Theodotion reading of Dan 7.13 (see Joseph Ziegler, *Susanna–Daniel–Bel et Draco* (Vandenhoeck & Ruprecht, 1954, *ad loc*). It is certain that the reference is to the Messiah, but it is impossible to know exactly to what extent the expression was· a veiled one for the first receptors, since no one can precisely tell how much of the rabbinic teachings with regard to ὁ ἐρχόμενος were common knowledge at that time. For these teachings see especially H. L. Strack and P. Billerbeck, *Kommentar zum Neuen Testament aus Talmud und Midrasch* (C. H. Beck'sche Verlagsbuchhandlung, 1956), 4:872ff.

[27] The fact that the invitation is fully lacking in the Lucan parallel and that the character of v. 27 is so distinct, has led to the assumption that the three strophes of vv. 25–30 did not belong together originally. So v. 27 has been attributed to a Hellenistic source (see, among oth-

the same crowds are still involved is not clear. Anyway, vv. 28–30 presuppose listeners, despite the apparent ignoring of them in vv. 25–27.

The first part, vv. 7b–19, falls into two paragraphs. The first discusses, in continuingly cryptic terms, the significance of John, and attributes to him a unique role in the *Heilsgeschichte*. He is a prophet, and more; he is apparently the one whose coming signals the end of the old era. In v. 15 Jesus challenges his hearers to try to grasp the inner import of his words. 11.16–19 reproaches the inconsistency of hearers who manufacture excuses for rejecting the spiritual challenge both of John's asceticism and of Jesus' liberal associations. Verses 18–19 are broadly parallel in structure, the main divergence coming in the quoted words δαιμόνιον ἔχει (v. 18) and ἰδοὺ ... ἁμαρτωλῶν (v. 19). This could be because the words are actual verbatim quotes rather than summaries of typical excuses. The final sentence of v. 19 ἐδικαιώθη ἡ σοφία ἀπὸ τῶν ἔργων αὐτῆς evaluates the ministry of both John and Jesus in figurative terms.

The second part of the monologue, 11.20–24, leads on from the reproaches of vv. 16–19. Specific towns are castigated for their failure to understand and respond to the miracles done within them. Verses 21–22 are closely parallel to vv. 23–24. In the first, Chorazin and Bethsaida are contrasted with Tyre and Sidon, and in the second Capernaum is contrasted with Sodom. The asymmetry of having pairs of names followed by single names, rather than two sets of pairs or a series of three is perhaps suggestive of something approaching verbatim recollections. At any rate, it does not seem to be the most artistically elaborated approach.[28]

Whereas in v. 20 the τότε[29] presumably gives a reasonably close temporal

---

ers, M. Dibelius, *Die Formgeschichte des Evangeliums* [Mohr Siebeck, 1933], 88–92) and vv. 28–30 to a Jewish one. Black (*Aramaic Approach,* 183–184) tries to reconstruct the Aramaic source text of vv. 28–30.

[28] For Bultmann (*Geschichte*, 117–118), Mt 11.21–24 is a creation of the church because it presupposes the preaching of the gospel by Christians and its failure. In this he is followed by E. Käsemann ("Die Anfänge christlicher Theologie," *Zeitschrift für Theologie und Kirche* 57 [1960]: 178) and D. Lührmann (*Die Redaktion der Logienquelle* [Neukirchener Verlag, 1969], 60–64) who thinks that the primitive church adopts the OT form of the oracle against the nations in order to use it against Israel. On the other hand, F. Hahn (*Das Verständnis der Mission im Neuen Testament* [Neukirchener Verlag, 1965], 27) defends the authenticity of the saying. However, it should be noted that even Bultmann does not disagree with K. L. Schmidt's observation (in *Die Religion in Geseichichte und Gegenwart,* Band III, Spalte 125) that the place indications, even if they belong to the redaction, may contain historical recollections.

[29] For the extremely frequent and unclassical use of τότε in Matthew see Nigel Turner, *Syntax*, A Grammar of New Testament Greek (T&T Clark, 1963), 3:341.

link with what preceded, the ἐν ἐκείνῳ τῷ καιρῷ of v. 25 appears to reflect a looser connection. The content of vv. 25–30 is also less obviously linked with the early part of the chapter. Possibly the failure of the privileged cities of vv. 21 and 23 is the link with the response of the less privileged of v. 25. Thus the ἔκρυψας (v. 25) reflects the failure of the cities, and offers the euphonic contrast with ἀπεκάλυψας. This in turn supplies the link with the new thought of v. 27 – as the Father reveals spiritual truth to the νηπίοις, so the Son can reveal himself ᾧ ἐὰν βούληται. In this fact lies the rationale for the offer of vv. 28–30. It is almost as though these few verses are intended to reflect an expansion of Jesus' awareness of what is involved in his Messianic office. The prayer of vv. 25–26 is directed to God and speaks of him revealing truth. The meditation of v. 27 shows that what God wants to reveal concerns the Son, and that conversely the Son alone is the source of knowledge of the Father. From this realization there springs the offer of vv. 28–30 to those who are burdened, to come to the Son and through him to experience something of the quality of life that emanates from the Father.[30] If John the Baptist closed the old era, here is something of what the new era holds.

The next two episodes are short and both concerned with Sabbath observance. In episode 2 (12.1–8) the issue is plucking grain (i.e., working) on the Sabbath. The Pharisees objected to the disciples doing this, but Jesus justifies it on two different grounds. Within the OT, its own rules were broken, both regularly by the priests in the course of their duties (v. 5), and exceptionally by David and his men in a case of extreme need (v. 4). And now, in the new era there is something here greater than the temple (i.e., the old era). Whereas the temple required sacrifice, the something greater requires the higher quality of mercy. This too was foreseen by the prophets (cf. 9.13).

Episode 3 gives an example of how this mercy works (12.9–14). Faced with the question of whether to heal on the Sabbath (and thus defile it with work) Jesus confutes his adversaries on the ground that people are more important than the animals whom their casuistry permitted them to help on the Sabbath. After this, the Pharisees can only plot to do away with Jesus, and thus remove the now overt challenge to their authority (v. 14). Here is both the logical outcome of the attitude that crowned Act 1 (9.34), and a forward look to the climax of the gospel in Act 3. (Jesus had of course already seen this, for in 10.25, 28 he implicitly links those who call him Beelzebub with those who

---

[30] Compare the scheme praise of God—seeking and finding wisdom—appeal to the unwise, which E. Norden thinks to be dependent on Ecclus 51 (*Agnostos Theos* [Darmstadt, 1956], 277–308).

kill the body.)

In these two episodes, it is interesting to observe that the narrative is no more than the line on which the discussion is pegged. In contrast with several of the healing miracles of chs. 8 and 9, the man healed in episode 3 is never fully in focus. His plight is viewed as no more than the occasion for a clash between Jesus and the Pharisees. This is probably symptomatic of a change of emphasis between Act 1 and Act 2. In Act 1, Jesus' character and powers of teaching and healing are being established, but in Act 2, they are already accepted, and their implications for the old order are being explored.

Since episode 2 and episode 3 both deal with Sabbath observance, it might be preferable to link them into one episode. They have been retained as separate because of the clearly "new setting" nature of 12.9. Since this is an N Block, the attempt continues to treat the narrative seriously as a framework even though the discussion is now semantically more important.

Next comes the interlude, or editorial comment (12.15–21). Because of the Pharisees' plot, Jesus departs, healing numerous people on the way. His charge to them to keep quiet about his activities is now linked to prophecy, in this case Isa 42.1–4. This passage is without further explanation stated to be fulfilled in the ministry of Jesus. It contains various phrases which suggest links with other parts of the gospel. Verse 18 looks back to the baptism, while v. 19 is presumably the link with the present context. Verse 20a and b is of general applicability to Jesus' dealings with people, while vv. 20c–21 point forward to the cross and the eventual gentile influx into the church. This is the second time in this gospel that one of the Servant Songs of Isaiah has been applied to Jesus, the previous occasion being in 8.17. It was often noticed in Act 1 that a citation from the OT was the climax and closure of an episode. In keeping with this, it would be possible to take the whole of 12.1–21 as one episode, with a clinching citation as before. This has not been done because the OT passage seems to have no connection with the topic of Sabbath observance which dominates 12.1–14.[31]

Episode 4 runs from 12.22–37. There is no great need to break it there, since the same discussion appears to continue in the following episode (12.38–45). The topic of Beelzebul has already occurred in 9.34, and is clearly not unrelated to the hypocritical demand for a sign in Episode 5. If 12.22–45

---

[31] In fact, the only link with the present context is formed by the interpretation ἐν ταῖς πλατείαις in v. 19b which is peculiar to Matthew and which fits very well into a context stressing the reluctant attitude of Jesus to publicity. But this is a link with the immediate context (vv. 15–21) and not with the wider one.

is regarded as all one episode, this will then be of comparable length with 11.2–30, and may indicate the treatment of 12.1–21 as another longer episode. This would perhaps give a better balanced division to the whole scene, but is not to be dogmatically asserted in case it looks like forcing the material into a predetermined mould.

Episode 4, then, will be taken as vv. 22–37. The blind and dumb man is healed and removed all in one verse (v. 22). The rest of the episode is again concerned with implications rather than facts. The crowds suggest from the miracle that Jesus may well be the Son of David of their Messianic expectations. (Note the contrast between this politically inflammatory expression and the careful language of John and Jesus in ch. 11. Even Peter in ch. 16 does not use this expression in his recognition of the Messiah.) The Pharisees, seeing their own position threatened by the presence of such a figure, at once do their best to scotch the idea, and assert that any supernatural power Jesus has is derived from below rather than from above. But even against such plain blasphemy, Jesus gives a soft answer, arguing by analogies. The divided kingdom and the divided city plainly show the fate of Satan if he is divided (vv. 25–26). Not only is the Pharisees' reasoning false, but they do not apply it consistently (v. 27); if they did, their own exorcists would have to go out of business. Then in v. 28 Jesus introduces the opposite possibility, that he is the agent of God. If this is true, then his powers are direct evidence of the presence of the kingdom of God (v. 28). The supporting argument for this view is again analogical rather than assertive (v. 29). The conclusion (v. 30) is that a decision is called for. In the light of the evidence, people must decide whether they are for Jesus or against him. There is no neutral ground.

It seems that a section break would come more appropriately after v. 30 than after v. 32, since the argument reaches a conclusion there. Verses 31–37 can well hold together as a sense unit. This unit as a whole derives from the view put forward by Jesus in v. 28. If his power comes by God's Spirit, then the Pharisees are blaspheming against God's Spirit. And while rejection of Jesus' person could find forgiveness, rejection of the Spirit's work could not, because it is only through the work of the Spirit that people's attitudes towards Jesus can be changed. Verse 33 picks up the metaphor of 7.16–20. Just as trees can produce only fruit which reflects their own inner nature, so the Pharisees can speak only words which match their evil hearts. The section ends, like the sections of ch. 10, on an eschatological note. Because men's words are an accurate reflection of their hearts, their words will constitute evidence on the day of judgement. It may be noted in passing that in v. 34

the expression γεννήματα ἐχιδνῶν is identical with John's language in 3.7, and that the assumption πονηροὶ ὄντες also occurred in 7.11 in a different context.

Next, in episode 5 (12.38–45) we reach the climax of the scene in the demand for a sign. Following the Beelzebul charge of 9.34 and 12.24 and the incipient murder plot (12.14), this is very plainly hypocritical, and evokes a correspondingly scathing reply from Jesus. In this he links two themes which have been increasingly prominent in this scene, namely the superiority of the new over the old (ἰδοὺ πλεῖον Ἰωνᾶ ὧδε [v. 41] and ἰδοὺ πλεῖον Σολομῶνος ὧδε [v. 42]) and the certainty of future judgement. (Judgment has been mentioned specifically in 10.15, 11.22, 24; 12.36, 41 and 42, and referred to also in 10.23, 26, 32–33, 42; 12.32. The superiority of the new over the old has occurred in 11.11–14, 21, 23, 12.6, 8, 28; this theme can also be traced in Act 1, e.g. at 3.11 and 9.16–17, as well as the six ἐρρέθη ... ἐγὼ δὲ λέγω ὑμῖν occurrences in ch. 5.) The heinousness of the Pharisaic attitude is thrown into higher relief by the choice of gentiles (the men of Nineveh and the Queen from the South) to put their unbelief to shame. They were like the demon-possessed man of vv. 43–45. Whereas their lives should have been purified and adorned by their religion, they had in fact become worse than those who knew nothing of it. And through their influence the whole nation/generation (γενεά) had become similarly infected.

Thus the scene ends with a head-on confrontation between the old and the new. From here the account moves into the somewhat calmer waters of the next D Block, which elaborates on the spread of the new.

How is Scene 1 to be summed up? The first episode deals broadly with the position and rejection of John (11.2–30). The next two episodes deal with the true purpose of the Sabbath, and the interlude emphasizes the true nature of its Lord (12.1–21). The remaining two episodes place in sharp focus the need to recognize clearly who Jesus is, and the resulting détente with the vested interests of the establishment (12.22–45). We may diagram thus:

Episode 1	Episodes 2–3	Episodes 4–5
11.2–30: John – the end of the old era	12.1–21: Jesus – The Lord of the new era	12.22–45 – The break between old and new

3.3. Formal Division of the 2nd D Block

This block, including both the discourse and its setting material extends from 12.46–13.58. The wider setting consists of 12.46–50 and 13.53–58, as argued previously. On the basis of its internal setting material, the remainder of the block, 13.1–52, can be divided as follows:

Setting 1–3a	Setting 24a	
Parable 3b–9	Parable 24b–30	Parables 44–48
Setting 10–11a	Setting 31a	Interpretation 49–50
Comment 11b–17	Parable 31b–32	Setting 51–52a
Interpretation 18–23	Setting 33a	Comment 52b
	Parable 33b	
	Comment 34–35	
	Setting 36–37a	
	Interpretation 37b–43	

Why there is so much apparently trivial setting material is hard to determine. If we omit it and concentrate on the rest, something of a pattern becomes more visible.

Parable	Parables	Parables
Comment	Editorial comment	Interpretation
Interpretation	Interpretation	Comment

This is the first use of parables in this gospel (cf. their introduction at relatively earlier points in the framework of Mark and Luke). It seems possible that the deliberate gathering together of a whole group of them at this point in Matthew made the author feel the need for the comment sections on their nature and use. Though these sections have some parallels in Mark and Luke, they are more extended here. It is interesting to note that the first and third comment sections are from the mouth of Jesus, while the middle section is a comment from the editor.

The first parable is given to the crowds (v. 2) whereas the interpretation is for the disciples alone (v. 10). In v. 24 we are given the impression that the next three parables are for the disciples alone, but v. 34 makes it clear that the crowds have been in view again. The interpretation is again only for the disciples (v. 36), and so it seems, in the light of v. 51, are the final three short parables. The setting pieces are then much more concerned in this block with audience than with location and time as is usual elsewhere. The frequent change of audience perhaps accounts in part for the frequency of the setting pieces, though in vv. 31 and 33 they seem simply to mark the end of one parable and the beginning of the next.

The first parable is that of the sower. It contains one sentence of initial setting (v. 3b) and one of final challenge (v. 9). The four different results of sowing are formally linked by ἃ μὲν (v. 4) and ἄλλα δὲ (vv. 5, 7, and 8), but the descriptions of what happened to the seed are not particularly parallel either in form or meaning.

The comment section (vv. 10–17) answers the question of the disciples as to why Jesus used parables – a question many modern readers would surely echo. The answer is in some ways no clearer than the parables themselves. Parables, it appears, are transparent only to those who are predisposed not merely to look but to see, not merely to hear, but to understand. Without this predisposition, they remain opaque. In terms of the socio-political situation in which they were given, this meant that those who were truly sons of Abraham would learn more of God, while those who were merely hotheaded insurrectionists would dismiss them as irrelevant. In this way, Jesus would gain adherents who were concerned with God rather than with Roman domination. Thus the parables would be not only self-revealing, but also self-fulfilling. The supporting citation from Isa 6 leads on to the assertion that Jesus' ministry is the culmination of the highest hopes of the saints of the old era.[32]

The interpretation (vv. 18–23) is, like the parable, fourfold – οὗτός (v. 19), ὁ δὲ (v. 20), ὁ δὲ (v. 22), ὁ δὲ (v. 23), but beyond this there again seems to be no clear parallelism of form or meaning.

The second section of the chapter (vv. 24–43) is parallel to the first, except that the first part of it gives three parables instead of just one. Unlike the parable of the sower, they all begin with a statement of their figurative nature, ὡμοιώθη ἡ βασιλεία τῶν οὐρανῶν ... (v. 24) ὁμοία ἐστὶν ἡ βασιλεία τῶν οὐρανῶν ... (vv. 31, 33). The parable of the mustard seed seems to emphasize the irresistible effect of the teaching of Jesus, while the parable of the yeast emphasizes its all-pervasive nature. The editorial comment emphasizes the low-key teaching method of Jesus in using parables, with another supporting

---

[32] C. C. Torrey (*Documents of the Primitive Church* [Harper & Brothers, 1941], 66–68) has rightly argued that this quotation has been interpolated at a later stage than the properly Matthaean. Its most remakable features are the pure LXX form and the full agreement in length and detail with the text of the same quotation in Acts 28.26–27. Moreover, the introductory formula is quite un-Matthaean in that it shows the use of two *hapax legomena* in Matthew: ἀναπληροῦται and προφητεία. See also the discussion by Stendahl (*Matthew*, 129ff.).

OT quote.[33] Then in vv. 36–43 comes the interpretation of the parable of the weeds. If the parable of the sower showed how mixed the response is, this parable emphasizes the difficulty of identifying a genuine response and warns against the premature identification of a false response. It also has a marked eschatological element which is absent from the parable of the sower.

In the third section there are three very short parables. The first two (twin parables) apparently both emphasize the surpassing value of the kingdom of heaven, while the third is given an explicit eschatological interpretation. In the position it is in, following the parables showing the value of the kingdom, the eschatological note is perhaps intended as a challenge to get out of the fire (v. 50) into the frying pan, if we may so paraphrase ἄγγος (v. 48)! Following the disciples' claim to have understood what the parables are about, Jesus adds that those learned in the wisdom of the new era will be able to bring out far more than Judaism had to give men.

The wider setting of these parables is the two incidents of 12.46–50 and 13.53–58. As commented previously, these show on the one hand the way in which a close relationship with Jesus is open to anyone willing to obey God (12.50); and on the other hand how a superficial familiarity with Jesus may hinder the development of a close relationship. In this way these setting pieces offer examples of the parables in action. Response is open to all, but some choose to reject (cf. 13.10–17, 34–35). Finally, a link may be noted between ἐσκανδαλίζοντο in 13.57 and the further recurrences of this term in the next D Block in 17.27 and 18.6–9. In summing up this D Block, we can say that it contains a long didactic section embedded in briefer narrative setting. Thus there is a key pattern:

Setting	Teaching	Setting
12.46–13.3a	13.3b–52	13.53–58

Within the teaching matter (omitting the minor internal setting pieces), there are three roughly parallel sections each containing parables, comment and interpretation. In the third section the order is varied to parables, interpretation and comment. This gives on a smaller scale the same pattern as that suggested for the whole Act, where the order of N and D sections is re-

---

[33] Again a formula quotation peculiar to Matthew which shows in its second half an intentional interpretation of the Hebrew text expressing more clearly than the LXX the aspect of sacred history.

versed in the third part.

3.4. Formal Division of the Second N Block

This block is taken as stretching from 14.1–17.23. It has already been argued that it breaks into two halves, 14.1–15.39 and 16.1–17.23, each half constituting a scene. We proceed with the analysis on this assumption.

3.4.1. The First Half (Scene 2)

This section is taken as a unit because, so far as the N Block material goes, it is enclosed by the two demands for a sign. It falls into 6 episodes, all but the first marked off by a change of location (14.13, 22, 34; 15.21, 29).

The first episode (14.1–12) reintroduces John the Baptist and in a series of flashbacks unique in the gospel, relates his death at the hands of Herod Antipas. Perhaps the purpose of setting this pericope at this particular point is to suggest that the death of John signifies the end of the old era. This is implied in Jesus' comments of 11.11–14 and 17.12–13.

On hearing the news of John's murder, Jesus goes to seek solitude and this move forms the setting for episode 2 (14.13–21). The pursuing crowds excite Jesus' pity (cf. 9.36) and he performs various unspecified healing miracles. The genitive absolute in 14.15 introduces the main topic of the episode, the hunger of the crowds and their miraculous feeding. It seems that Jesus did not up to this point get the solitude he wanted, and after the departure of the disciples by boat, he dismissed the crowds and remained alone to pray (episode 3, 14.22–33).

The significance in the context of walking on the sea of the words "ἐγώ εἰμι" (cf. Exod 3.14 LXX) was apparently not lost on the disciples. Peter's response "εἰ σὺ εἶ" seems to imply more than just Jesus' identity, in the light of the request to share the experience of walking on the sea. The fact that his achievement was limited did not obscure from the other disciples its implications. They were able to say to Jesus "You really are the Son of God" (v. 33), which seems to be connected with the implicit claim of ἐγώ εἰμι in v. 27.

The fourth episode is taken to extend from 14.34 to 15.20. It may seem odd to include 14.34–36, but there are several reasons for doing so. First of all, the change of location which seems to be a constant episode initial marker in this section, occurs there. Secondly, the three verses are hardly enough to constitute an episode on their own. Thirdly, they form an appropriate contrastive setting to the discussion of true purity which is the main topic of the episode. Following the evidential miracles of episodes 2 and 3, these verses resume in miniature Jesus' healing abilities and their widespread value. It is in spite of all this that the Pharisees draw attention to pettifogging rules about handwashing (15.2). Jesus points out to them that their scrupulosity over external minutiae blinded them to the inner purpose of the Law they were so proud of. Thus did they fulfil Isaiah's prophecy and deserve his strictures on their hypocrisy.

The second part of this episode begins (v. 10) with Jesus giving to the crowds some semi-figurative teaching on purity arising from the Pharisees' complaint. Though sufficiently clear to annoy the Pharisees (v. 12), it was sufficiently obscure to warrant the label of a parable (v. 15) and to require explanation (vv. 17–20), somewhat to Jesus' surprise (v. 16). In vv. 13–14 Jesus speaks in strong, though still metaphorical terms of the spiritual blindness of the Pharisees. If despite the evidence before them, they could still think of nothing but externals, their ultimate rejection by God was assured. Perhaps in this assessment, we have a semi-humorous adumbration of the teaching of the parable of the vineyard (21.33–45).

In contrast with this rather despondent note, the fifth episode (15.21–28) gives an example of outstanding faith, and that on the part of a Gentile. This episode is reminiscent of the healing miracles of chs. 8 and 9, but here the emphasis is on the Canaanite woman's faith, as shown in her exchange with Jesus, rather than on the healing itself. In this respect, it has most in common with the episode of the healing of the centurion's servant (8.5–13). Here even more than there, the recognition of faith is the climax of the episode. Surely it is no accident that this episode is juxtaposed to the previous one that highlights the obtuseness of the religious authorities, and that both come among the miracles that are enclosed between the two demands for a sign. Finally, we may note the contrast between the impatient embarrassment of the disciples (v. 23) and the patient forbearance of Jesus himself, towards the woman's noisy importunity.

The sixth and last episode (15.29–39) combines a rehearsal of Jesus' general healing powers with another feeding miracle. The first part (vv. 29–31) is the most detailed and wide-ranging of all the general summaries of healing (4.23–24; 8.16; 9.35; 14.34–36; partly perhaps because this summary uses and replaces the Marcan story of the healing of the deaf and dumb man [Mk 7.31–37]). Since it is the last such summary to appear in the gospel, this is appropriate, as is the recording of the general attitude of the common people (v.

31b). Here is a further contrast with the hardened unbelief of the establishment. The presence of the multitudes for healing is the cue for the feeding miracle in the second half of the episode. In the previous feeding miracle, it was the disciples who initiated the train of events (14.15); here it is Jesus himself, motivated by pity (σπλαγχνίζομαι v. 32, cf. 14.14, 9.36) and humanitarian concern. The events themselves are naturally similar to those of the previous account, and conclude with a further change of location (v. 39). The repetition of a feeding miracle, combined with the final summary of the healing miracles thus forms a suitable culmination to the section on signs, and a poignant contrast with the renewed demand for a sign which follows.

To sum up Scene 2, we must acknowledge thematic links of various "distance" from the scene itself. Episodes 2 and 6 have a clear connection of topic, and can be seen as balancing elements of a somewhat subdued key pattern. Episodes 3 and 5 may perhaps be linked in their emphasis on faith (cf. ὀλιγόπιστε 14.31 and ... πίστις 15.28) while episode 4 stands out starkly. Its thematic connections are rather with the demands for a sign which enclose this whole section. The remaining episode, episode 1, we have previously suggested to be linked with other episodes concerning John the Baptist in Act 1, Scene 2 and Act 2, Scene 1 as well as subsequent mentions in chs. 17 and 21. We may diagram as follows with arrows representing connections of theme outside the present scene.

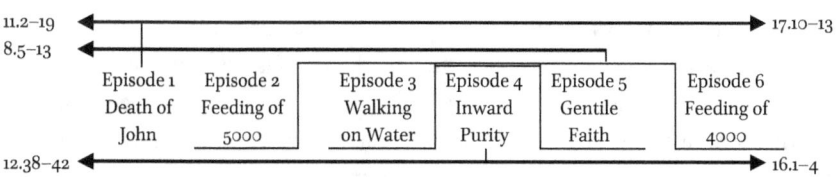

3.4.2. The Second Half (Scene 3)

As previously argued, this section is taken as running from 16.1–17.23. It is difficult to divide it convincingly into episodes; to take changes of location or sense breaks as definitive would yield a high number of short episodes. The approach taken here therefore is to speak of four episodes, each falling into two phases. This allows for the maximum number of possible breaks, but does not fragment the narrative excessively, though it is admittedly somewhat arbitrary.

The four divisions are as follows: 16.1–12; 16.13–28; 17.1–13; 17.14–23.

In the first half of the first episode the demand for a sign is repeated in language very similar to that of 12.38–39. The significance of this repetition has already been suggested, and the arguments will not be repeated. It is perhaps worth noting that the Sadducees are associated with the demand on this occasion, whereas previously it was only the Pharisees. This unholy union of political opponents (not mentioned together since 3.7) is an indication of the buildup of opposition to Jesus. When the exchange is completed, Jesus leaves and the change of location is a convenient watershed for the episode. Once alone with the disciples, Jesus warns them to avoid the attitude of unbelief that characterized the corrupting teaching of the Pharisees and Sadducees,[34] about which he had evidently been thinking. The disciples' failure to grasp his point showed that they were in measure infected by this faithless attitude, and merited the rebuke of ὀλιγόπιστοι (v. 8). That they were not beyond help, however, is shown in that the point was finally taken (v. 12).

A further change in location brings us into the second, long and important episode. After the busy times in the area of Galilee, Jesus retreated to the relative peace and anonymity of Caesarea Philippi. The teaching and healing of Act 1 is now well known, especially to the disciples. The "signs" of Act 2, Scene 2 have been given, and, so far as the establishment is concerned, rejected. The time is now ripe to see whether the inner circle of disciples have pierced the veil of mystery that surrounds Jesus. The popular rumours and assessments are elicited, and though they are in some ways more perceptive than the views of the religious leaders, they are quietly placed on one side. They are inadequate, but the full truth of Jesus' identity had evidently penetrated to at least one of the disciples, for Peter acknowledges both the Messiahship and the divine Sonship of Jesus. This insight is a direct revelation from God, Jesus asserts, and in some way confers a special privilege upon Peter. (The specific problems of vv. 18–19 need not detain us). For the

---

[34] It is interesting to note the differences between the synoptic parallels. Though the implicit ground of the comparison is the same, namely 'corrupting,' the implicit object differs. In the Matthew text, the editor adds an explanation in v. 12 in which the object is explicitly stated: 'teaching.' The Lucan text (12:1) reads, "Beware of the leaven of the Pharisees, which is hypocrisy" and provides thus a different explicit statement. Mk 8:15 has the reading; "beware of the leaven of the Pharisees and the leaven of Herod," and though no interpretation is given, the implicit object is very probably something like "evil disposition." See especially the discussion in V. Taylor, *The Gospel According to St. Mark* (MacMillan, 1959), 365–366. It is very probable that the saying was current as an isolated logion, though Bultmann (*Geschichte*, 139) is certainly right in observing that its original form and meaning can scarcely be determined. καὶ Σαδδουκαίων in Matthew is secondary. Is it a connecting link with the first half of this episode?

time being the truth about Jesus is to remain confined to the disciples (v. 20) and the reason for this becomes apparent in the second phase of the episode (vv. 21–28). Though the disciples now knew of Jesus' Messiahship, they needed some radical re-education as to its implications. Premature and ill-informed publicity would do nothing but harm. Whereas the disciples seem to have thought of Messiahship in terms of glory and perhaps military conquest, Jesus shows that the glory will be truly manifested only through rejection, suffering and death. The shock of this was way too much for the disciples, who seem to neglect the promise of resurrection. Peter's no doubt representative reaction merits a stern rebuke from Jesus, which contrasts markedly with the praise given in v. 17. The word σκάνδαλον here alone applied to Peter, and its related verb seems to be key words in this Act (cf. 11.6; 13.21, 41, 57; 15.12; 17.27; 18.6–9). In the remaining verses (vv. 24–28) there is a strong thematic link with ch. 10. The principle of 10.24–25 is applied in the light of the clearer teaching just given about the cross. The fate of the master is always an open possibility for the servants. The words of 10.37–39 are now seen to have one interpretation which is unpleasantly literal (16.24–26). In 16.27–28 the atmosphere of ch. 10 is retained by a closing eschatological note, and in the final sentence a repetition of the ἀμὴν λέγω ὑμῖν which was there taken as a closing formula.

This episode marks a new stage in the thematic development of the gospel as a whole. Whereas in Act 1 Jesus is depicted as a teacher and healer and up to this point in Act 2 he is rejected as such by the religious leaders, here he is shown explicitly to be the key figure in God's saving purposes (cf. 1.21). This new step is presented not as an abstract conclusion at the end of a reasoned argument, but as a dramatic insight on the part of one of the characters in the narrative. Presumably this helps to stimulate reader involvement, and self-identification with Peter.[35] In one way then, this episode is in its first phase a climax to all that has preceded. In its second phase, with the freshly emphasized theme of suffering and death, it is the opening to all that follows, in which the defeat and victory of the cross are made increasingly plain. The centrality of this episode has long been recognised in gospel studies, but the study of thematic interweaving may show more clearly something of how this effect is achieved.

The third episode begins in an unusually precise way with a setting that

---

[35] In this connection the peculiar and emotive use of direct speech in 16.22 should especially be noted.

specifies both time, place and participants. The first phase of the episode (17.1–8) has some link with the preceding confession in 16.16. Now that Jesus' true nature has been recognised by revelation (16.17) it can be at least in measure seen directly. The mention of Moses and Elijah is a clear connection with God's purposes as carried out in the old era, and the voice from the cloud gives divine approval to the course of the ministry, as in 3.17 it gave approval to its inception. We may note the recurrence of ἰδοὺ in this section, as frequently in the more obviously supernatural events recorded in chs. 1–3.

The second phase of the episode relates the conversation on the descent from the mountain (17.9–13). The presence of Elijah in the transfiguration scene raises the question of his eschatological role as popularly understood. Jesus' assertion that this role has already been fulfilled is an indication of the end of the old era. Only in Matthew is the "Elijah" overtly identified as John the Baptist, and the obscurities of Mark skillfully ironed out. Jesus uses the disciples' questions to remind them that his own fate will involve suffering as John's did, and thus to counteract any false messianic hopes which may have been stimulated by the glory of the transfiguration scene (v. 12). And again they are given the encouragement of the resurrection hope (v. 9).

The fourth episode is thematically somewhat puzzling, and structurally rather unsatisfactory. The first phase of the episode is vv. 14–20, and the second vv. 22–23. Under this scheme the main emphasis of the incident with the demoniac boy is faith (ἄπιστος v. 17 and ὀλιγοπιστία v. 20). This fits into the broader picture of the block, yet it is hard not to see this pericope as something of an anticlimax after the transfiguration. The γενεά of v. 17 may be the people at large, the disciples, or both.[36] Is the incident intended to show that the disciples now have some true faith, even if not enough, or to show their slowness to believe despite all they had seen and heard? Probably the latter, since elsewhere ὀλιγόπιστος is used only in reproach. As noted in other healing miracles in this Act, the focus of attention seems to be on the discussion (vv. 19–20) rather than the facts (vv. 14–18). The closing statement which shows the boundless potential of faith, is again prefaced by ἀμὴν ... λέγω ὑμῖν (v. 20).

The second phase of the episode is very short and consists of the second passion prediction. Thematically its links and relevance are obvious, but structurally it is too short to give a convincing balance to the episode as a

---

[36] On the other hand, the tone of the saying may generally be described as "celui d'un maître fatigué de jouer un rôle ingrat, et déjà pénétré de la pensée de sa mort prochaine" (M. J. Lagrange, *Evangile selon Saint Marc* [Librairie Lecoffre, 1929], 239).

whole. Its opening genitive absolute seems to be dealing purely with setting rather than with a switch of focus. The gloomy reaction of the disciples shows how very far they still were from understanding the true nature of Jesus' Messiahship. Perhaps we can take this as a further example of their "little faith," and if so, it would go some way towards explaining the location of the second passion prediction at this point.[37]

To sum up Scene 3 then, it may be viewed as four episodes which give something of a subdued mirror image. The first and last episodes are both concerned with lack of adequate faith (10.8; 17.20), while the two central episodes are both concerned with various aspects of Messiahship. This can be diagrammed as follows on the next page, with the lines showing some of the main thematic links. Arrows indicate links with passages outside this scene.

This diagram is rather oversimplified, but the number and interconnection of themes of various degrees of importance is now sufficiently large that it cannot be comprehensively shown on one diagram without becoming hopelessly obscure.

3.5. Formal Division of the Third D Block

This Block, including setting material, extends from 17.24 to 19.2. The incident of the temple tax (17.24–27) is unique to Matthew. Jesus submits to the temple tax voluntarily rather than as of duty, and this attitude sets the key for the teaching on the values of the kingdom of heaven which follows in the discourse. Furthermore, Peter is singled out by the tax collectors as though he were in some way the representative of Christ's followers. This would afford an occasion for the question: "Who then is the greater?" i.e., "Why is Peter assumed to be the chief among us?" There is also, as previously noted, the verbal link (σκανδαλ-) between 17.27 and 18.6–9, and the link of thought between the "Sons of the king" of 17.25–26 and the question about greatness in the kingdom of 18.1. There is also a link between the ἄρα γε of 17.26 and the ἄρα of the 18.1. The RV is the only English translation that makes this connection. Perhaps the paragraph breaks of the printed texts are misleading. A check of the 20 occurrences of ἄρα in Mt, Mk, Lk and Acts shows that in 17 cases ἄρα refers backwards to a previous point in the argument, or draws a

---

[37] One can, of course, explain this location by the simple presence of the prediction at this point in the Marcan source. However, this only means that the question why the prediction has been inserted at this particular point now has to be raised with regard to Mark.

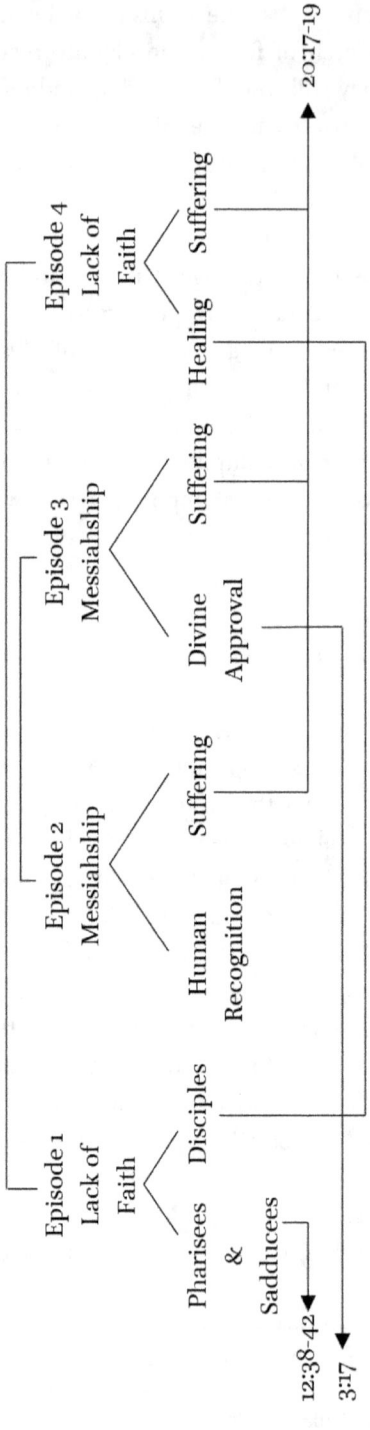

conclusion from a set of events or circumstances. In the three residual examples, the ἄρα follows εἰ in the protasis of a conditional clause, but even in these places, the condition is based on information given in the earlier part of the same sentence. The six other instances of ἄρα in Mt all contain a clear reference to what has preceded (7.20; 12.28; 17.26; 19.25, 27; 24.45) and it is probable therefore that the same is true here. The ἄρα in 18.1 looks back not only to the ἄρα of 17.26, but to the whole argument of 17.25–27, which, as suggested before, provides the setting for the question in 18.1.

The monologue section of this block, 18.3–35, is dominated by two questions, the first posed by the disciples in 18:1, and the second by Peter in 18.21. It is quite hard to disentangle the train of thought in the answer to the first question, and perhaps the paragraph breaks in the UBS edition of the Greek text are not very helpful. It seems best to regard the answer to the first question as given on two levels, the first in a broad generalization, dealing with greatness in relation to God, and the second dealing with greatness in relation to other people. To this division correspond the conditionals ἐὰν (v. 3) and ἐὰν δὲ (v. 15). Within the first section, vv. 3–4 are regarded as laying down a principle which answers the question of v. 1; vv. 5–10 as examining some implications of the principle; and vv. 12–14 as illustrating the principle. However, the profusion of imagery renders this analysis less than certain!

The "secondary setting" of v. 2 (i.e., Jesus' non-verbal response to the question) is crucial for the whole of this first section of the monologue. The presence of the child is assumed at least until v. 14. To the question then of who is greatest in the kingdom of heaven, Jesus says that people who do not become like children will not be included in the kingdom at all. Those who come closest to the humility of the child will be greatest in the kingdom. In some way it then seems that the adults' approximation to childhood virtues is measured by their treatment of children. The ὅς ἐὰν of v. 5a and ὅς δ' ἂν of v. 6a put forward alternative responses to children. The apodosis of the first condition is very simple (v. 5b), but the apodosis of the second (v. 6b) is elaborated in the following verses (v. 7–10). These verses contain a general principle (v. 7); two specific ways of applying that principle to oneself (or rather three ways expressed through only two parallel clauses, vv. 8–9, cf. 6.19–21); and a concluding summary and justification (v. 10). (Verses 8 and 9 are closely parallel in expression with 5.29–30, but the context is very different.)

In vv. 12–14 the picture of the lost sheep (which is here neither called a parable as in Lk 15.3, nor introduced by the verb ὁμοιόω frequent in Mt 13) illustrates God's care even for the least (self-)important, such as the child whose very presence was an object lesson. It is thus different in purpose from the similar passage in Lk 15.[38] Jesus for the second time in this D Block invites the disciples' opinion (18.12 cf. 17.25) before suggesting an analogy to guide its formation. This may again be an oblique form of reader involvement.

The second section, vv. 15–20 appears to be tangential to the original question of v. 1. It may be suggested that it deals with the question of greatness as shown by the handling of discord in personal relationships. Every effort is to be made to effect reconciliation. If a personal attempt fails, a delegation should try. If they fail, the whole ἐκκλησία (whatever that means in this context) is to be involved. And the decisions of such a believing community have in some way a binding force which is not merely earthly (cf. 16.19). Verse 18 seems to make better sense if taken with vv. 15–17 than with vv. 19–20. In favour of this is the initial ἀμὴν λέγω ὑμῖν which as we have seen, often ends a section.[39]

Verses 19–20 seem to explore the spiritual potential latent in a reconciliation such as that desire in v. 15. If this is so, the περὶ παντὸς πράγματος would refer to any matter under dispute, as in v. 15, and the thrust of the passage would be that where people are humble enough to be reconciled, their meeting together is in Jesus' name and presence. In this the true greatness of God's kingdom is revealed.

The second half of the chapter is mercifully more straightforward. Peter's question of v. 21 constitutes internal setting, and receives from Jesus a direct, though surprising answer (v. 22). The question arises from Jesus' teaching in vv. 15–16 above. The answer of v. 22 is elaborated in explicitly parabolic fashion in the rest of the chapter. In some ways, the parable pulls together the threads of the earlier part of the block, in that it shows not only the need for people to forgive each other, but also the reason, namely, that one owes to God an incalculable debt. The mention of the kingdom of heaven in 18.23, and the identification of the king with the *heavenly* father in 18.35 give a link with the original question of v. 1, which was about greatness in the *kingdom of heaven*. In comparison with the king, none of the servants is great. Such greatness as any attain is but a reflection of the values and attitudes of the king himself.

---

[38] It has generally been observed that Matthew's readings are more original than the Lucan ones. See Bultmann, *Geschichte*, 184–185 and especially E. Linnemann, *Gleichnisse Jesu* (Vanderhoeck & Ruprecht, 1966), 70–79, 150–155.

[39] This is the division that normally has been made by form criticism. See Bultmann, *Geschichte*, 150–151, 156; L. Brun, *Segen und Fluch im Urchristentum* (J. Dybwad, 1931), 93ff.

Within the parable, v. 23 is the opening setting and v. 35 gives concluding application. The story has three scenes, the first (vv. 24–27) between the king and the first debtor, the second (vv. 28–30) between the two debtors, and the third (vv. 32–34) between the king and the first debtor again. Verse 31 is transitional between Scenes 2 and 3.

The three scenes have a measure of both parallelism and contrast. The first involves a good deed to an unworthy man, the second a bad deed to a worthy man, and the third the application of his own standards to the unworthy man. It is thus aesthetically pleasing in structure, and morally satisfying in theme. It may be noted that apart from the genitive absolute of vv. 24–25, almost every verse begins with a nominative participle.

Verses 34–35 may include an eschatological tinge, but if so, it does not have the same prominence as the eschatology in the two previous D Blocks.

The terminal setting (19.1–2) contains the D-Block closing formula, and the important change of location which is taken as marking the end of Act 2. Involved in the journey from Galilee to Transjordan are crowds still seeking healing. Thus is the stage set for the third and final act.

We may summarize this D Block in the following simple diagram, where arrows show the links of thought.

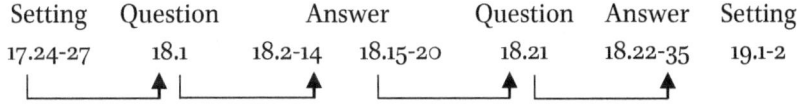

| Setting | Question | Answer | Question | Answer | Setting |
| 17.24-27 | 18.1 | 18.2-14   18.15-20 | 18.21 | 18.22-35 | 19.1-2 |

3.6. Summary of Act 2

Once again, a brief summary in diagram form may be helpful. The verbal labels under each section may be of some mnemonic value, but are not of great importance. They may just help to clarify a diagram that is becoming too complicated for comfort. The boxes in which episodes or D Block sections are placed are not significant in themselves—they serve to join those episodes or sections which seem to be more closely linked. The abbreviations P, C, and I stand for Parable, Comment, and Interpretation. The lines with arrows link sections thematically related. More could be put in, e.g., to show the occurrence of σκανδαλ-, ὀλιγόπιστος etc., but such complexity seems better avoided. To save space, D Block settings are indicated only when they are more than minimal.

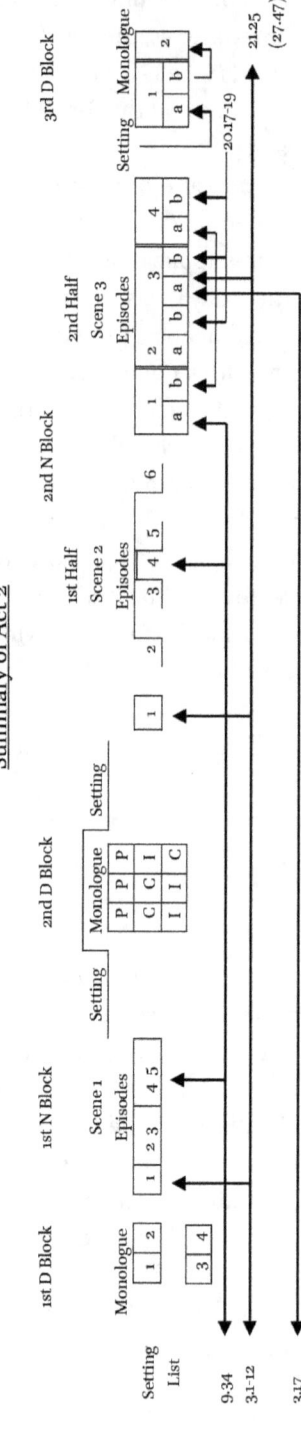

It is interesting to observe the heavy bunching of the thematic lines in Scene Three, which perhaps helps to show why this passage has always been regarded as an important one. It is also worth noting that no thematic lines link to the first section of Episode 2—Peter's confession. Perhaps this is an indication of its "new information" value.

4. Act 3

This Act embraces the rest of the gospel, chs. 19–28. It consists of an N Block (chs. 19–22), a D Block (chs. 23–25), and another N Block (chs. 26–28). All three are considerably longer than any previous block and give a total of 450 verses, as against approximately 350 for Act 2 and 270 for Act 1. In purely quantitative terms, this may seem rather unbalanced, but presumably it reflects the author's estimate of the importance of the last period of Jesus' ministry.

It will be recalled that the second N Block in Act 2 (chs. 14–17) was divided into two halves, so that within the whole Act it was possible to see three sections each containing some discourse and some narrative material. This was diagrammed as

(Blocks)	D	+	N	D +	½ N	½ N	+	D
(Chapters)	10	11–12		13	14–15	16–17		18

The reversal of the elements in the third section seemed curiously asymmetrical, so the possibility was investigated that some similar secondary division of the Act 3 blocks might serve to restore the balance somehow. It does indeed seem that such a division is feasible. In the D Block of Act 3 (chs. 23–25) there is a very obvious break at the end of ch. 23, where a change of theme from denunciation to eschatology is overtly marked by internal setting material. The change is such that at first it seemed doubtful whether ch. 23 should be included in the D Block at all. In the end it seemed best to include it, but to allow a secondary division between chs. 23 and 24.

Then there was the question of whether the first N Block (chs. 19–22) permitted a secondary division like that of chs. 14–17. It seems not unreasonable to posit such a division at the end of ch. 20, for in chs. 19 and 20 there is largely "the mixture as before" of general teaching, and one healing miracle. At the beginning of ch. 21, Jesus enters Jerusalem where the climax of the story is set, and the events and disputes take on a different character. In terms of the formal flow of the narrative there is no major break at the end of ch. 20, but the switch of emphasis after that point is sufficient to justify a secondary division.

What is the effect of making such a division anyway? First let us give a diagrammatic summary of the main division of the gospel into Acts, indicating the result of key patterns.

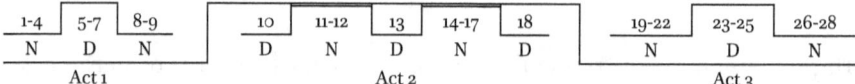

Now by linking chs. 19–20 with chs. 16–18 and linking chs. 21–22 with ch. 23, a further set of key patterns can be derived from the secondary divisions.

Chs	1-4	5-7	8-9	10	11-12	13	14-15	16-17	18	19-20	21-22	23	24-25	26-28
	N + D		N	D	N	D + ½N		½N + D + ½N			½N + ½D		½D + N	
No. of Verses	87	114	68	47	74	63	75	51	41	62	91	39	97	161

We cannot build too much on this since it deals only with the gross division of the Gospel according to the broad types of material contained in it. But a couple of features seem worth pointing out. One is that the new patterns paper over the major breaks in the old patterns, so to speak. The other is that in purely quantitative terms, various units in the secondary patterns seem remarkably well balanced. The number of verses in (1/2)N or (1/2)D Block is indicated in the second diagram.

When a piece of writing shows clear major divisions, it is quite likely that secondary divisions can be found which tend to offset the major divisions by showing links across their boundaries. As a type of analogy, we might consider the division of e.g., a Latin hexameter into feet. The caesura, a secondary division, has to come in the middle of one of the feet. In detail, this is a secondary feature breaking up a primary unit, whereas we are arguing above for a secondary pattern running across a primary boundary. But the general picture of secondary features tending to subdue and balance out primary ones seems broadly comparable.

Perhaps one of the ways in which good writing is good, is that patterns at different levels of analysis should *not* coincide – at least not all the time. If they did, the result would be too obvious and too dull. Could it be that the writer's artistry depends on the way in which he interweaves patterns at different levels so that they sometimes coincide and sometimes do not?[40]

There remains one more general topic to be discussed before the detailed analysis is begun. It is obvious even on a casual reading that the three synoptic accounts are closer to each other in the passion narrative than elsewhere. It therefore seemed a reasonable assumption that the structural divisions and the semantic purposes of the individual writers would show up most where their accounts are unique either in order or in content. The unique parts of Matthew do tend to have a patterned distribution which will be noted as we proceed.

4.1. Formal Division of the First N Block

The block runs from 19.3–22.46. It is divided into six scenes, each containing three or four episodes. The first extends from 19.3–15 and contains teaching on human relationships centered round family life. The second embraces 19.16–20.16 and holds teaching on wealth and rewards. The third runs from 20.17–34 and relates final incidents before reaching Jerusalem. In the fourth (21.1–22) Jesus' activities in the city are described, while the fifth (21.23–22.14) and sixth (22.15–46) focus on the reactions of the religious authorities to Jesus.

4.1.1. Scene 1

The topic of divorce (19.3–9) is introduced by a group of Pharisees attempting to get Jesus to align himself with one or other of the views then current. As often, Jesus parried a tendentious question by referring not to party traditions but to scriptural principles; he pointed out that, whereas their interest lay in evaluating various grounds of divorce, in God's purpose, marriage was to be an indissoluble union. The disciples were evidently so steeped in popular views that they overreacted by asserting that in the face of such strictness, it would be better not to marry.

Jesus uses this statement to give further teaching in the second 'episode' 19.10–12 (though this is hardly an appropriate label here) on the positive value of celibacy. While some people through congenital defect or human cruelty are unable to marry, there are others who voluntarily forego the privilege for the sake of God's kingdom. Such sacrifice is a challenge for anyone who

---

[40] Cf. the discussion in fn 23.

can accept it.

The third episode (19.13–15) comes apparently to counterbalance any false exaltation of celibacy that may have arisen from the second. Though celibacy may have its purpose for some, marriage is evidently the normal state, and as if to emphasize this, Jesus goes out of his way to bless the children, who are the usual result of marriage. As he had stated before (18.3), such children are an object-lesson on the attitudes required for entry to God's kingdom.

4.1.2. Scene 2

Following the change of location in 19.15, the question from the rich young man opens up a new set of topics. Legalistic observance had left the questioner with an abiding sense of need (19.20). Jesus' reply is neither a call to make a histrionic gesture, nor a programme for economic reform, but rather an *ad hominem* challenge to break down the barriers which prevented full commitment. This seems to be the point of the command not only to sell all, but also to come and follow. The young man's failure to accept the challenge (19.22) closes the first episode.

In 19.23–30 the second episode yields the teaching that arose from the previous incident. Jesus' comment on the young man reversed the popular estimate of wealth as an overt mark of God's blessing, and this, reinforced by the comical figure of v. 24, evoked the astonishment of the disciples, which was perhaps not fully assuaged by the reassurance of v. 26. Peter's thoughts remained very much on the material plane and his blunt "What do we get out of it?" must have been a disappointment to Jesus. Jesus meets him on his own level with the promise of a real reward, yet tries to lift Peter to a higher level by reminding him of the future and spiritual nature of that reward. The closing epigram (19.30) seems intended to provide a link both backwards to Peter's question, and forwards to the parable that follows as the third episode/topic. Peter was apparently considering himself and the other disciples as among the πρῶτοι, and Jesus is reminding him that God's estimate may reverse human estimate.[41]

---

[41] This double function of the epigram on the level of the scene becomes also clear from the doublet in 20:16. It is, of course, true that the connection of this epigram with the preceding remains obscure both in Matthew and in Mk 10:23–31. It is possible to state that the disciples are the last who are to be the first (so J. Wellhausen, *Das Evangelium Marci* [G. Reimer, 1909], 82). But it is equally possible to take the saying as a warning to the disciples (so, among

In the parable that follows Jesus illustrates how those in Peter's position, with good reason to consider themselves πρῶτοι, found their self-estimate cut down to size by their employer's generosity (20.15). In the same way Peter is warned, the allotment of rewards in God's kingdom may hold surprises for those with high expectations. The parable itself calls for little comment, but the repetition of the epigram of 19.30 in 20.16 serves to bind the parable closely to what preceded rather than leaving it isolated. The addition of οὕτως and the reversal of the word order in 20.16 make it seem unlikely that the repetition is erroneous or accidental. This parable is unique to Matthew, and as with other such pericopes in this block, comes at the end of a scene.

4.1.3. Scene 3

This scene is in some ways the most heterogenous in the Act; it opens with a change of location (20.17) and consists of three discrete episodes that do not seem to have a close connection with each other. In the first of these (20.17-19) there is the third passion prediction, which looks back to 17.22-23 and 16.21, but is more detailed and specific.

In the second episode (20.20-28) there is the request on behalf of James and John by their mother and the teaching arising from it. And in the third (20.29-34) there is the healing of the two blind men at Jericho.

There is, however, some degree of unity in terms of the various estimates given about the person and purpose of Jesus. In the first episode, Jesus reinforces his own teaching on the Son of Man coming to victory through suffering and death. In the second, the two disciples emphasize the glory at the expense of the suffering and Jesus has both to remind them that to share the glory they must first share the suffering, and to remind the other ten that true greatness in the new era lies in sacrificial service. In the third episode the blind men again address Jesus as "Son of David" (cf. 9.27) with its overtones of Messianic Kingship. The interesting feature is that whereas in 9.30

---

others, H. B. Swete, *The Gospel according to St. Mark* (Macmillan & Co., 1920), 233. C. H. Turner, *The Gospel according to St. Mark* (SPCK, 1928), 50; Allen, *Matthew, ad loc*). The choice can hardly be decided on the level of the clause, since it is hard to know whether δέ has the meaning of γάρ (this is the reading of 237, 259, sy^s, geo', arm in Mark according to S. C. E. Legg, *Novum Testamentum Graece: Euangelium secundum Marcum* (Clarendon, 1935) and of the Itala ms Petropolitanus and the Coptic version in Matthew according to C. Tischendorf, *Novum Testamentum Graece*, Editio octava critica maior (Hinrichs, 1869) or whether it is sharply adversative. However, on the level of the scene, the latter interpretation seems to be the best.

Jesus had tried to suppress this term, here in ch. 20 he does nothing of the kind, but rather goes on at once to substantiate it in the triumphal entry.

It has been previously noted how the Beelzebul charge at the end of Act 1 (9.34) was taken up and amplified in Act 2 (10.25, 12.24). The first incident with the two blind men in ch. 9 immediately preceded the Beelzebul affair, and just as the latter was expanded in Act 2, so the former is resumed and given a different twist here in Act 3. It is again the final episode of a scene which shows something of Matthew's unique approach, though in this case it is not the content which is peculiar (20.29–34 is paralleled in Mark and Luke) but the repetition (9.27–31 is not in any other gospel).

To sum up the thematic structure of this scene then, we could suggest that the first and third (short) episodes give estimates of Jesus which he accepted while the second (longer) episode gives a view which needed radical modification.

4.1.4. Scene 4

This scene (21.1–22) includes three episodes linked to Jesus' ministry in Jerusalem. They are obviously related in theme, but only Matthew records them in this particular order and juxtaposition.

The first episode (21.1–11) shows how in the triumphal entry, Jesus openly received the title "Son of David," and indeed symbolically encouraged it by his mode of travel, which fulfilled the prophecy of Zech 9.9.[42] This seems to have been planned well in advance, with careful arrangements made beforehand. As a result, the words of the pilgrims from Ps 118 took on a new meaning. Consequently the crowds in the city showed themselves willing to recognize Jesus at least as a prophet (21.11).

The second episode (21.12–17) contains an act of symbolic significance in keeping with the prophetic tradition. The temple, which had become polluted with mundane concerns, was cleansed and its spiritual purpose brought

---

[42] This formula quotation combines Is 62:11 with Zech 9:9. In fact the quotation from Isaiah serves to introduce the quotation from Zech and this text has been somewhat abbreviated. Interestingly, both the adjectives δίκαιος and σῴζων, which would have been so appropriate to Matthew, have been omitted. So the focus is fully on "poor and riding on an ass." However, Matthew shares this particular focus with rabbinic texts which use Zech 9:9 as a messianic prophecy. See especially Strack and Billerbeck, *Kommentar*, 1:842–843; J. Klausner, *Die messianischen Vorstellungen des jüdischen Volkes im Zeitalter der Tannaiten* (J. Klausner, 1904), 45–46; O. Michel, s.v. ὄνος, in *Theologisches Wörterbuch*, ed. Kittel, 5:284ff.

to the fore again (v. 13). The open display in Jerusalem both of Jesus' miraculous powers and his regal aspirations provoked the anger of the authorities, who confronted him especially on the latter point. In v. 16 Jesus explicitly accepts the title 'Son of David' even though given by those unaware of its implications. This presumably was the point of no return, both for him and for the authorities. His claims of kingly status were dangerous to their vested interests and he would therefore have to be removed if they were to retain their political positions. Thus prudence as well as convenience suggested Jesus' retirement to Bethany for the night (v. 17).

In the third episode (21.18–22) concerning the cursing of the fig tree, Jesus used the wonder of the disciples to teach a lesson on the potential of believing prayer.

The three episodes of this scene, all heavy with both political and spiritual symbolism, represent the climax of this block so far as action goes. The remaining scenes consist almost entirely of a dialogue in which Jesus and his opponents are in open confrontation. This has been foreshadowed in 9.1–17 and developed in 12.1–14, 22–45, 15.1–20, and 16.1–4. The activities of Scene 4 here trigger the climax of the verbal duels in Scenes 5 and 6.

4.1.5. Scene 5

This scene runs from 21.23–22.14. It contains four episodes, the first an attack by the establishment and the others a three-pronged reply by Jesus.

In the first episode (21.23–27) the high priests and elders demand to know Jesus' authority for his actions. The question is asked in the temple, the same location where Jesus had caused such a disturbance only the previous day. The point of Jesus' answer, or rather his refusal to answer, seems to be that his questioners had already by their attitude to John the Baptist shown themselves incapable of recognizing spiritual authority; they would therefore not acknowledge the source of Jesus' authority even if told it.

The second and third 'episodes' (21.28–32 and 21.33–46) reinforce the point. The parable of the two sons show the religious leaders that despite their professed devotion to God, they in reality did nothing to obey him whereas the tax-collectors and prostitutes, though lacking a façade of religious observance, nevertheless responded to John's call to repentance. The obstinacy of the hierarchy was compounded by their failure even to accept the results of John's ministry as evidence of his divine authority. (The complex textual problems of vv. 29–31 do not affect the overall thrust of the episode.)

The parable of the vineyard tenants in the third episode is common to the three synoptics. Its emphasis is made clear in the editorial comment of v. 43.[43] Abuse of privilege must lead to loss of privilege. The nation which, through its leaders, was about to reject God's representative, would find itself rejected by God. The hearers clearly saw that this lesson was directed against them, but instead of learning from it, they simply became even more set in their opposition (vv. 45–46).

In the fourth episode (22.1–14), Jesus adds another parable, that of the wedding feast, which drives home the point that the rejection of the Jews is no hasty or capricious action by God but rather is caused by their own willful and persistent refusal to accept God's invitation. A variant form of this parable occurs at an earlier point in the narrative of Luke (Lk 14.15–24) and lacks anything parallel to vv. 11–14, the section about the guest with no wedding garment. It is very hard to understand the inclusion of this section in Matthew, as it does not seem to have any obvious interpretation, nor any clear relevance to the context. Indeed it appears rather to spoil the climax of the parable without any compensating value. Verse 22.13b and c contains phrases repeated elsewhere in Mt, but even these do not seem to shed any light.[44]

The order and juxtaposition of these three parables is unique to Matthew and the first is also unique in content. We can diagram the episodes of this section as follows:

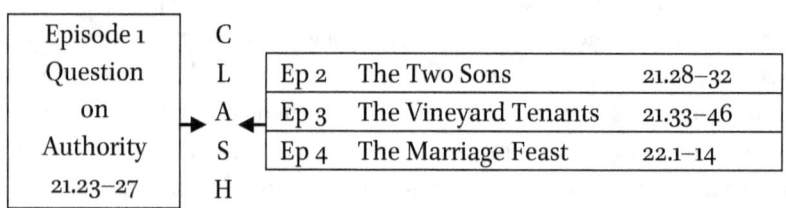

---

[43] This verse which is not in Mark, should be regarded as an expository comment of the editor on the meaning of the parable. For the use of βασιλεία τοῦ θεοῦ compare the rabbinical expression "the sovereignty of the heavens" to which βασιλεία τοῦ θεοῦ may allude. See G. Dalman, *The Words of Jesus Considered in the Light of Post-Biblical Jewish Wrirings and the Aramaic Language*, trans. D. M. Kay (T&T Clark, 1902), 97.

[44] Verses 11–14 may have been added for such reasons as similarity of subject matter and verbal connection between κλητοί (v. 14) and κεκλημένοι (vv. 3, 4 and 8). Perhaps vv. 11–14 can be considered as a fragment of a Jewish parable. The same kind of parable is attributed to Jochanan ben Zaccai in the Babylonian Talmud Shabbath 153a and to Judah ha Nasi in Midrash Koh 9.8.

4.1.6. Scene 6

The final scene extends over 22.15–46. Like the previous scene it falls into four episodes, of which the first three recount questions put to Jesus by his enemies, and the last a question put by him to them.

Each of these three questions put to Jesus was an attempt to trap him. In the first episode (22.15–22) the Pharisees linked with their opponents the Herodians to try and bring Jesus into political disrepute. Jesus neatly turned their attack into an unforgettable lesson on the twin responsibilities of man to God and to society.

In the second episode (22.23–33), the Sadducees concoct an improbable situation with metaphysical implications, aimed at embroiling Jesus in doctrinal controversy. Jesus sidesteps their question, declaring it to reveal the defectiveness of their knowledge both scripturally and experimentally. The false premises of the Sadducean view are shown up plainly even in that part of the OT whose authority they did purport to acknowledge.

The third episode (22.34–40) records a question which was presumably aimed at making Jesus align himself with some sectarian position. In an answer that is thematically somewhat akin to that in the first episode, Jesus states the pith of the law and the prophets to be the twofold duty of love to God and to man.

Finally, Jesus puts a question to his interrogators (22.41–46) which even at this late stage seems designed to bring a change of heart. It is indeed of David's line that the Messiah should come, but such is the Messiah that even David called him 'Lord.' That Jesus was the Son of David the crowds had already proclaimed; could the religious powers overcome their prejudice enough to perceive his Lordship? Apparently not, but at least they recognized their impotence against such a skilled teacher, and their subtle questions were stopped.

In some ways then, this scene is a mirror image of the previous one and could be diagrammed thus:

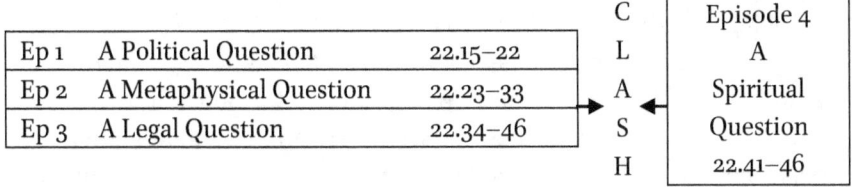

4.1.7. Summary of the First N Block

This block comprises six scenes, whose internal coherence is topical rather than formal. In the first, Jesus deals with various aspects of family life, and in the second with the rewards of devotion to God. The third gives various assessments of Jesus, while the fourth makes overt his Messianic claim. In the fifth Jesus warns the Jews of the dangers of rejecting him, and in the sixth they try to compromise him verbally. We may diagram as follows:

Scene 1	Scene 2	Scene 3	Scene 4
Divorce	Wealth	The Suffering Servant	Triumphal Entry
Celibacy	Its Significance	The Serving Lord	Cleansed Temple
Children	Rewards	The Coming King	Cursed Fig Tree

Scene 5		Scene 6	
	Obedience	Taxes	
Authority	Fruitfulness	Resurrection	The Messiah
	Responsiveness	Love	

This summary is oversimplified more than most, but it may still be of some value. In some ways the scenes seem to fall into pairs, 1 and 2, 3 and 4, 5 and 6, but the links do not seem close enough to be of great importance. There is overall a loose chain of connection between all of the scenes.

4.2. Formal Division of the D Block

This Block (23.1–26.2) is marked by minimal external setting material. From 21.23 we know that this section is set in the temple in the last week of Jesus' ministry and here in 23.1 Matthew adds that the audience initially included both disciples and "the crowds." In 26.1 the discourse closing formula occurs, and is linked with an announcement of the imminence of the passion. This serves both as a backward glance to the three passion predictions, and as a topical link with the plot against Jesus that immediately follows.

In 24.1–4a, by contrast, there is a more substantial piece of internal setting material which, as previously noted, divides this block into two, and marks a change of topic. In these verses we are given the information that Jesus comes out of the temple and goes to the Mount of Olives and that the audience is narrowed down to the disciples. According to the placement of this material, we shall examine the block in two halves.

4.2.1. *The First Half*

This section runs from 23.2–39 and in broad structure is not unlike the Sermon on the Mount. There is an introductory section (vv. 2–12) giving a general description of Pharisaic hypocrisy; then a longer central section (vv. 13–36) giving, if we follow the UBS text in omitting v. 14,[45] seven specific examples of the Pharisees' misdeeds; and finally a brief lament over Jerusalem (vv. 37–39). In the first section the crowds are addressed in the second person, in the second the scribes and Pharisees are so addressed, and in the third the apostrophised city.

A detailed examination reveals that the structure is again very dense. The introduction opens with a general statement (v. 2) about the relationship of the scribes and Pharisees to Moses. They are the "authorised interpreters" (TEV) of the Law. The deductions from this (οὖν, v. 3a) are firstly that their instructions, which rest on valid authority, are to be followed, but secondly their example is to be avoided. The reason for this second part is again twofold and introduced by γάρ (v. 3b); their actions do not match their words (v. 3b) and are merely for outward show (v. 5). The first of these charges is illustrated in v. 4 and the second in vv. 5b–7.

In vv. 8–10 Jesus sets out a contrasting behaviour pattern for his followers, first negatively with three types of activity which they are to avoid, each for its own reason; and second, positively, in a simple statement of the principle they are to follow. Finally, in v. 12, there is a summary of the passage giving God's evaluation of the actual behaviour of the scribes and Pharisees and of the expected behaviour of Jesus' followers.

The semantic relationships in vv. 2–12 are more clearly discernible in the diagram below, in which cola with the same degree of indentation have the same degree of semantic (*not* syntactic) subordination, or, to use a term that may be less ambiguous, involvement.

---

[45] Verse 14 has to be considered as an interpolation inspired by the Marcan (12.40) and Lukan (20.47) parallel. It is absent from the earliest and best authorities of the Alexandrian, Western and Caesarean types of text and the manuscripts including v. 14 have it in different places (either following or preceding v. 13). So Bruce Metzger, *A Textual Commentary on the Greek New Testament* (United Bible Societies, 1971), 60.

Verse	Degree of Semantic Involvement	
2	1	GENERAL STATEMENT (asyndetic)
3a	2	DEDUCTIONS (οὖν)
		(i) Positive (ποιήσατε καὶ τηρεῖτε)
		(ii) δὲ Negative (μὴ ποιεῖτε)
3b	3	REASONS (γάρ)
		(a) Words without deeds
4	4	EXAMPLES
		(i) δεσμεύουσιν δὲ ...
		(ii) καὶ ἐπιτιθέασιν
		(iii) αὐτοὶ δὲ ... οὐ θέλουσιν
5a	3	(b) Actions merely for show (δὲ)
5b–7	4	EXAMPLES (see next two diagrams)
8	2	CONTRAST (ὑμεῖς δὲ)
		(i) Negative
	3	(a) μὴ κληθῆτε ...
	4	REASON (γάρ)
9	3	(b) μὴ καλέσητε ...
	4	REASON (γάρ)
10	3	(c) μηδὲ κληθῆτε ...
	4	REASON (ὅτι)
11	2	(ii) Positive (δὲ)
12	1	SUMMARY (δὲ)

This diagram calls for a number of comments. The overall flow of the argument falls into two halves, with the second beginning at v. 8. The number of degrees of semantic involvement are the same in each half, so that there is a broad semantic symmetry about the whole. The final summary is at the same degree as the opening statement, so that the whole paragraph has an aesthetically satisfying balance, with the second half unwinding the convolutions of the first. The semantic involvement increases only by one degree at a time, but may decrease by more than one degree at a time. In the present paragraph there are two occasions when it decreases by two degrees (from 4 to 2 at the beginning of vv. 8 and 11), and on both occasions this 2-degree shift signifies a major step in the flow of the argument. In the former instance it shows that the second section is beginning and in the latter it shows that the final wind-down has begun.

Next it must be noticed that particles, to use a rather loose term, do not always indicate coordinate degrees of involvement. Thus the first reason (degree 3, v. 3b) is introduced by γάρ, but the second by δέ (degree 3, v. 5a). In vv. 8 and 11 δέ marks degree 2, whereas this is marked by οὖν in v. 3a. Reason at degree 4 is marked by γάρ in vv. 8, 9 but by ὅτι in v. 10. This is only to be expected, as such particles as οὖν and γάρ mark a relationship between statements rather than the degree of involvement of an argument.

In the overall layout of the argument there is a large scale chiasmus centred on degree 2. In the DEDUCTION (v. 3a) a positive aspect is first stated in simple form. Then a coordinate negative aspect is added. This is elaborated by degrees 3 and 4 in vv. 3b–7. In the CONTRAST the negative aspect is first stated (v. 8a), with elaboration at degrees 3 and 4 in vv. 8b–10; the positive aspect comes in v. 11 without elaboration.

The two degree shift between the first and second halves of the argument is 'toned down' by the recurrence of the catch word 'Rabbi' in vv. 7b, 8. This may be another instance on a small scale of papering over the cracks as suggested earlier.

In v. 8 there is what may be termed a telescoping of the semantics in the syntax. The opening clause ὑμεῖς δὲ μὴ κληθῆτε, 'Ραββί is syntactically only one clause, and is coordinate with πατέρα μὴ καλέσητε … (v. 9) and μηδὲ κληθῆτε … (v. 10). After deliberation, this is analysed as manifesting *two* degrees of semantic involvement. The ὑμεῖς δέ is taken to be alone on degree 2, and the μὴ κληθῆτε etc. to be on degree 3 with the coordinate parts of vv. 9 and 10. The reason is that the full pronoun form ὑμεῖς is used only in the first clause. Its emphatic nature and its being followed by δέ seem to set it up in contrast with the DEDUCTION in v. 3a. Its absence from the parallel imperative clauses of vv. 9 and 10 seems to support this. The whole of vv. 8–11 derive some unity from the emphasis on "you," despite the different degrees of involvement. The double occurrence of ὑμῶν in vv. 10, 11 strengthens the case, since none of the other records of this sentiment listed in the UBS text margin have exactly this form. Further support for putting ὑμεῖς δέ on a separate degree is that it leaves a neat and unobtrusive key pattern in the verbs on the third degree. The alternation here is

passive	Active	passive
κληθῆτε	καλέσητε	κληθῆτε

We have previously noted similar arrangements in the beatitudes and part of the Lord's Prayer (6.9b–10). This may be a feature of Matthew's individual style.

The change from the second person in v. 11 to the indefinite ὅστις in v. 12 serves to mark the decrease in degree of involvement from 2 back to 1 at the conclusion of the paragraph. Incidentally, v. 12 shows an interesting clash between linguistic levels. Lexically, it has a chiastic structure, but semantically its elements are simply polar.

In vv. 5b–7 there is an interesting contrast of syntax and semantics. Syntactically there is a string of three co-ordinate verbs, the first two governing one noun each and the last governing a string of three nouns and a further verb in the infinitive. This could be set up as follows.

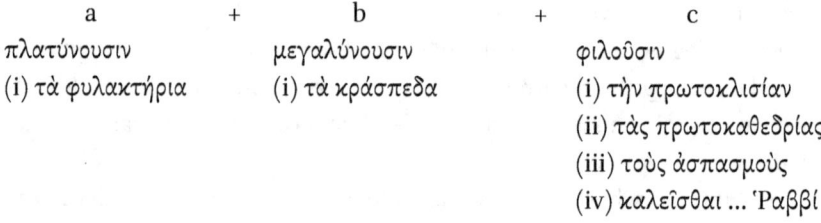

However, semantically, the particles appear to indicate a rather different structure. The γάρ links the whole sentence to degree 3 in v. 5a. The first two verbs πλαντύνουσιν and μεγαλύνουσιν are linked by καί, and thus form a pair with both morphological and phonological parallelism. The third verb is linked to these not by καί but by δέ, and does not share the parallelism. Of the items which it governs, the first two πρωτοκλισίαν and πρωτοκαθεδρίας again share morphological and to some extent phonological parallelism; thus they form another pair and are, we suggest, the items which are semantically coordinate with the first two verbs. The verbs express two aspects of clothing, and the nouns two aspects of position. This leaves the third noun ἀσπασμούς (which does not share the morphological or phonological features of the first two) and the infinitive verb. The difference in their word class, coming at the end of such a carefully balanced list makes it likely that this is a hendiadys, with the καλεῖσθαι ... Ῥαββί as the content of the ἀσπασμούς. If this is so there would be three types of ostentation which are semantically coordinate and could be set out in the following diagram.

	Type 1 Clothing			Type 2 Position		Type 3 Deference		
a	+	b	(c)	(i)	+	(ii)	(iii) = (iv)
πλατύνουσιν		μεγαλύνουσιν		πρωτοκλισίαν		πρωτοκαθεδρίας	ἀσπασμοὺς	καλεῖσθαι ... 'Ραββί

Thus the third verb φιλοῦσιν ends up semantically as a dummy item which is required in the syntax to carry the switch of word classes which is necessitated by the lexical structure of Greek at this point. We could say that φιλοῦσιν or something like it is implicit in the first two verbs, but does not need to be made overt because they are verbs.

The conclusion that there are basically three units semantically coordinate explains why despite the structural complexities, the whole of vv. 5b–7 have been kept at the same degree of involvement in the above diagram.

So much then for the introduction to the first half of this D Block! Fortunately the remainder is not quite so intricate. The main section (23.13–36), like the main section of the Sermon on the Mount, has seven parts. This section is usually called "The Seven Woes" from the formulaic opening Οὐαὶ ὑμῖν, γραμματεῖς καὶ Φαρισαῖοι ὑποκριταί. This occurs in each instance except the third where the variant form Οὐαὶ ὑμῖν, ὁδηγοὶ τυφλοὶ οἱ λέγοντες is found. Each Woe formula except the third is followed by a reason introduced by ὅτι. The 1st, 2nd, 4th, 5th and 6th Woe formulas are of comparable length, with the 3rd and especially the 7th much longer. The 7th Woe formula is rather different in content from the others and gradually changes from denunciation to prediction of punishment.

As things stand there is no obvious significant pattern. It is interesting to see, however, that if v. 14 is reinstated as the 2nd Woe formula and each of the following ones moved up a number, then something of a clearer pattern does emerge, as shown below.

Woes	1	2	3	4	5	6	7	8
Verses	13	14	15	16-22	23-24	25-26	27-28	29-36

Of the longer Woes, the one with the variant formula is now the central one, and is balanced by three shorter ones on either side. The last Woe, which we have already noticed to be somewhat divergent in content as well as in length, now stands apart as a conclusion and climax to the whole section. Considerations of discourse structure should not of course influence the evaluation of manuscript evidence,[46] but on the other hand it is hard to deny that a more convincing pattern is evident if v. 14 were included before v. 13, as in some manuscripts.

The final Woe (vv. 29–36) calls for a few comments. The logic of v. 31 does not seem too clear but presumably would have been acceptable in Rabbinic reasoning. Exactly where the theme moves from denunciation to prediction is hard to determine; v. 33 has an eschatological ring, but is taken with the preceding verses, as the conclusion of a denunciation with a vocative is paralleled in vv. 24 and 26. This would leave vv. 34–36 as the predictive climax.[47] These verses are also united by the use of the first person which starts in v. 34. As we have often remarked before, the final sentence of the section opens with ἀμὴν λέγω ὑμῖν, and the use of τὴν γενεὰν ταύτην (cf. 24.34) seems to make the passage refer primarily to the fall of Jerusalem.

This interpretation gains some support from the immediate switch to the lament over the city (vv. 37–39). Verse 37 has three verbal links with v. 34 (ἀποστέλλω, ἀποκτείνω, and προφήτας), but otherwise this section requires little comment. It does appear however that v. 39 would have sounded more appropriate if it had come in before the triumphal entry in ch. 21. In its present position it must refer to the parousia. At least it forms a fitting connec-

---

[46] On the other hand, considerations of discourse structure may be one of the reasons why v. 14 has been interpolated!

[47] For the very complex relationships between Mt 23:34–36, Lk 11:49–51 and the Logia see the observations by E. Haenchen, "Matthäus 23," *Zeitschrift für Theologie und Kirche* 48 (1951): 38–63; S. Légasse, "Scribes et disciples de Jésus," *Revue Biblique* 68 (1961): 323–333; and E. E. Ellis, "Luke 11:49-51: An Oracle of a Christian Prophet?" *The Expository Times* 74 (1963): 157–158. Compare further D. Lührmann, *Die Redaktion der Logienquelle*, 43–48; O. H. Steck, *Israel und das gewaltsame Geschick der Propheten* (Neukirchen Vluyn, 1967), 26–34, 50–53, 222–227. In the text of Matthew these words are spoken by Christ himself. On the other hand, in Luke the introductory formula shows that this is a quotation from an unknown writing. The particular enumeration προφήτας καὶ σοφοὺς καὶ γραμματεῖς, in Matthew may be an indication that the writing in question was a Jewish one. See especially A. Merx, *Das Evangelium Matthäus* (Reimer, 1902), 336ff., A. Harnack, *Sprüche und Reden Jesu* (J. C. Hinrichs, 1907), 72; R. Reitzenstein, *Das mandäische Buch des Herrn der Größe die Evangelienüberlieferung* (Carl Winters Universitätsbuchhandlung), 1919, 41ff.

tion with the eschatological material in the following chapter.[48]

We can sum up this half of the block then in the following simple diagram

Introduction	Main Section	Conclusion
Pharisee/Disciples	7/8 Woes	Lament
vv. 2–12	vv. 13–36	vv. 37–39

Any overall pattern would seem to be a loose chain connection rather than a key, unless the Lament is taken as dealing with the result of the Pharisaic behavior of the Introduction.

4.2.2. The Second Half

This section extends from 24.1–25.46. It is the most difficult section of the gospel to interpret and the more one brings a preconceived eschatological scheme to its interpretation, the more difficult it becomes. However some of the details are to be interpreted, this section does have a reasonably clear thematic structure and this will be kept in focus.

We have already noted the internal setting of 24.1–4a, in which the scene is changed from the Temple to the Mount of Olives. Jesus' words on the destruction of the Temple (v. 2) seem to provoke the disciples' question in v. 3, and it is this verse which is the key to the structure of the next two chapters. The disciples ask two questions, this first is simple in form (πότε ταῦτα ἔσται), and the second complex (τί τὸ σημεῖον τῆς σῆς παρουσίας καὶ συντελείας τοῦ αἰῶνος). Chiastically, the second question is taken up first (24.36–25.30). The change of topic is marked by the περὶ δὲ of 24.36. (Cf. Paul's constant use of this phrase in 1 Cor 7.1, 25; 8.1, 12.1; 16.1, 12.)

The second question as framed by the disciples seems to anticipate that *one* sign will indicate both the parousia and the end of the age. This seems to be the force of the omission of the article before συντελείας.[49] Perhaps the σῆς

---

[48] Verses 37–39 often have been considered as the original continuation of the quotation vv. 34–35. Verse 39 has been taken as a Christian addition either as a whole (so among others E. Klostermann, *Das Matthäusevangelium* [J. C. B. Mohr, 1927], *ad loc*) or in part (λέγω ... ἄρτι).

[49] It should, however, be noted that the article is not omitted in the Antiochian Recension, D,W,Δ,Φ, 0138, fam 13, 700, 1241 and the majority of the other witnesses. συντελεία τοῦ αἰῶνος is a technical apocalyptic expression. See P. Volz, *Jüdische Eschatologie von Daniel bis Akiba* (J. C. B. Mohr, 1903), 166. Compare, for example, T. Levi 10.2: ἐπὶ συντελείᾳ τῶν αἰώνων.

should also be understood before συντελείας. If so, this would seem to imply a transitive event, so that we might have to translate "What is the sign for your coming and bringing the age to a close?" This view seems to harmonise with the final judgement of 24.31–46, but is not required by anything in the answer of 24.4–35. Indeed within this answer (again chiastic) the end of the age and the parousia seem to be dealt with separately, though it is not clear whether or not Jesus is deliberately dissociating them. We may also note that Jesus uses the word τέλος (not συντέλεια) in 24.6, 14, though presumably these words refer to the same event.

Let us now proceed to analyse the text. Jesus does not state explicitly which question he is answering first, but the expressions οὔπω...τὸ τέλος of v. 6 and τότε ἥξει τὸ τέλος of v. 14 show that he is dealing first with the end of the age. Its negative indications are given first (vv. 4–6), then its positive one (vv. 7–14). Neither are spectacularly apocalyptic. Rather are they practical in nature and ethical in import. False Messianic claimants and the battles they cause show that the end is not yet (v. 6), and the followers of Jesus must not be deceived (v. 4) or anxious (v. 6). However, international strife and natural disasters (v. 7), persecution (vv. 8–10) and apostasy (vv. 11–12) show that the end is near and form a challenge to the believer's endurance (v. 13). Enough people will endure to ensure the worldwide spread of the gospel before the end (v. 14).

Now in vv. 15–31 there is a kind of zoom lens effect. After giving some broad general features in vv. 6–14, the focus is narrowed down to one of these features (θλῖψις vv. 9, 21, 29) and its after-effects. In those verses we have a description which is more spectacular and apocalyptic. It seems to begin with material fairly readily applicable to the siege of Jerusalem in AD 66–70, and end with material which can only be futuristic. Exactly where the change comes is hard to say. Verses 15–20 seem to refer primarily to the fall of Jerusalem and vv. 23–27 primarily to the future. Verses 21–22 could refer to either or both. Such deliberate ambivalence is one of the distinctive marks of this type of topic. The exact relevance of v. 28 is difficult to determine. It seems hard to connect it with v. 27, but if taken to refer to the false prophets of vv. 24–26 (cf. vv. 5 and 11), it could mean that it is where society is rotten that there will be many charlatans preying on it.[50]

---

[50] Part of the problem is that v. 28 probably is a profane proverb which has been made Jesus' word by tradition. Compare Job 39:30 and the parallel in Lk 17:37b. If connected nevertheless with v. 27, the application could be: "when the world has become rotten with evil, the Son of Man and his angels will come to execute the divine judgement" (Allen, *Matthew, ad loc*). In

The contrast of the unmistakable evidence of the parousia (v. 27) with the secret promises of the false Messiahs leads into a fuller description of the true parousia. At least vv. 29–31 appear to refer to the parousia, though the word does not occur in these verses. Astronomical phenomena of OT prophecy will be fulfilled, and the Son of Man will come in glory on the clouds, gathering his followers. This will happen immediately after the θλῖψις (v. 29), but it is not clear whether the σημεῖον of v. 30 precedes the parousia, accompanies it, or is identical with it.

Verse 31 seems to conclude the "close-up," and in vv. 32–35 we are given a summary which takes the long-distance, more generalised view again. Just as in nature there are clear signs of the advancing temporal seasons, so the discerning should be able to detect signs of the spiritual season. Verse 33 however is very vague, presumably on purpose, both about the signs (πάντα ταῦτα) and their meaning (is the subject of ἐγγύς ἐστιν masculine or neuter?).[51] The reference to ἡ γενεὰ αὕτη in v. 34 (cf. 23.36) appears to bring the fall of Jerusalem into the picture again, despite the futuristic import of the paragraph immediately preceding. This section is closed with the ἀμὴν λέγω ὑμῖν formula, and an assertion of the permanence of Christ's words. The very vagueness of these verses suggest that the fig tree of v. 32 (unlike that of 21.18) carries no particular symbolic reference, but is just a typical annually budding tree. The addition in Lk 21.29 of καὶ πάντα τὰ δένδρα supports this view.

Verse 36a marks a resumption of the first question of v. 3, πότε ταῦτα ἔσται, but we should notice that whereas in v. 3 the disciples seemed to be asking when the destruction of the Temple (v. 2) would take place, in his answer Jesus seems to be dealing with when the parousia will take place (vv. 37, 39, 44). If the fall of Jerusalem is somehow symbolic of the end time (as it seems to be in vv. 15–27), then the switch is understandable, though it is not explained. This change of perspective is only to be expected in apocalyptic material. As before, the answer to the question is first dealt with negatively. Jesus can give no answer, since the time is known to the Father alone. Never-

---

this case ἀετοί are the ministers of judgement. It cannot be completely excluded that the ἀετοί contain a reference to the eagles of the Roman standards. The patristic interpretation of the saints gathering round the glorified body of Christ did not take the context into account. See e.g. Cyr. Alex.: ὅταν ὁ υἱὸς τοῦ ἀνθρώπου παραγένηται τότε δὴ πάντες οἱ ἀετοί, τουτέστιν οἱ τὰ ὑψηλὰ πετόμενοι, καὶ τῶν ἐπιγείων καὶ κοσμικῶν ἀνενηγμένοι πραγμάτων, ἐπ' αὐτὸν συνδραμοῦνται (text in J. P. Migne, *Patrologiae Cursus Completus: Series Patrum Graecorum*, LXII, 848, Paris, 1857–1866).

[51] The vagueness in both Mark and Matthew contrasts remarkably with the explicit statement of the subject in Lk 21:31: ὅτι ἐγγύς ἐστιν ἡ βασιλεία τοῦ θεοῦ.

theless certain general characteristics can be given, in a parallel drawn from the flood. Not that they are very illuminating, for the physical and social behaviour mentioned is both normal and necessary in any age. Work in the field or in the home will be in its usual groove when the end comes and the elect are removed, presumably by the angels of v. 31. This very ordinariness seems to mean that the end could come at any time, which is consistent with the morals drawn. These dominate the rest of the section up to 25.30, and are two in number. The first is that the believer must be watchful (γρηγορεῖτε v. 42 and ἕτοιμοι v. 44), and the second is that he must be faithful (πιστός...καὶ φρόνιμος v. 45). Each requirement is fortified by an analogy; just as the householder does not know when the burglar will come, so the believer does not know when the Son of Man will come. Hence the need to be constantly watchful. And just as the servants do not know when their κύριος will return to evaluate their work, so the believers do not know when their κύριος will return in judgment. Hence the need to be constantly faithful and not presume upon delay.

These two needs are taken up in a parable. That of the ten girls (25.1–13) emphasizes watchfulness (γρηγορεῖτε, 25.13, cf. 24.42), and that of the talents faithfulness (πιστός 25.21, 23; cf. 24.45). The link of these two parables with 24.42–51 is further reinforced by the repetition of ἐκεῖ ἔσται ὁ κλαυθμὸς καὶ ὁ βρυγμὸς τῶν ὀδόντων 24.51 and 25.30. (The occurrence of this expression here perhaps throws back some more light on its earlier use in 13.42, 50; 22.13).

There is no need to go into the details of the parables, since each makes but one main point. We may notice in passing that the first gives a simple contrast of the wise and the foolish, whereas in the second there are two examples of faithfulness and only one of wickedness. The second parable is thus a little more complex in formal structure.

In 25.31–46 Jesus adds this information which goes beyond what the disciples had originally asked, though it certainly arises from the answers to their questions. The theme of the coming of the Son of Man (24.30–31, cf. 25.31–32) provides the jumping off point for the material on the final judgement, and the theme of separation (24.46ff.) gives a link of content. We may notice the tacit identification of the Son of Man of 25.31 with the King in 25.34. The judgement scene is in two contrasting and closely parallel halves, though the second is slightly reduced by comparison (e.g., 25.44 is shorter than 25.37–39). Both halves of the judgement are ended with a sentence beginning with ἀμὴν λέγω ὑμῖν (vv. 40, 45) and the concluding verse gives the (definitive!) closing setting.

Though these chapters have often been used in the construction of programmes for the end-time, we should note again the heavy ethical emphasis that pervades them (24.4, 6, 13, 23, 42, 44, 46; 25.13, 21, 23, 35, 36, 42, 43). It can hardly be repeated too often that what Scripture says about the future, it says so that we may be equipped with right attitudes rather than right answers.

A summary of these chapters is aided by the diagram below.

Each question is first answered negatively and then positively, and in each answer the second half expands on some particular feature(s) of the first. The first answer (to the second question) contains a brief summary to which there is no parallel in the second answer. The final section on the judgment draws together themes from both answers, and goes beyond what the questions originally asked.

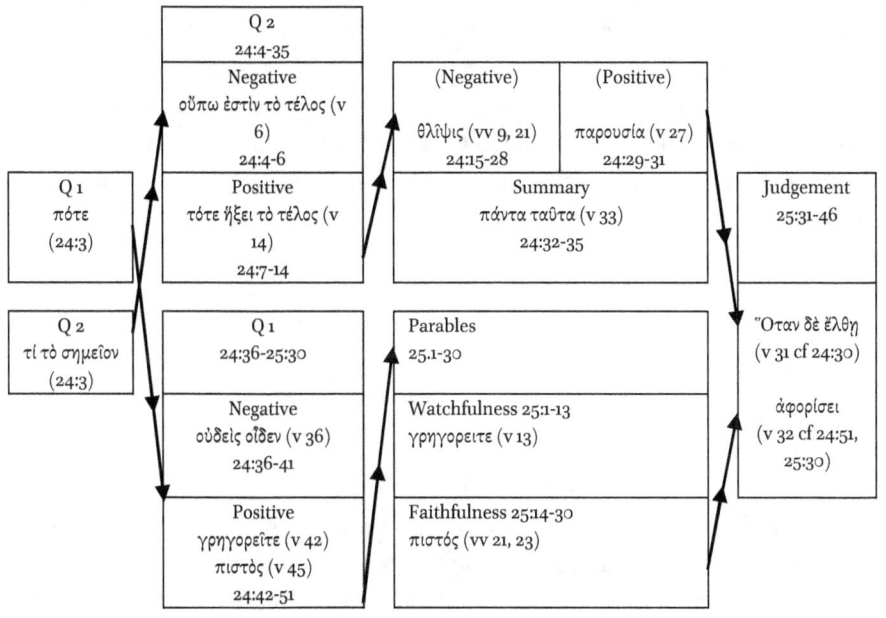

The arrows indicate the connections of thought.

4.3. Formal Division of the Second N Block

This block covers the remainder of the book, chs. 26–28, and may be analyzed as six scenes (numbered 7–12) with a short epilogue. The narrative is much more continuous in this section than in any previous section and, to that extent, any division into scenes is rather more arbitrary than previous divisions. However, in most cases there is some credible unity of theme to hold the scene together and the key pattern is often in evidence again. The scene division is as follows: Scene 7, 26.1–16; Scene 8, 26.17–30; Scene 9, 26.31–75; Scene 10, 27.1–14; Scene 11, 27.15–61; Scene 12, 27.62–28.15; Epilogue, 28.16–20.

4.3.1. Scene 7

After the brief introduction in 26.1–2, this scene embraces 26.3–16 and holds three episodes. The first of these (vv. 3–5) is closely linked in sense with the παραδίδοται of v. 2, and gives the definite decision of the authorities to take action against Jesus. The third (26.14–16) shows how their opportunity arose through the treacherous greed of Judas. The middle episode (26.6–13) is in stark contrast with this dismal background and reveals the costly devotion of the unnamed woman. Despite the disciples' objections, Jesus accepts the gift and relates it to his coming death. (And again, the concluding sentence of his remarks is introduced by ἀμὴν λέγω ὑμῖν.) The inclusion of this incident between the two references to the plot on Jesus' life seems quite deliberate and of high dramatic effect. Thematically, it gives the scene a key pattern.

Plot	Anointing	Plot
Ep. 1, 26.3–5	Ep. 2, 26.6–13	Ep. 3, 26.14–16

4.3.2. Scene 8

This scene, covering 26.17–30, deals with the Last Supper and is in some ways the thematic converse of the previous scene. The first episode (26.17–19) deals with the preparations for the Passover and the third (26.26–30) with the Last Supper. Between these, we are taken again to the theme of the plot (26.20–25) in which Jesus shows his knowledge of the treachery of Judas and relates it to God's purpose as revealed in scripture (v. 24). The resumption of the ἐσθιόντων αὐτῶν of v. 21 in v. 26 is a formal bracketing of the plot theme in this scene.

Passover Preparation	Plot	The Last Supper
Ep. 1, 26.17–19	Ep. 2, 26.20–25	Ep. 3, 26.26–30

4.3.3. Scene 9

This scene is taken to run from 26.31–75; it thus embraces all the material between the prediction of Peter's denial and its occurrence. The scene is thus considerably longer than the two previous scenes and can be divided into five episodes. The first of these (26.31–35) takes place on the journey from the house where the Passover was celebrated to the Mount of Olives. Jesus' attempt to lift the disciples' eyes past the crucifixion to the resurrection (v. 32) evokes a protest of loyalty from Peter which Jesus firmly sets aside (v. 34). The formula ἀμὴν λέγω ὑμῖν here (as in v. 21 above) seems to be used purely for emphasis and not to be of significance for the discourse flow.

Episode 2 (26.36–46) takes us into Gethsemane where there is the thrice offered prayer of Jesus and the thrice lost opportunity for the disciples to support him at this hour of great stress. If the transfiguration revealed the divine glory underlying the humanity, this passage shows more fully than any other the humanity quailing at the divine task that lay just ahead. There is almost a sense of physical relief when the tension breaks and the action is resumed (v. 46).

The third episode (26.47–56) outlines the betrayal (v. 47), the token resistance by the disciples (v. 51) and its rejection by Jesus (v. 52), and emphasizes the divine purpose behind the untoward arrest (vv. 54, 56). When the note of fulfilled prophecy is sounded (v. 56), then the disciples' flight is recorded, just as Jesus had predicted. The uncertain meaning of v. 50 does not affect the discourse flow.[52]

In the fourth episode (26.57–68) the scene moves to the High Priest's residence where the council was waiting. With Peter in the shadows (v. 58) and

---

[52] Verse 50 has been translated in very different ways. NEB: "Friend, do what you are here to do" (marginal reading: "Friend, what are you here for?"); TEV: "Be quick about it, friend!" Gute Nachricht: "Freund, worauf wartest du noch?" When one does not take into account certain transformations within receptor languages, it can be said that the use of ὅς in direct questions is generally rejected by NT philology. See F. Blass and A. Debrunner, *Grammatik des neutestamentlichen Griechisch*, trans. R. Funk (University of Chicago Press, 1961), §300.2 and P. Maas' observations in *Byzantinisch-Neugriechisches Jahrbuch* 8 (1931): 90 and 9 (1932): 64; Edwin A. Abbott, *Johannine Grammar* (Macmillan, 1906), §2231e. However, A. Deissmann (*Licht vom Osten* [J. C. B. Mohr, 1923], 100–105) has made a rather strong defence of the interrogative status and Turner (*Matthew*, 50) takes this possibility into account. So it is hard to arrive at any certainty. If ὅ is taken as a relative, the simplest solution is to supply a verb: "Do that for which you are here." See especially E. C. E. Owen's remarks in "St Matthew xxvi 50," *The Journal of Theological Studies*, 29 (1928): 384–386.

the false witnesses failing to produce adequate evidence, the main focus is on the clash between Jesus and the High Priest. Here Jesus accepts (v. 64, cf. v. 25) the claim of Messiahship thrust on him by Caiaphas, and is thereupon condemned to death (v. 66) and subjected to the humiliation of a condemned man (vv. 67–68).

The fifth and final episode details Peter's threefold denial, in progressively stronger terms, of his connection with Jesus. The cock crow made Peter's memory overcome his sense of self-preservation and, in the bitter realization of his failure, he departed in tears.

To sum up this scene then, the first and last episode deal with Peter and the puncture of his self-image. The second and fourth episodes show Jesus in different relationships to God and man, with some thematic contrast between them. In Scene 2, Jesus is accompanied by his friends and shown on his face before God in private supplication as a Son. In Scene 4, he is surrounded by his enemies and shown on his feet before men in public declaration of his Sonship. The earlier episode is a sort of spiritual preparation for the latter. The third, or central episode highlights Judas' treachery in bringing about Jesus' arrest. We could diagram the scene as follows:

> Peter's denial predicted
> Ep. 1, 26.31–35
> > Prayer in Gethsemane
> > Ep. 2, 26.36–46
> > > Arrest
> > > Ep. 3, 26.47–56
> > Trial before Caiaphas
> > Ep. 4, 26.57–68
> Peter's denial performed
> Ep. 5, 26.69–75.

4.3.4. Scene 10

This scene (27.1–14), containing the account of Judas' death unique to Matthew, is plainly and artificially formed on a key pattern. In the first episode (vv. 1–2) Jesus is taken to Pilate, and in the third (vv. 11–14) is interrogated by him. The intervening verses of the middle episode (vv. 3–10) relating Judas' remorse and suicide are deliberately inserted at this point (by contrast with Mark and Luke who do not have this Palestinian tradition). This may be intended to signify some slight delay before the interrogation took place, but another possible explanation is suggested below in Appendix C. Even the traitor's conduct and demise is seen to be related to God's purposes, as shown by the citation from Zechariah and the allusion to Jeremiah in vv. 9–10.[53] We may finally note the change from the Jewish capital charge of blasphemy in 26.65 to the Roman capital charge of sedition in 27.11. The diagram of the scene is again simple:

Transfer to Pilate	Death of Judas	Interrogation by Pilate
Ep. 1, 27.1–2	Ep. 2, 27.3–10	Ep. 3, 27.11–14

4.3.5. Scene 11

This scene is taken to extend from 27.15–61 and is the most continuous in narrative and loosely knit in theme. It is here regarded as comprising five episodes, though other divisions are possible.

The first episode (27.15–26) deals with the release of Barabbas and seems at first an aside from the main theme of the fate of Jesus. It does however serve to emphasize both the determination of the authorities to have Jesus executed (v. 20) and Pilate's reluctance to do so (v. 24). Political expediency (θόρυβος γίνεται v. 24) eventually overcame both his own conscience and his wife's superstition (v. 19) and secured Jesus' condemnation (v. 26).

The details of the dream and the handwashing peculiar to Matthew, undoubtedly heighten the effect of the account.[54]

In the second episode (27.27–31) Jesus is handed over to the governor's soldiers for further degradation prior to the crucifixion. Not surprisingly, it is the political side of the accusation against Jesus which forms the focus of the soldiers' mockery. The "king" is decked out with the imitation trappings of royalty – the robe, crown and scepter. When finally sated with their cruelty,

---

[53] Compare H. F. D. Sparks, "St. Matthew's References to Jeremiah," *Journal of Theological Studies, New Series* 1, no. 2 (1950): 155–156. For the targumizing procedure in Matthew and the relationship between formula quotation and context (vv. 5–9a) see especially Stendahl, *Matthew*, 120–127.

[54] These details probably belong to Palestinian traditions. The short note in v. 19 recapitulates a more elaborate legend according to M. Dibelius's views (in "Zur Formgeschichte der Evangelien," *Theologische Rundschau*, Neue Folge I [1929]: 207). Compare also his *Formgeschichte*, 113–114 and R. H. Lightfoot, *History and Interpretation in the Gospels* (Hodder & Stoughton, 1935), 160.

they returned to Jesus his own clothes (v. 31).

Episode 3 (27.32–44) gives a brief but poignant picture of the actual crucifixion. Being already in a weak condition after the flogging of v. 26, Jesus needed help with the task of carrying the cross and an unfortunate foreigner was pressed into service for this (v. 32). The widespread use of bold face type in the 1st and 2nd editions of the UBS Greek text between vv. 34 and 48 shows how very much the suffering and death of Jesus is seen by the evangelist as linked with God's purpose as revealed in the OT. Psalms 22 and 69 are especially echoed. The charge over Jesus' head relates to his alleged royal claims (v. 37) and it was thus appropriate for him to be executed along with a pair of bandits who had probably been involved in political insurrection (cf. Mk 15.7, Lk 23.19). The mockery of the onlookers centers rather on his claims to divine Sonship (v. 40), while that of the authorities takes up both aspects (vv. 42–43). No detail of the physical suffering of Jesus is given, nor any indication of his reaction to the insults flung at him.

The fourth episode (27.45–56) relates the death of Jesus with minimal detail, for the interest is heavily upon its significance and interpretation. The darkness (v. 45) may be seen as an echo of Ex 10.22 and Amos 8.9–10 and indicates the wrath of God. The torn temple curtain (v. 51) shows that entry to God's presence is no longer barred and Matthew alone adds the cryptic account of the resurrection of the (? recently) dead saints.[55] The strange phenomena of the darkness and the earthquake are evidently seen by the centurion in charge of the execution squad as related to Jesus' death, and wring from him an acknowledgement at least of Jesus' supernatural powers and perhaps of his deity (v. 54). The whole chain of events was watched from a distance by some women who had evidently been among Jesus' followers for a considerable time (vv. 55–56).

The fifth and last episode (27.57–61) relates how Joseph of Arimathea obtained the body of Jesus and gave it respectable burial. The stone across the grave entrance must have given the setting an air of awesome finality as the two Marys took up their lonely vigil (v. 61).

In summing up this scene, it is hard to find any diagram scheme that is very helpful. We might see some thematic balance between episode one, where the mob's howls obtain the release of Barabbas, and episode 5, where

---

[55] It is still an open question whether these miracles are of Jewish-Palestinian or Christian-Hellenistic origin. For parallels see especially G. Dalman, *Jesus-Jeshua, Studies in the Gospels* (Ktav Pub. House, 1922), 198; P. Saintyves, *Essais de Folklore Biblique: Magie, Mythes et Miracles dans L'Ancien et le Nouveau Testament* (Emile Nourry, 1923), 423–463.

Joseph's request secures the body of Jesus, but it is hard to see any patterning in episodes 2, 3 and 4, which might even be regarded as one long climactic episode. They are certainly more closely bound together in terms of their unity and continuity of narrative than any other three episodes in the gospel. In the diagram below the broken line indicates a possible key pattern and the square with dotted internal lines indicates the close unity of the scene. It is interesting to observe that it is here at the climax of the story that the patterns that emerge fairly readily elsewhere are hardest to find.

Release of Barabbas Episode 1 27.15–26	Mockery by Soldiers Episode 2 27.27–31	The Crucifixion Episode 3 27.32–44	Death of Jesus Episode 4 27.45–56	Burial of Jesus Episode 5 27.57–61

4.3.6. Scene 12

This scene runs from 27.62–28.15 and gives a rather clear key pattern with the resurrection in the second episode set between the dispatch of the guards to the tomb and their support. Both the pericopes involving the guards are unique to Matthew and their placement seems a deliberate means of throwing the resurrection into higher relief.[56]

In the first episode (27.62–66) the Jewish authorities are represented as anxious to prevent the spreading of any resurrection story, which presumably shows that Jesus' teaching to the disciples on this had not gone entirely neglected by a wider audience. They are even able to specify that the third day is the crucial time. Pilate somewhat curtly accedes to their request for a detachment of soldiers for guard duty at the tomb.

Episode 2 (28.1–10) opens with the loyal women at the tomb again early in the morning. How different things were from their previous visit! The angelic presence paralysed the guard (οἱ τηροῦντες v. 4) but by contrast brought reassurance to the women (the emphatic ὑμεῖς of v. 5 is unique to Matthew).

---

[56] There can be no doubt that both pericopes stem from the same Palestinian source. Whether one wants to speak of an "apologetische Legende" with Bultmann (*Geschichte*, 310) or to construct with F. Cumont ("Un Rescrit Impérial sur la Violation de Sepulture," in *Revue Historique* 163 [1930]: 241–266) a historical relationship with the διάταγμα Καίσαρος inscription from Nazareth is not pertinent to the present study.

The resurrection is asserted, and a meeting with Jesus promised for the disciples in their familiar Galilean homeland. The women themselves did not have to wait for this but met Jesus while on the way to spread their news to the other disciples. Again the promise of a meeting in Galilee was given.

The third episode (28.11–15) shows the guards sufficiently recovered to report to the high priests, who make one last desperate attempt to discredit Jesus. No doubt the soldiers were more than willing to cover themselves and make some extra money in the process. In relating these two incidents involving the guard, Matthew is clearly giving the lie to the official Jewish version of what happened.

We may represent this scene with a simple key diagram.

The Guard Set	The Resurrection	The Guard Bribed
Ep. 1, 27.62–66	Ep. 2, 28.1–10	Ep. 3, 28.11–15

4.3.7. *The Epilogue*

Why treat the last five verses of the gospel (28.16–20) as an epilogue rather than just another episode in the previous scene? There are several reasons. Firstly, there is a clear break of time and (more prominently) place, from the events of 21.1–28.15; the location is moved from Jerusalem back to Galilee. Secondly, these verses have the typical function of an epilogue in that they pull together some loose ends, notably the thrice repeated promise of the resurrection (16.21; 17.23; 20.19). These are here fulfilled not only to the women (as in 28.9–10) but to the very disciples to whom the promises were given. Thirdly, the inclusion of these verses with the previous scene would not simply fail to yield a coherent pattern, but would actually obscure the one which is otherwise there. The fourth reason is in a way the converse of the third; taking these verses as an epilogue gives the whole gospel a nicely rounded balance both of structure and of theme. The Prologue of 1.1–17 links Jesus as the central character of the gospel with Israel's historic past; this epilogue, especially in its closing words, links him with the open-ended future of the new community which his ministry has brought into being. Whereas before Jesus' birth, God's purposes were narrowly channeled through one particular nation and through successive members of it, now in the resurrection era, they can embrace all nations through the authority and perpetual presence of the one representative Man. Thus will come the completion of God's purposes in the consummation of the age.

4.3.8. Summary of the Second N Block

This block holds six scenes in whose thematic structure Matthew's careful arrangement can frequently be observed. Scenes 9 and 11 each have 5 episodes and the other scenes have 3 episodes each. The longer scenes hold the crucial events of the arrest, trial, crucifixion and death of Jesus and the shorter scenes give the related and supporting events.

In the seventh scene the devotion of the woman at Bethany is contrasted with the crystallization of the plot on Jesus' life, and in the eighth the betrayal prediction is contrasted with the solemn celebration of the Passover. Scene 9 covers events from the prediction of Peter's denial to its occurrence, with Peter (anonymously) active again in the 3rd and central episode of Jesus' arrest. Scene 10 sets Judas' death (a flashforward?) between Jesus' transfer to Pilate and Pilate's interrogation. Scene 11, in a continuous narrative, moves from the release of Barabbas and condemnation of Jesus through his mockery, crucifixion and death to the burial in Joseph's tomb. Scene 12 uses the appointment and bribing of the guards as a foil for the great discovery of the empty tomb. The Epilogue rounds off the immediately preceding narrative with the promised resurrection appearance and links Jesus with the future as the Prologue did with the past.

We may diagram the block as below.

Diagram for Summary of 2nd N Block

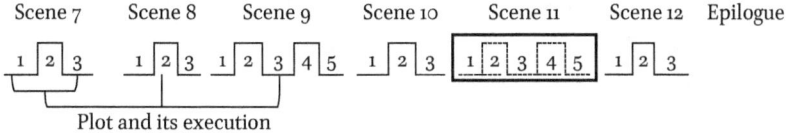

As already noted, the key pattern is much in evidence again, but in contrast with the diagram for Act 2, there is relatively little thematic complexity. The plot and its execution stand out, but are clearly integrally related to the main part of the narrative. The themes laid down in Act 1 and developed in Act 2, are brought to a conclusion through one clear and dominant train of events.

In the diagram the left-hand forking of the line linking the occurrences of the plot motif is intended to indicate how the plot moves from the peripheral episode of Scene 7 to the central episodes of Scenes 8 and 9.

4.4. Summary of Act 3

Again, a diagram may be helpful (see p. 99). In this case it is complicated by the large number of scenes, so, in order to keep it on one page, the episodes have been written vertically. This gives the key patterns in the 2nd N Block a curious appearance, but they mean the same as before. Rings around groups of episodes indicate a chain link of varying degrees of closeness. The one or two word summaries under the scenes give some minimal assistance to the memory about the content.

5. Summary of the Gospel

In this final section an attempt must be made to outline the overall development of themes in the gospel. This will inevitably involve some overgeneralization, and if only because of the limited length of the page, labels must be used which do not embrace the whole content of the sections to which they are attached.

The overall balance of the N and D Blocks has been amply noted before. We might pause to add that certain features such as the use of the key pattern and the frequency of genitive absolutes and ἰδού are much more characteristic of Acts 1 and 3 than of Act 2, but focus will be mainly on the themes. Perhaps somewhat unexpectedly one can usefully separate the N Blocks from the D Blocks, as the subject matter of the D Blocks is not closely related to the unfolding of the story.

5.1. The N Blocks

Perhaps we can diagram some of the main N Block themes as on p. 100.

It must be emphasized that these are main themes only and cannot do full justice to the complexity of the gospel. In Act 1 the first N Block is now seen to be the *setting* for the whole gospel, but setting in which both opposition (derived ultimately from Satan) and human response (e.g. from Herod, the Magi, or the first four disciples) are latent. The second N Block gives the *establishment* of the main themes, with the healings bringing a challenge that evokes varying reactions from the beholders. The opposition from the establishment begins to make itself felt.

In Act 2 Jesus is led, through the questions from John the Baptist, to make a private but explicit self-identification. The opposition to his ministry grows

DISCOURSE STRUCTURE IN MATTHEW'S GOSPEL

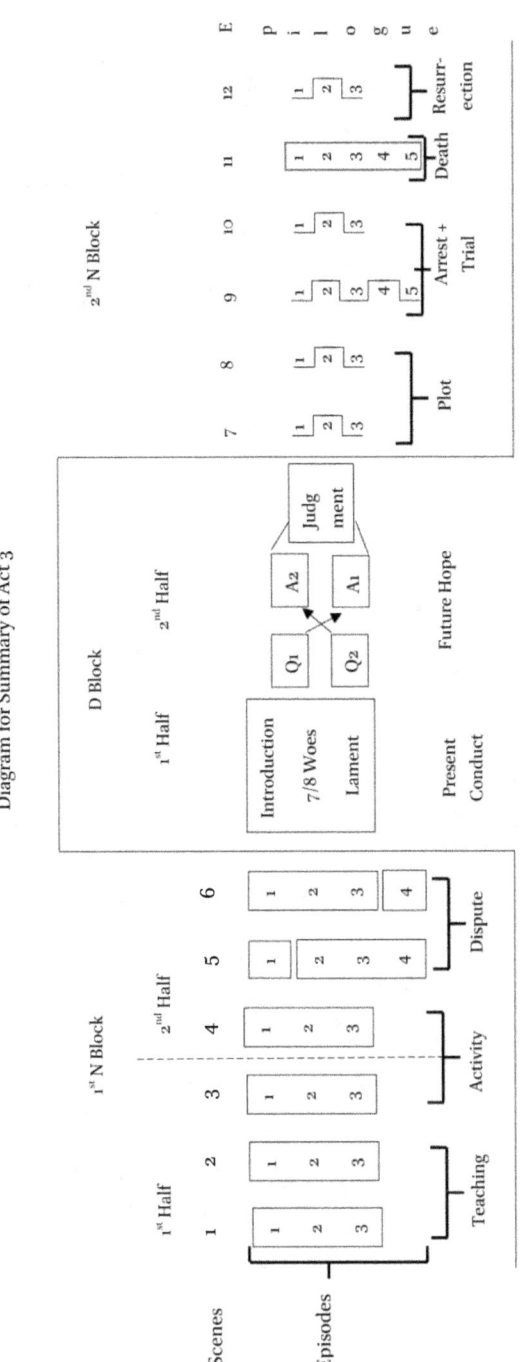

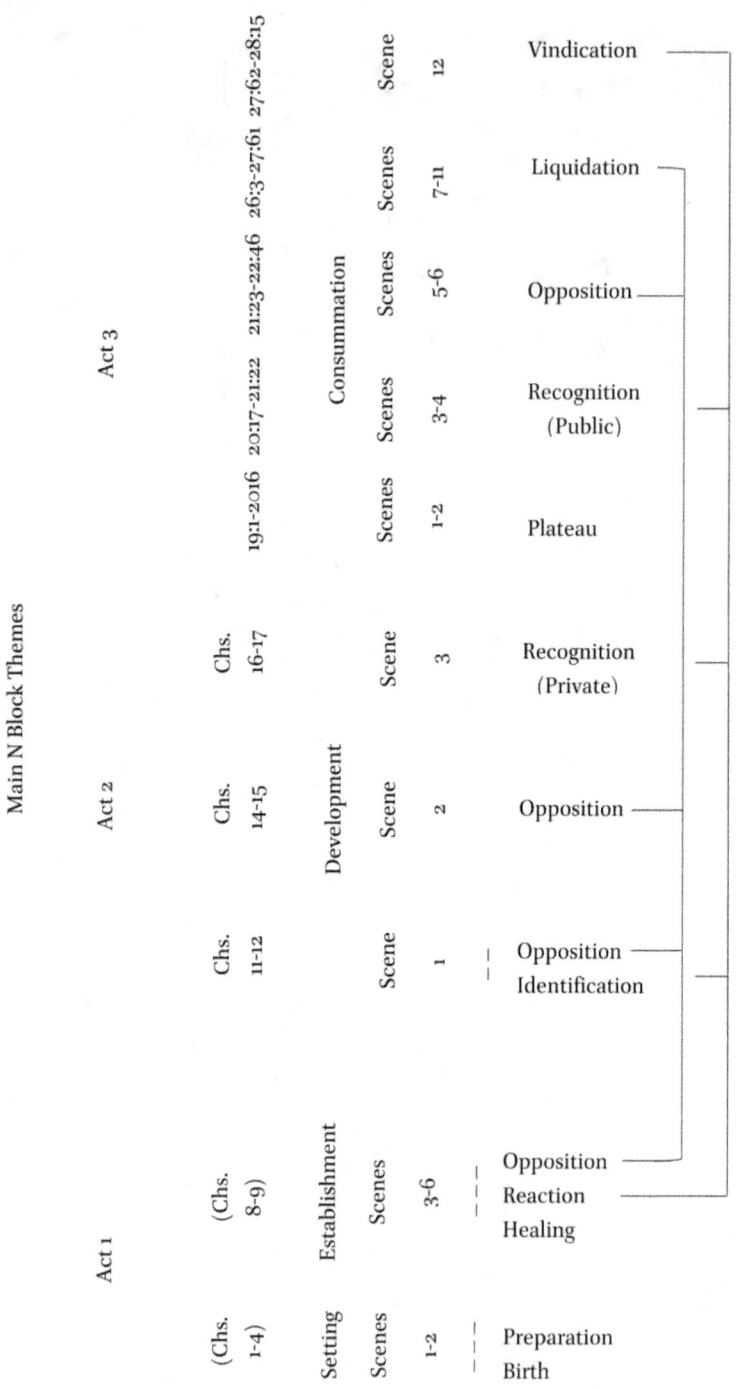

and hardens, but through the confession at Caesarea Philippi and the transfiguration, there is a corresponding growth in understanding and conviction on the part of at least some of the disciples. Thus Act 2 can be said to give the *development* of the main themes.

Act 3 sees the culmination of the ministry in the public recognition of Jesus at the triumphal entry. This naturally brings the opposition to a head and leads to its final action in the crucifixion. In the resurrection, however, God gives an open vindication of Jesus' life and work which is of universal and eternal application. Thus, the gospel reaches its *consummation*.

If the above outline is a reasonable presentation of the gospel themes, then we can categorize Matthew as being basically polar in its outlook. Jesus' life and ministry provoke fundamentally only two types of response, acceptance or rejection. Both are manifested in different ways, but the variety of expression conceals what is essentially a dichotomy.

A general movement forward from the setting, through the establishment and the development to the consummation is now visible. The only large break in this scheme comes in chs. 19 and 20 at the beginning of Act 3. Until the healing of the two blind men at the end of ch. 20, this section does not carry the action forward at all. Rather, we are simply given more examples of Jesus' teaching on such specific issues as family life and wealth. If this section is to be integrated into the outline, it has to be regarded as a sort of plateau (the label in the diagram), a pause before the final climax begins. Such a device would not be without literary parallels.

This outline is painted with broad strokes only, but does seem to yield a coherent direction and purpose behind the gospel as a whole, into which the various sections fit fairly readily, each making its contribution.

5.2. The D Blocks

Now we must look at the D Blocks and here again the labels can only be rather general. All the D Blocks make considerable mention of the Kingdom of Heaven, and we might use this as a basis for labelling them as in the diagram on p. 102.

The first D Block, the Sermon on the Mount, with its frequent "You have heard ... but I say to you ..." sets up the Kingdom of Heaven in contrast with life under the Law as in the past. They are in contrast, but not in opposition, since in Jesus' ministry, the Law is not destroyed but fulfilled.

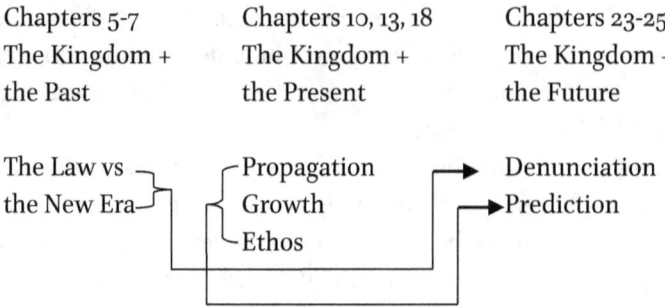

The three separate D Blocks in Act 2 give three windows into the Kingdom as Jesus expounds it. Its manner of propagation, growth and conduct are each dealt with. Since they embody principles which are as relevant today as when Jesus taught, the label "The Kingdom and the *Present*" seems not inappropriate.

In the final D Block, with its two distinct parts, the two previous aspects of teaching are picked up. The practical rejection of the New Era by those who preferred life under the Law leads to the denunciations of ch. 23. The spread of the Kingdom through the life and witness of its members leads naturally to teaching on its consummation as found in the predictions of chs. 24 and 25. The future reference of this gives rise to the label in the diagram.

5.3. Integration of the N and D Blocks

Now though the N and D Blocks have been considered separately with regard to their themes, and though the removal of the D Blocks would still leave an orderly narrative, we can see that the D Blocks hold material which is appropriate to the stage of the narrative where each is placed. The Sermon on the Mount, with its broad contrast of old and new, is consonant with its position in the section where the narrative is being *established*. Considerations of the propagation, growth and ethos of the Kingdom are fittingly set amid the *development* of the narrative themes. And to set teaching on the future fulfillment of the Kingdom in the *consummation* of the narrative is natural and congruent.

We have already noticed some of the use made in this gospel of repetition. It is interesting to observe a rather consistent patterning in the placement of repeated motifs in relation to the discourse blocks. Each block has a distinct motif occurring both before and after it. The distance of the repeated motif from the D Block itself is variable, but with under-the-surface patterning of this kind, complete symmetry is not to be expected. The first D Block (chs. 5–7) is preceded by the calling of the first four disciples (4.18–22) and followed by the calling of Matthew (9.9). The second D Block (ch. 10) is preceded and followed by a Beelzebub charge (9.34 and 12.22–24). The third (ch. 13) is enclosed by the demands for a sign (12.38–42 and 16.1–4) and the fourth (ch. 18) by passion predictions (17.22–23 and 20.17–19). References to the evil designs of the authorities (21.45–46 and 26.3–5) surround the fifth block (chs. 23–25). We may note furthermore that the two incidents involving two blind men (9.27–31 and 20.29–34) fit neatly into this pattern, since they enclose the three central discourses and their enclosing repetitions. This pattern may be represented diagrammatically:

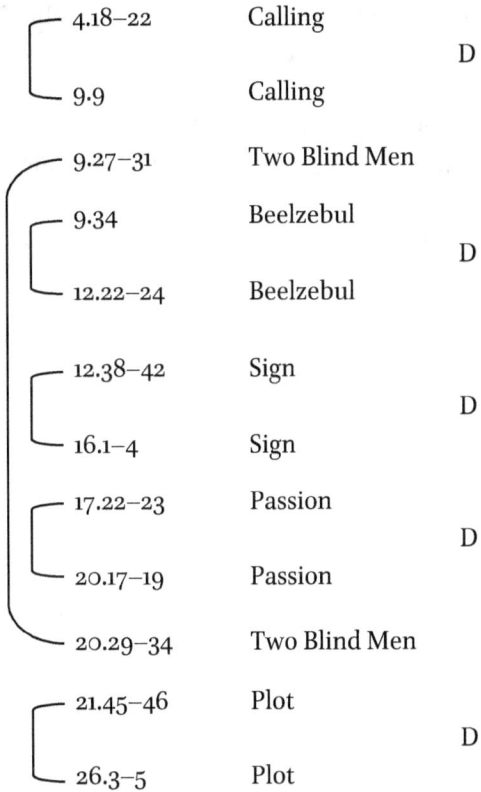

We may observe furthermore that the motif of John the Baptist interweaves and interpenetrates this whole pattern. References to John precede the first incident involving the two blind men, and follow the second (9.14 and 21.25–26, 32). Other references to John occur within the inclusions formed by the Beelzebul and sign-demand repetitions (11.2–19 and 14.1–12). The other references to John in Act 2 of the gospel (16.14 and 17.9–13) form their own inclusion of the first passion prediction (16.21), in some measure setting it off and highlighting it. There remains the further section 3.1–17 that deals with John. For the interweaving of John's appearances with the D Block inclusions to be complete, it would be necessary for another reference to John to come at some point after 26.5. There is no such reference, but there is the reference to Elijah in 27.47–49. Since elsewhere in the gospel Elijah is mentioned only in close connection with John (11.14; 16.14; 17.3–4, 10–12), it seems quite possible that the mention of him in 27.47–49 can be regarded as the completion of the pattern of references to John. If this is acceptable, the total interweaving of these motifs is as shown in the diagram on p. 105.

It appears that not all the motifs in Matthew exhibit this kind of distribution. For instance, references to gentiles, and to Jesus as the Davidic king, show no such patterning.

Thus the gospel as a whole has an impressive unity of structure, theme and movement which is not fully apparent when only shorter sections are under consideration.

Discourse Structure in Matthew's Gospel

```
Elijah      27:47-49
                            ┌ Plot        26:3-5  ┐
                            │ D                   │
                            │ Plot        21:45-46┘
John        21:25-26, 32 ───┤
                            │ Two Blind Men 20:29-34 ─────┐
                            │ Passion     20:17-19 ┐      │
                            │ D                    │      │
                            │ Passion     17:22-23 ┘      │
John*       17:9-13      ───┤                             │
Passion     16:21                                         │
John*       16:14        ───┤                             │
                            │ Sign        16:1-4 ┐        │
John        14:1-12      ───┤ D                  │        │
                            │ Sign        12:38-42┘       │
                            │ Beelzebul   12:22-24 ┐      │
John*       11:2-19      ───┤ D                    │      │
                            │ Beelzebul   9:34     ┘      │
                            │ Two Blind Men 9:27-31 ──────┘
John        9:14         ───┤
                            │ Calling     9:9  ┐
                            │ D                │
                            │ Calling     4:18-22┘
John        3:1-17       ───┘
```

* indicates those points where John is associated with Elijah. At 11:14 and 17:13, this explicit association of the two is peculiar to Matthew.

APPENDIX A

The Handling of Participants in Act 1, Scenes 1 and 2

The aim here is to make explicit the surprisingly patterned manner in which participants enter and leave the story, and to point out some of the syntactic devices by which focus is switched.

In Scene 1 episode 1 (1.18–25) the first sentence is a title for the whole scene. Although syntactically Jesus Christ is attributive to γένεσις, semantically it is in focus by virtue of the word order. The next sentence, structurally rather curious, introduces both Mary and Joseph, but by using oblique cases, sets both in the background and seems to focus on the event of the pregnancy. In v. 19 Joseph, now in the nominative, is brought into focus, but in v. 20 he is backgrounded again by a genitive absolute (a favourite device in this gospel for backgrounding). And as here, it is very often followed by ἰδού, bringing a new element into focus. In this instance it is the angel who makes a speech lasting through v. 21 and followed by editorial comment, vv. 22–23. Then Joseph is brought to the foreground again through a nominative participle. Mary is referred to obliquely in v. 25, and finally Jesus is mentioned once more. In terms of the participants then, we see once more what may be presented as a key pattern, but of a more complex nature than any of the key patterns that have been seen in the formal structure.

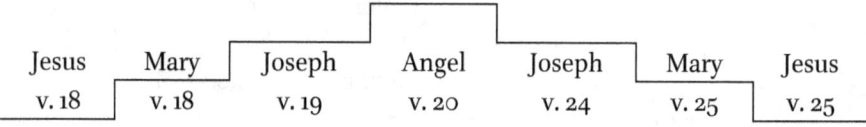

| Jesus | Mary | Joseph | Angel | Joseph | Mary | Jesus |
| v. 18 | v. 18 | v. 19 | v. 20 | v. 24 | v. 25 | v. 25 |

An alternative presentation is in terms of inverted parallelism, thus

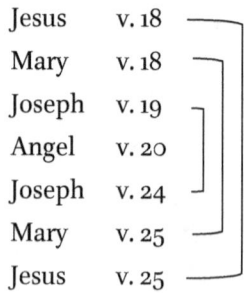

Jesus   v. 18
Mary   v. 18
Joseph v. 19
Angel   v. 20
Joseph v. 24
Mary   v. 25
Jesus   v. 25

Episode 2 opens (2.1) with the genitive absolute which sets the whole of episode 1 into the background and concentrates on a new section. Note that the genitive absolute also obliquely introduces Herod as a character to be prominent in what follows. But the focus is now on the Magi (observe the ἰδού) who come to the king's court with their question. Herod is foregrounded (2.3) with a nominative participle, and passes on the question to the religious authorities. These give their reply, but are not foregrounded in the way the Magi and Herod were. The focus is on their reply rather than on them. Herod resumes centrality in v. 7 and retains it through v. 8 (but note that, perhaps because he had not been backgrounded, the nominative participle in v. 7 follows the name rather than preceding it as in 1.24; 2.3). Then the Magi, who have been mentioned again in v. 7, come to the fore with another nominative participle in v. 9 and remain in focus to the end of the episode, though the star is syntactically subject in v. 9b. Nominative participles unobtrusively maintain the focus on the Magi in vv. 10, 11 and 12 and in this last verse there is another oblique reference to Herod. Participation thus again follows a key pattern.

Herod	Magi	Herod	Scribes	Herod	Magi	Herod
v. 1	v. 1	v. 3	v. 5	v. 7	v. 9	v. 12

The third episode is in three parts, of which the first and third are closely parallel. Both open with a genitive absolute (vv. 13, 19) the first of which puts episode 2 into the background, and the second of which treats the middle part of this episode likewise. Both are followed by ἰδού and the foregrounding of the angel with his message. Both continue by foregrounding Joseph with a nominative participle (vv. 14, 21), and both end with an OT reference (vv. 15, 23).

In the middle section Herod is the lone participant, and he is brought into focus with a nominative participle (v. 16). This section also closes with an OT reference (v. 18). The participants in the whole episode then run

Angel	Joseph	Herod	Angel	Joseph
v. 13	v. 14	v. 16	v. 19	v. 21

Here is a variation on the key pattern in which the first and third sections are identical rather than being mirror images.

In Scene 2 the first episode maintains throughout a focus on John the

Baptist (whose introduction is prepared by a new temporal setting [3.1]) though others are mentioned, e.g., the general populace in v. 5 and the Pharisees and Sadducees in v. 7.

In the second episode the participation is also simple. Jesus is re-introduced (v. 13); John with his initial refusal to baptize Jesus comes in (? abruptly) as the subject of a verb with no nominative participle (v. 14); and then Jesus is foregrounded again with a nominative participle (v. 15). Participation becomes somewhat obscure with the textual corruption and ambiguity of v. 16, but probably Jesus remains in focus until the voice is brought in in v. 17.

The second half of this second episode (4.1–11) probably exhibits a key pattern with the first and last verses balancing each other and a different structure in between. We may diagram vv. 1 and 11 and follows:

Jesus	Spirit	Devil	Devil	Angels	Jesus
	V. 1			V. 11	

In between there lie three utterance-response pairs, which perhaps show hostility through their asyndeton. In v. 3 the devil is foregrounded with a nominative participle and Jesus' reply is given via ὁ δὲ and a nominative participle (cf. 3.14). In the second pair the devil is brought back with τότε (v. 5) and Jesus rejects him with ἔφη αὐτῷ and no link (v. 7). In the third pair the devil returns with no connective (unless πάλιν [v. 8] is counted), and Jesus spurns him again with τότε λέγει αὐτῷ. Whether or not the linkage reflects the content, the three sharp utterance-response pairs probably do indicate something of the hostility between the participants. At any rate they are unlike any other participant alternation in the first N Block.

APPENDIX B

Transition Markers

Participial clauses account for a remarkably high proportion of episode-initial material. Matthew uses such participial links much more than Mark or Luke.

These participles fall into two groups with respect to their cases though there is a small residue. In many instances there is a nominative participle which is syntactically attributive to the subject of the main verb of the sentence (or the first main verb, if there is more than one). Rather rarely, the participle simply gives added information about an already named subject; 1.19 is the only clear example of this, and the participle there is the verb 'to be,' which may have a unique distribution.

In many cases, as already noted in section 3.2.1, a nominative participle has the effect of bringing an already named participant into the foreground in a narrative or dialogue passage. In Act 1 we may list examples in 1.24; 2.3, 14, 21; 3.7, 15; 4.21; 8.8, 10; 9.2, 4, 8, 11, 19, 23. It is interesting to observe that the participle in these examples always precedes the name of the participant if this is given. An exception is in 9.22, where the name comes first, but is followed by *two* participles. If the participant is already clear in the flow of the story, the name may be replaced by an article which then precedes the participle (2.9; 4.20, 22; 9.12, 31).

Many of the above examples are not episode initial. Where nominative participles do occur at the beginning of an episode, they seem to have a double function. In terms of the discourse flow, they mark some degree of transition and in terms of the participant alternation, they retain focus on the last major participant (4.12, 18; 8.14, 18; 9.1, 9; 12.9; 14.13; 15.29).

In a large number of other examples the participle is in the genitive, a "genitive absolute" construction. In many cases these have the effect of backgrounding a participant and switching focus on to another participant or event (1.18, 20; 5.1; 9.10, 33; 11.7). When in episode-initial position, a genitive absolute also has a double function. In terms of participants, it puts someone into the background and in terms of the discourse flow, by the very switch of focus, it marks a transition point (2.1, 13, 19; 8.1, 5, 28; 9.18). In quite a few cases, the genitive absolute is followed by ἰδού, which seems to emphasize the switch of focus (1.20; 2.1, 13, 19; 8.1; 9.18; 12.46; 20.29; 26.47; 28.11).

There are a few places where a genitive absolute does not involve a participant, but is a means of giving a temporal setting, e.g. 8.16; 27.1, 57.

The residue of participial forms show the dative case, as required by the following main verb (8.23; 9.27, 28). They also seem to involve a focus switch. But why the participle is in the dative in these examples, when it is in the genitive in the similar syntactic context of 1.20; 5.1; 8.1, 5, 28; 9.18 is hard to determine. By the canons of classical style the residual examples are more "correct."

Another item which is of frequent occurrence at transition points is τότε. Sometimes it seems to have the purpose of reintroducing a character who has not been mentioned for some time, or who has not been in focus for some time (e.g. 3.13; 9.14) but usually it seems to be just a vague link word without any very precise reference to time.

Finally a brief word about settings of time and place. In episode-initial position it is rare to have both specified. Chronological order was evidently not one of Matthew's primary interests, at least in the bulk of his narrative, for place settings are considerably more common at least in Act 1. Only in 2.1 and 3.1 are there time references to events outside the narrative itself, and these are not quite what a modern historian would wish to see. Events are often loosely related to each other by τότε, and occasionally by tighter links (e.g., 8.18, 23, 28; 9.18; 12.46).

APPENDIX C

Participants in Act 3, Scenes 7–12

In these scenes the participation of certain characters may be represented as follows:

```
Scenes        7           8            9           10          11             12
Episodes  1 2 3       1 2 3      1 2 3 4 5     1 2 3     1 2 3 4 5        1 2 3
Judas           └─────┴────────────┘
Pilate                                           └───┴─────┴─────────┘
Guards                                                                       └───┘
Chief
Priests,
etc.     └─────┘                              └──┴─┴─────┴──────────┘    └───┘
```

The Chief priests and their henchmen are present in each of the scenes marked, i.e., repeatedly right through the block from beginning to end. They are presented as the villains masterminding the whole disreputable business. But the other participants listed, Judas, Pilate and the guards, are only involved for limited parts of the time, and barely overlap each other. It is as though they are each in turn presented as the tools of the chief priests, each being laid aside as the next is taken up. Particularly is this so with Judas. No sooner has he served his purpose and Pilate has replaced him, than he is written out. The placement of Judas' death pericope (unique to Matthew) immediately after Jesus is in Pilate's hands, may be Matthew's way of closing off one aspect of his narrative as he takes up the next. And once Jesus is dead and Pilate has served his purpose, the guards (again unique to Matthew) are introduced as the instruments of the chief priests' machinations.

The appearances in this block of other characters, such as Peter and the women, do not show this patterned distribution.

4

VOCATIVE DISPLACEMENT IN THE GOSPELS: LEXICO-SYNTACTIC AND SOCIOLINGUISTIC INFLUENCES

Introduction

Vocatives are a frequent source of trouble for Bible translators. Not only do they appear in Hebrew and Greek at points where they are awkward in various receptor languages, but perhaps even more often they are absent from Hebrew and Greek when required by the normal rules of conversational interaction in many receptor languages. Furthermore a literal translation of a vocative term in Hebrew or Greek may produce sociolinguistic overtones in a receptor language which are completely out of place in the context. The classic case is Jn 2.4, where Jesus addresses his mother as *gunai*. To translate this into English (and many other languages) as "woman" sounds at the very least rude and uncouth.

Despite the frequency with which vocatives present a translation problem, remarkably little seems to have been written about them. Apart from the relevant section in Moulton/Turner, the only item I have been able to trace is Barnwell.[1] Barnwell's notes on vocatives used in the Gospels to address Jesus are concise and helpful, but her summary of the functions of the vocative is brief and rather impressionistic, with no distinction between the

---

[1] Katharine Barnwell, "Vocative Phrases," *Notes on Translation* 53 (1974): 9–15.

different genres in the NT. The present study is limited to the Gospels, for several reasons. First, they contain much direct speech and therefore offer many examples of vocatives. Second, their parallel passages show some interesting variations in the use and placement of vocatives. Third, the Gospels are all documents of similar genre, and therefore intrinsically likely to be worth comparing: vocative usage in the Epistles is almost bound to be different in some degree. Fourth, the time available for study was limited, and the Gospels are of manageable size. In due course it will be necessary to apply the conclusions reached in this study to Acts and perhaps Revelation to see what, if any, modifications need to be made. Then the Epistles can be tackled as a different genre. A preliminary investigation of Acts indicates that some additional explanatory categories will be needed to account for all its examples of vocatives.

An important point to note at the outset is that the choice of whether or not to use a vocative, and where to place it, is to a fair degree open to the writer or speaker. We are investigating an area of language use where constraints are often not strong enough to be called rules. It is more useful to think in terms of probabilities and tendencies rather than rules. It is also necessary to recognise that we are in an area of language use where syntax and sociolinguistics are closely intertwined, and conflicting pressures may be operating. We are working in a fuzzy-edged area, and a neat analysis with no residues is therefore an unlikely result of the investigation.

Method

All the occurrences of possible vocatives in the Gospels have been examined in UBS[4]=NA[27]. There are some structures which seem to fullfill the function expected of a vocative, but which nevertheless do not, strictly speaking, have the form of vocatives. Instances where a noun has a nominative case ending (with or without a definite article) in a semantically vocative function have been included. The rationale for this is that participial forms are used in a vocative function, but do not usually show a vocative case ending. Rather they have a nominative ending plus the definite article. Examples are *hoi ergazomenoi tēn anomian* (Mt 7.23), *pantes hoi kopiōntes kai pephortismenoi* (Mt 11.28), *hoi eulogēmenoi tou patros mou* (Mt 25.34), *hoi katēramenoi eis to pur to aiōnion* (Mt 25.41), *ho kataluōn ton naon* (Mt 27.40). (With Mt 7.23 compare Lk 13.27 *pantes ergatai adikias*, a genuine vocative.) Instances where an interjection plus a dative case have a vocative-like function are excluded for the purposes of this study, though in many receptor languages these instances may also need to be translated as vocatives. Examples are Lk 11.42, 43, 46, 52 (contrast Mt 23.13, 23, 27, 29).

The first point to note is that vocatives occur in indicative, imperative and interrogative sentences, both positive and negative. There are apparently no requirements or prohibitions related to these categories. Nor does it seem to make any difference whether the vocative is in a second degree quotation or in a quotation from the OT. The major observation arising from the data is that a vocative appears frequently at the beginning of its sentence, but not always. Allowing for the somewhat fluid boundaries in the definition of a vocative, the figures are as follows. In Matthew, there are 42 non-sentence initial vocatives out of 96 (44%); in Mark, 7 out of 32 (22%); in Luke, 26 out of 107 (24%); and in John, 12 out of 66 (18%). The total is 87 out of 301 or 29%. It is clear that a large majority of vocatives in the Gospels, in round figures seven out of every ten, occur in sentence initial position. This is therefore assumed to be the normal, or unmarked, position, and the challenge is to account for the three cases in every ten where the vocative is found in a non-initial or displaced position. Since the highest proportion of displaced vocatives occurs in Matthew, this Gospel was taken as a test case. The tentative results arising were cross-checked with the other Gospels, and the overall picture is summarised below.

Displaced Vocatives: Lexico-Syntactic Influence

First, a brief explanation of the label lexico-syntactic. It is used to include restricted groups of adverbs, fossilized imperatives and interjections. In that these items are based on word classes, a categorization according to linguistic function, they may be termed syntactic. But though in theory they are not necessarily closed classes, in practice their attested membership is very restricted, and they could thus be viewed as lexical. To sidestep such theoretical issues, the term lexico-syntactic is used for convenience.

Certain items are found to precede a vocative always or at least in a large majority of occurrences. It should be noted that *ō* is not included as an item that precedes (and displaces) a vocative. In classical times it was a regular accompaniment to a vocative, and on the five occasions when it occurs in the Gospels it is treated in the same way. It may be, as Turner suggests, a marker of heightened emotion, amazement in Mt 15.28 (*ō gunai, megalē sou hē pistis*) and exasperation in Mt 17.17 ‖ Mk 9.19 ‖ Lk 9.41 (*ō genea apistos [kai diestrammenē* added in Mt and Lk]) and in Lk 24.25 (*ō anoētoi kai bradeis tē kardia tou pisteuein*).[2] These items can be classified into three groups.

1) **One word adverbial phrases**, usually responses to a question or comment, always displace the vocative in the Gospels. Examples are:

> *nai kurie* (Mt 9.28; 15.27; Jn 11.27; 21.15, 16; also Mt 11.26; Lk 10.21b which are not responses but part of a continuing utterance)
> *ouchi, pater Abraam* (Lk 16.30)
> *eu, doule agathe kai piste* (Mt 25.21, 23)
> *euge, agathe doule* (Lk 19.17)
> *kalōs, didaskale* (Mk 12.32)
> *pou, kurie* (Lk 17.37)

It is interesting to observe the word order in Lk 20.39 (|| Mk 12.32), *didaskale, kalōs eipas*: where the adverb *kalōs* is subordinated to a verb as part of a clause rather than standing on its own as in Mk 12.32; the vocative occurs in unmarked initial position.

2) **Phrases**, often of one word, based on fossilized imperatives, always displace the vocative in the Gospels. Examples are:

> *deute pros me pantes hoi kopiōntes kai pephortismenoi* (Mt 11.28)
> *deute hoi eulogēmenoi tou patros mou* (Mt 25.34)
> *ea, tí hēmin kai soi, Iēsou Nazarēne?* (Lk 4.34; compare Mk 1.24 where *ea* is absent)
> *chaire, rabbi* (Mt 26.49)
> *chaire, basileu tōn Ioudaiōn* (Mt 27.29 || Mk 15.18 || Jn 19.3 where however the vocative becomes *ho basileus tōn Ioudaiōn*)
> *chaire, kecharitōmenē* (Lk 1.28)
> *idou ta hēmisia mou tōn huparchontōn, kurie, tois ptōchois didōmi* (Lk 19.8).

There are probably focus factors in play in the last example, as *idou* occurs elsewhere after a vocative, for example *kurie, idou hē mna sou* (Lk 19.20); *Simōn Simōn, idou ho Satanas exētēsato humas* (Lk 22.31).

3) **Interjections** (or expletives?), often followed by a dative. Examples are:

---

[2] Nigel Turner, *Syntax*, Grammar of New Testament Greek (Edinburgh, 1963), 3:33.

> *oua ho kataluōn ton naon kai oikodomōn en trisin hēmerais* (Mk 15.29;
> the parallel in Mt 27.40 lacks *oua*)
> *ouai soi, Chorazin, ouai soi Bēthsaida* (Mt 11.21 ‖ Lk 10.13)
> *ouai (de) humin, grammateis kai Pharisaioi hupokritai* (Mt 23.13, 15, 23,
> 25, 27, 29)
> *ouai humin, hodēgoi tuphloi* (Mt 23.16)

A fourth group of examples where the vocative is displaced have in common the occurrence of a personal pronoun. This is by no means a factor which *compels* the vocative to leave the initial position, and there are plenty of cases where a vocative precedes a phrase or clause that includes a pronoun. In cases where the vocative is displaced from the initial position there is often a sociolinguistic influence present as well as a pronoun. See the discussion of sociolinguistic influences below. Selected examples are:

> *tí hēmin kai soi, huie tou theou* (Mt 8.29)
> *kai su, Kapharnaoum* (Mt 11.23 ‖ Lk 10.15)
> *exomologoumai soi, pater, kurie tou ouranou kai tēs gēs* (Mt 11.25 ‖ Lk
> 10.21a)
> *eleēson me, kurie, huios Dauid* (Mt 15.22).

It is curious that the vocative *kurie* is followed in apposition by the nominative *huios Dauid*; perhaps once the vocative function was established by the form of the first noun it was felt unnecessary to repeat the form since the function of the noun in apposition is unmistakeable.

> *tí soi dokei, Simōn?* (Mt 17.25)
> *egō, kurie* (Mt 21.30)
> *mēti egō eimi, kurie/rabbi?* (Mt 26.22, 25)
> *tí hēmin kai soi, Iēsou Nazarēne?* (Mk 1.24)
> *tí emoi kai soi, Iēsou huie tou theou tou hupsistou?* (Mk 5.7 ‖ Lk 8.28)
> *kai su de, paidion* (Lk 1.76)
> *erōtō se oun, pater* (Lk 16.27)
> *ek tou stomatos sou krinō se, ponēre doule* (Lk 19.22)
> *tí emoi kai soi, gunai?* (Jn 2.4)
> *oudeis, kurie* (Jn 8.11)
> *kai nun doxason me su, pater* (Jn 17.5)
> *...kathōs su, pater* (Jn 17.21)

Displaced Vocatives: Sociolinguistic Influences

Frequently the displacement of a vocative from sentence initial position is correlated with increased social distance between the interlocutors. In many cases the sentence conveys a strong rebuke from the speaker to the hearer. In most a pronoun is also present, so that it is arguable whether the social distance or the presence of the pronoun is the dominant factor in the displacement of the vocative. But since there are clear examples of a rebuke where no pronoun is present, there are firm enough grounds for establishing the category of "rebuke" as a factor in displacement. Examples are:

> *hupage Satana* (Mt 4.10)
> *apochōreite ap' emou, hoi ergazomenoi tēn anomian* (Mt 7.23)
> *tí deiloi este, oligopistoi?* (Mt 8.26)
> *hileōs soi, kurie* (Mt 16.22)
> *hupage opisō mou, Satana* (Mt 16.23 ‖ Mk 8.33)
> *tí me peirazete, hupokritai?* (Mt 22.18)
> *poreuesthe ap' emou hoi katēramenoi eis to pur to aiōnion* (Mt 25.41)
> *prophēteuson hēmin, Christe* (Mt 26.68)
> *apostēte ap' emou pantes ergatai adikias* (Lk 13.27)
> *legō soi, Petre* (Lk 22.34)
> *ouk oida auton, gunai* (Lk 22.57)
> *tosoutō chronō meth' humōn eimi kai ouk egnōkas me, Philippe?* (Jn 14.9).

It is worth noting that all the occurrences of the phrase *tí hēmin/emoi kai soi* could also be included in the category of rebuke (Mt 8.29; Mk 1.24; 5.7; Lk 4.34; 8.28; Jn 2.4). In this phrase syntactic and sociolinguistic influences are mutually reinforcing.

A second set of occurrences involve social distance between the interlocutors but no rebuke. A convenient label for this group of examples is "superior to inferior." Example are as follows:

> *tharsei, teknon* (Mt 9.2)
> *tharsei, thugater* (Mt 9.22)
> *makarios ei, Simōn Bariōna* (Mt 16.17)
> *akoue, Israēl* (Mk 12.29)
> *mē phobou, Zacharia* (Lk 1.13)

mē phobou, Mariam (Lk 1.30)
mē phobou, to mikron poimnion (Lk 12.32)
pisteue moi, gunai (Jn 4.21).

Although there is some overlap between these two categories in that a rebuke is normally from a superior to an inferior, they must be kept separate because in some cases a rebuke is administered by a speaker of socially lower status to a speaker of higher status. The classic case is *hileōs soi, kurie* in Mt 16.22, but Mt 22.18 and Mt 26.68 are other probable examples.

Summary of Syntactic and Sociolinguistic Influences

The explanatory categories listed above seem to be sufficient to account for the vast majority of the examples of displaced vocatives in the Gospels. We shall now present the categories in diagram form to try to give some indication of their interrelations, and discuss a few residual cases and possible counter-examples.

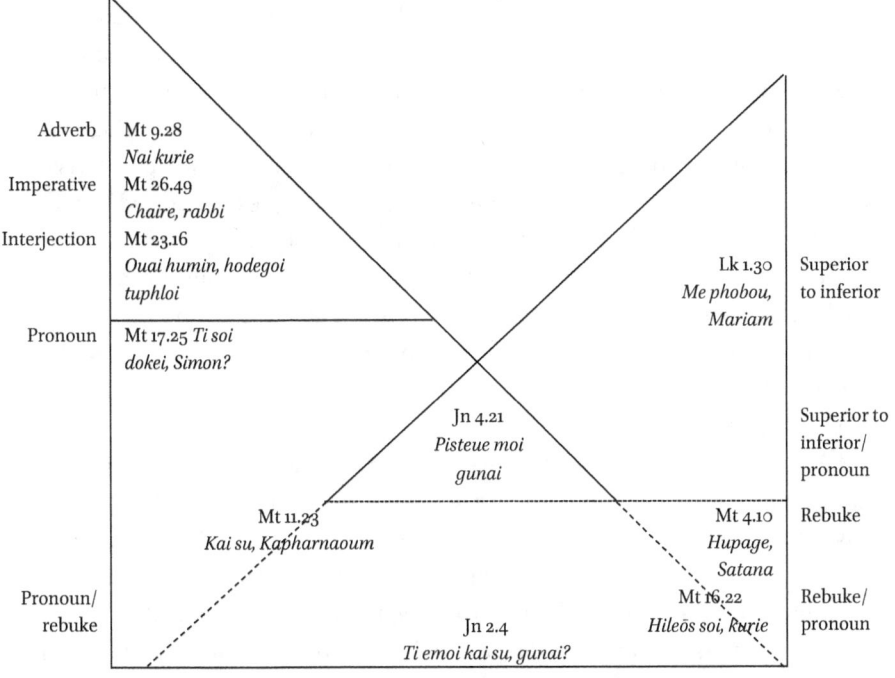

Figure 4.1: Interrelations of Categories of Displaced Vocatives

Then we shall look at some parallel passages in the synoptics, and try to discern the different nuances carried by the presence or absence of vocatives, and their relative positions. Finally, we shall try to assess possible implications of this study for translators.

Figure 4.1 above consists of two right-angled triangles. The larger triangle at the left stands for syntactic influences on vocative displacement, and the smaller triangle at the right for sociolinguistic influences. The two triangles overlap to a considerable extent. The upper part of the left-hand triangle (above the solid horizontal line) represents those lexico-syntactic items which seem to require vocative displacement irrespective of sociolinguistic considerations. These are one word adverbial phrases, interjections, and phrases based on fossilized imperatives. The larger part of the left-hand triangle (below the solid horizontal line) represents the pronouns which, often in combination with sociolinguistic factors, seem to predispose towards the displacement of a vocative.

The upper part of the right-hand triangle (above the dotted horizontal line) represents the sociolinguistic category of "superior to inferior" which has some but not much overlap with the pronoun category. The lower part of the right-hand triangle (below the dotted horizontal line) represents the sociolinguistic category of "rebuke," which overlaps extensively but not completely with the pronoun category. The horizontal line in the right-hand triangle is dotted rather than solid as the boundary between the sociolinguistic categories seems more fluid than that between the lexico-syntactic categories. The lower parts of the long sides of the two triangles are dotted to indicate that boundaries between lexico-syntactic and sociolinguistic categories are increasingly fuzzy the nearer they get to the base. A typical example of each category of displaced vocative is written in at the appropriate point in the figure. Where the example crosses a dotted line, this is an indication that more than one type of factor may be involved, and category boundaries are becoming blurred.

Among possible residues are several examples including the vocative *oligopistoi* (Mt 6.30; 8.26; 16.8; Lk 12.28). They are distinctive in that in each case, this vocative is actually a covert predicate rather than a form of address. That is to say it introduces new information which could be expressed as "you have too little faith." The vocative *oligopistoi* in Mt 8.26 is absent from the parallel passages in Mk 4.38; Lk 8.24, but its content is represented as an explicit predicate in Mk 4.40 *oupō ekhete pistin?* and Lk 8.25 *pou hē pistis humōn*. The feature of covert predication may be a factor in the displaced position of the vocative. Indeed in Mt 6.30; Lk 12.28, the vocative is the final item in a lengthy sentence, and is in effect its climax. However, it does not seem necessary to set up a separate category to account for these occurrences, as in all cases, pronouns precede the vocative and they can be accounted for under the pronoun category. It may be noted that there is one instance of *oligopiste* in sentence initial position (Mt 14.31).

The one vocative which may fall outside this article's categories is *kratiste Theophile* in Lk 1.3. It is in fact preceded by several pronouns (*en hēmin... hēmin... k' amoi... soi*), but the paragraph Lk 1.1–4 is so different from all the rest of the material in the synoptic Gospels, that it should probably be treated as belonging to a different genre. The only comparable paragraph in the NT is Acts 1.1–5, and there *ō Theophile* is displaced without any preceding pronoun.

There are a few cases in John where the categories established above may seem barely adequate. In Jn 8.11 the adulterous woman responds to Jesus' question with *oudeis, kurie*. This is only accounted for by defining the pronoun category to include *oudeis* as a negative equivalent of *tis*, though such a definition is within the bounds of linguistic acceptability. The more interesting and tricky examples are in Jn 9.35–38. The man who had been born blind responds to both of Jesus' questions with displaced vocatives. The first one *kai tís estin, kurie, hina pisteusō eis auton?* may be accounted for on the grounds that the interrogative pronoun *tís* occurs. The second one *pisteuō, kurie* is harder to deal with, and taken on its own falls outside the established categories. There are two possible ways in which this may be accounted for. It should be noted that the interchange between Jesus and the man is chiastic. Jesus' initial question is answered by another question. Jesus then answers this second question, and the man's second response is in fact an answer to Jesus' original question. It is conceivable that the vocative is displaced in order to put the focus on the verb *pisteuō* as a way of showing within the paragraph that this response goes back to the initial question.

Another possibility is to regard *kurie* here as an example of a covert predicate, and to say that in view of the semantic content of the paragraph, the man is now with his confession of faith attributing to Jesus the full theological meaning of *kurie*. This would give *kurie* different meanings in 9.36 and 9.38, a very subtle nuance which may have more appeal to preachers than to linguists. Nevertheless, some English translations accept that this is the intended distinction. Both TEV and NRSV for instance, render *kurie* as "sir" in 9.36 and "Lord" in 9.38, NRSV adding a footnote to indicate that the Greek word is the same in both verses. If *kurie* in 9.38 is indeed a covert predicate, then covert predication would need to be recognised as a separate category in accounting for vocative displacement, since none of the other categories is adequate here. We leave the question open.

Under the heading of possible counter-examples we may mention that there are numerous places where pronouns occur but do not displace a vocative from sentence initial position. It seems that displacement is more likely to occur when the pronoun is not part of a long and complex clause. We may note for instance that displacement does not occur in the following three complex sentences:

> *kurie, epitrepson moi prōton apelthein kai thapsai ton patera mou* (Mt 8.21; similarly Lk 9.59)
> *kurie, ei su ei, keleuson me elthein pros se epi ta hudata* (Mt 14.28)
> *kurie, ou melei soi hoti hē adelphē mou monēn me katelipen diakonein?* (Lk 10.40).

It is perhaps more surprising that displacement does not occur in *kurie, sōson me* (Mt 14.30), but the occurrence of a pronoun does not compel displacement; as noted before, it simply increases the likelihood of it. We may further note that in Lk 15.31, *teknon, su pantote met' emou ei* displacement does not take place despite the presence of pronouns. Though undoubtedly in a superior-inferior relationship to his elder son, the father in the parable does not assert his status and talk down to the son. This is completely in keeping with the conduct of the father throughout the parable, and is another very subtle nuance.

Parallel Passages in the Synoptics

The assertion that the presence or absence of a vocative is to a large degree at the discretion of the writer can be easily supported from synoptic parallels. Most permutations of two writers against a third are found, as in the following examples. Where a vocative is marked as omitted, the passage is sometimes rendered in indirect speech.

Matthew and Luke include a vocative where Mark omits: Mt 8.2 ‖ Lk 5.12; contrast Mk 1.40.

Mark and Luke include a vocative where Matthew omits: Mk 5.41 ‖ Lk 8.54; contrast Mt 9.25.

Matthew and Mark omit a vocative where Luke includes: Lk 21.7; contrast Mt 24.3 ‖ Mk 13.4; also Lk 22.58, 60; contrast Mt 26.72, 74 ‖ Mk 14.70, 71.

Matthew and Luke omit a vocative where Mark includes: Mk 10.20; contrast Mt 19.20 ‖ Lk 18.21.

Mark and Luke omit a vocative where Matthew includes: Mt 26.68; contrast Mk 14.65 ‖ Lk 22.64.

The only missing permutation is Matthew and Mark including a vocative where Luke omits. The absence of this particular combination seems to be accidental.

Of more interest are parallel passages with minor variations between the synoptics which may reflect subtle differences in nuance, perhaps related to the writer's control over the finer points of Greek. In Mt 8.25 ‖ Mk 4.38 ‖ Lk 8.24, the pericope of the stilling of the storm, all three synoptics include a vocative form. Matthew has the generic *kurie*, Mark the more specific *didaskale* and Luke the specific but probably somewhat higher level *epistata*. It is noteworthy that in Luke the vocative is repeated. Repeated vocatives in Luke carry a reproachful tone, and Mark, who does not repeat the vocative, makes the reproach explicit with the words *ou melei soi hoti...* For repeated vocatives compare Lk 10.41 *Martha, Martha*: Lk 13.34 *Ierousalēm, Ierousalēm* (‖ Mt 23.37); Lk 22.31 *Simōn, Simōn*. Possibly Mt 25.11 *kurie kurie, anoixon hēmin* carries the overtone of reproach, though it is not clear whether this holds in cases where *kurie kurie* is the entire content of an utterance (Mt 7.21, 22; Lk 6.46).

Matthew in 9.2 and 9.22, includes the imperative *tharsei* before the vocative, whereas Mark (2.5 and 5.34) and Luke (5.20 and 8.48) omit the imperative and begin Jesus' utterance with the vocative in initial position. The effect of the displacement of the vocative in Matthew is to emphasize the authority of Jesus by having him speak with a superior/inferior nuance to the people he is healing. It is noteworthy that whereas in Mt 9.2 ‖ Mk 2.5 the vocative is *teknon*, in Lk 5.20 it is *anthrōpe*. This may be Luke's way of hinting at the status difference between Jesus and the paralysed man, since Luke elsewhere uses *anthrōpe* in situations where there is some social distancing between the interlocutors: compare Lk 12.14; 22.58, 60.

Another small point is that whereas Mt 9.22 has the genuine vocative form *thugater*, both Mk 5.34 and Lk 8.48 have the nominative *thugatēr* in a vocative position and function. The opposite situation prevails in Mt 20.30, 31 ‖ Mk 10.47, 48 ‖ Lk 18.38, 39, where Matthew has the nominative form *huios* in a vocative position and function whereas Mark and Luke have the genuine vocative form *huie*. Since there is considerable manuscript fluctuation in all these occurrences, the question is probably textual rather than syntactic or sociolinguistic.

In the transfiguration scene Mt 17.4 ‖ Mk 9.5 ‖ Lk 9.33, we find *kurie* ‖ *rabbi* ‖ *epistata*. As with Mt 8.25 ‖ Mk 4.38 ‖ Lk 8.24, Matthew is generic and Luke higher level, but in this case Mark has *rabbi*, which according to Barnwell indicates a special "sense of awe and reverence."[3]

In Mt 20.33 ‖ Mk 10.51 ‖ Lk 18.41 Matthew and Luke both have *kurie* where Mark has *rabbouni*, whereas in Mt 22.16 ‖ Mk 12.14 ‖ Lk 20.21 all three have *didaskale*. It is hard to discern any significance in these variants, underlining the writer's freedom of choice.

One could also compare Mt 26.39 (*pater mou*) ‖ Lk 22.42 (*pater*) with Mk 14.36 (*abba ho patēr*); and Mt 27.29 ‖ Mk 15.18 (*chaire, basileu tōn Ioudaiōn*) with Jn 19.3 (*chaire ho basileus tōn Ioudaiōn*). As N. Turner observes, the occurrence of the article and nominative may be due to influence from Hebrew or Aramaic, as also in Mk 5.41 (*to korasion* ‖ *talitha*) ‖ Lk 8.54 (*hē pais*).[4] But compare Mt 27.46 (*thee mou thee mou*) with Mk 15.34 (*ho theos mou ho theos mou*), both being translations of the Aramaic form of Ps 22.1. Vocative and nominative forms occur in the same utterance in Mt 11.25–26, and in Lk 10.21, so it is hard to believe that there can be any difference of connotation intended.

Finally, it is worth noting that Matthew uses the vocative *hetaire* only in contexts where it carries a sense of distance and reproach (Mt 20.13; 22.12). So when Jesus addresses Judas as *hetaire* in Mt 26.50, he is obliquely indicating his disapproval of Judas' action in betraying him. In Lk 22.48 Jesus uses the personal name *Iouda* which does not carry the same overtones. Thus Luke, who at this point is parallel to Matthew in general structure rather than in detail, also gives a different nuance to his portrayal of the interaction between Jesus and Judas.

Implications for Translators

It seems clear that there is more to vocatives than at first meets the eye. Where subtle nuances can be established with reasonable probability, translators should be made aware of them, and encouraged to reproduce them in

---

[3] Barnwell, "Vocative Phrases," 14.
[4] Turner, *Syntax*, 34.

receptor languages. Of course the linguistic devices by which nuances may be conveyed will vary widely according to the resources of the receptor language. In a number of languages a vocative may occur only at the beginning of a sentence, and in such languages, any attempt to imitate Greek displacement would merely sound unnatural, and would completely fail to indicate the appropriate nuance.

In general, lexico-syntactic displacement of vocatives is likely to hold fewer implications for translators than sociolinguistic displacement, because it appears to operate in a more mechanical way. Sociolinguistic nuances are more important to a translator, and are more likely to be found where the writer has more choice on how to formulate his sentence. In many languages of South East Asia for instance, social standing and social distance are usually conveyed more by the choice of pronouns in the clauses containing a vocative than by the form or position of the vocative itself.[5]

---

[5] For further observations and suggestions see Barnwell, "Vocative Phrases," 10–12.

5

THE SERMON ON THE PLAIN: STRUCTURE AND THEME IN LUKE 6.20–49

A careful study of the discourse structure of the so-called Sermon on the Plain in Luke 6.20–49 suggests two things that are significant for the translator, and indeed for the interpreter and the preacher. The first is that in many modern versions some of the section headings and paragraph breaks are not at the places where the structure of the Greek indicates that they should be. The second is that misplaced section headings actually obscure the real point of the last part of the sermon. In this article I will examine the discourse structure of the sermon, and also propose a theme which unifies the apparently haphazard subsections in vv. 39–49. All quotations in the article will be from the RSV.

The Good New Bible, the Contemporary English Version, and the Common Language versions in French, German, Italian, and Spanish all have section headings at vv. 17, 20, 27, 37, 43 and 46. The New International Version differs only in omitting the heading at v. 20. The New Jerusalem Bible (NJB) is the only available modern version that departs from this pattern: it has section headings at vv. 17, 20, 24, 27, 36, 39 and 46. I will examine what this means later. The UBS *Translator's Handbook on the Gospel of Luke* was published as long ago as 1971, in the days before anyone paid much attention to discourse structure, and it does not discuss the issues involved. The UBS *Translator's Guide to Luke* (1982) simply follows the GNB section headings, though its comment on the heading at v. 37, that the illustrations in vv. 39–

40 "do not fit too well in the context of judgment" shows that the author may have had some questions about the headings. However the Guide fails to examine the possibility that it is the section headings rather than the illustrations that "do not fit too well"!

The Sermon on the Plain has many similarities with the Sermon on the Mount in Matthew 5–7, but I will not discuss these here. I intend to treat the Sermon on the Plain as a discourse in its own right, with its own independent structure and its own internal logic.

Structure of the Sermon on the Plain

In 6.17–20a, Luke gives the narrative setting for the sermon that follows. The words translated "on a level place" in v. 17 give the basis for the usual name "the Sermon on the Plain." In v. 20 it is not certain whether "his disciples" refers to the "great crowd" of v. 17 or to the twelve named in vv. 14–16. Since the twelve are called "apostles" in v. 13, it seems more likely that the large crowd is in view in v. 20.

The sermon falls into three main sections which are each indicated by words introducing a quotation; two of these are from the gospel writer (vv. 20–39) and one is from the mouth of Jesus himself (v. 27). We might expect that translators of the major English versions would have readily recognized these quotation formulas as markers of new sections; but as noted above, the one at v. 39 has been largely ignored. NJB rightly respects the Greek in putting a section heading there. The main sections, then, comprise vv. 20–26, 27–38, and 39–49.

The First Section (Verses 20–26)

Many commentators have observed that the three blessings of vv. 20b–21 are paralleled by the three curses of vv. 24–25. NJB is fully justified in printing them as two paragraphs with the parallels shown in the layout of lines. Indeed many translations use a similar layout.

What has not been so widely noticed is the partial nature of the parallel between vv. 22–23 and v. 26. Verse 22 ("Blessed are you when men hate you, and when they exclude you and revile you, and cast out your name as evil, on account of the Son of man!") is parallel with v. 26a ("Woe to you when all men speak well of you"). Verse 23b ("for so their fathers did to the prophets") is parallel with v. 26b ("for so their fathers did to the false prophets"). On the other hand v. 23a ("Rejoice in that day, and leap for joy, for behold your reward is great in heaven") has no parallel in v. 26.

It is not uncommon that in passages where there is extensive parallelism, the units that are without parallel are the ones in focus, and that is very probably the case here also. This view is supported by the occurrence of the Greek focus-marking particle *idou* ("behold") in v. 23a. The paragraph consisting of vv. 20b–26 as a whole makes a series of shocking and exaggerated statements that reverse commonly held earthly values. It is wholly appropriate that these statements should be justified by reference to reward in heaven. Verse 23a, coming as it does at the very centre of the pattern of parallel lines, gives the key to understanding the entire paragraph. Only in relation to a reward in heaven do the challenging statements make sense. It is no surprise that a further and more detailed reference to rewards comes in v. 35 at the climax of the second section of the sermon.

The Second Section (Verses 27–38)

The beginning of this section is marked by Jesus' own quotation formula, "But I say to you [who] hear..." The presence of the next quotation formula at the beginning of v. 39 clearly indicates that the section extends to the end of v. 38.

The structural framework of vv. 27–38 is indicated by the verbs. The section begins with four imperatives, each at the beginning of its clause: "Love...do good...bless...pray..." (vv. 27b–28). How to carry out these commands is then illustrated by four further imperative verbs that do not come at the beginning of their clauses. They are paired, with the second member of each pair restating the first in a negative form: "offer...do not withhold; give...do not ask again" (vv. 29–30). These illustrations would also be shocking to us and difficult to understand if they were not so familiar. This unit is rounded off with a fourth imperative that summarizes its content by a general command in language which is not pictorial: "as you wish that men would do to you, do so to them" (v. 31). In NA[27] a new paragraph begins with this verse, but such a layout does not reflect the Greek discourse structure. If a new paragraph is to be shown at all, it should begin at v. 32, not v. 31. But it is better to continue the same paragraph, as in UBS[4].

In vv. 32–34 there are three conditional sentences, which are linked by the features that each ends with the same question and comment: "what credit is that to you? For even sinners..." The three conditions echo verbs from the earlier part of the paragraph: "If you love" (v. 32, repeating the identical verb from v. 27), "if you do good" (v. 33, repeating a similar but not identical verb from v. 27), and "if you lend" (v. 34, repeating the general thought but not the wording of v. 30). The question forms in vv. 32–34 are a way of stimulating the involvement of the hearers, and come again in vv. 39, 41, 42, and 46. The Greek word translated "credit" is *charis*, and it is possible that there is a wordplay intended. The word *charis* can mean both "thanks" and "grace," but RSV takes it in the first sense. This is probably the primary meaning intended in this context, though perhaps the meaning of "grace" is present under the surface, so to speak. People who offer only a love that depends on the hope of getting something back deserves no *charis* ("thanks") because they show no *charis* ("grace," that is, "undeserved kindness"). It is unlikely that such a double meaning could be preserved in translation.

In v. 35 there are three more imperatives, repeating the verbs of vv. 32–34, "love...do good...and lend..." This sentence functions as a summary and climax to vv. 27–34, repeating the main themes and linking them with the first section by stating again that "your reward will be great" (compare v. 23). This time the nature of the reward is explained as "you will be sons of the Most High; for he is kind to the ungrateful and the selfish." Those who practice the values of the heavenly kingdom will show by that that they share the character of the king.

Verses 36–38 form a further unit which enlarges on the idea of showing the character of the heavenly Father. Its structure is broadly similar to that of vv. 29–31. It opens with a general statement, then has four imperative verbs (two negative and two positive) and an explanatory concluding statement. This statement, "For the measure you give will be the measure you get back," is in effect another summary, stating the summary in v. 31 in other words: God will treat us as we treat others. This means that it is in our own interests to treat other people as we would like them to treat us, because God will treat us as we treat them. If this unit is printed as a separate paragraph, the paragraph should begin at v. 36 where there is no connective particle, and not at v. 37 where there is one (*kai*). But since the theme is closely linked with v. 35, it is probably better not to print a new paragraph at all.

The Third Section (Verses 39–49)

The opening quotation formula gives a hint of the unity of this section: "He also told them a parable." Luke regarded the section as "a parable" in the singular, despite the fact that half a dozen different metaphors are used, none of them having much in common with the typical parable form in his gospel. This suggests that section headings within these verses, such as are commonly found at both vv. 43 and 46, are likely to be misleading. They fragment the passage and prevent readers from seeing its unity of theme.

The theme focus of the section is in fact indicated in the opening two verses. Verse 39 gives a picture which is interpreted in v. 40. The picture is of one blind man leading another and both falling into a ditch. Though familiarity may make it hard for us to realize, this picture is certainly intended to be humorous (even if the humour is not in a form that meets the standards of modern "political correctness!"). The picture is immediately explained as referring to a teacher and a disciple. Just as a blind person cannot be led by someone else who cannot see, so a disciple cannot learn what his teacher does not know. The highest value for the disciple of Jesus is to be "like his teacher" (v. 40). The relation of teacher and disciple is the theme which underlies and binds together the whole section.

In vv. 41 and 42, the second person verbs are in the singular rather than the plural. Why are second person singular forms found only here in the sermon? In a context dealing with relations between teachers and disciples, these verses may best be understood as a conversation between an individual teacher and an individual disciple, that is, a piece of play acting within the sermon. This could originally have been indicated also by other features such as gesture and change in tone of voice, but in writing only the switch to second person singular verbs survives. Jesus is in effect telling those who claim to be his disciples not to look at one another's faults ("the speck" and "the log": compare the theme of v. 37), but to keep their eyes on the teacher, Jesus himself.

The point is reinforced by another somewhat humorous picture (vv. 43–44) which is again immediately interpreted (compare vv. 39–40). Just as trees can bear fruit only according to their nature, so people can produce teaching only according to their real character. In this paragraph Jesus is holding himself up as the supreme teacher, who is not blind, does not have the faults of his disciples, and does not teach anything evil. The theme is a development of that in vv. 39–42, not a new and different one as a section heading at v. 43 would suggest.

Verses 46–49 challenge the hearers or readers (the second person verbs are now plural again) to respond to Jesus as the ultimate teacher. It is debatable whether the question in v. 46 ("Why do you call me 'Lord, Lord,' and not do what I tell you?") is to be included in the same paragraph as vv. 43–45 or taken with vv. 47–49. The French *Traduction Oecuménique de la Bible* takes the first option and most other versions the second. If put in a paragraph with the verses before it, the question sharpens the interpretation that Jesus is there presenting himself as the supreme teacher. If put in a paragraph with the following verses, it forms a very suitable introduction to the house-building illustration. On the whole a question seems more likely to open a paragraph than to close one, and the view of the majority of versions appears preferable.

Verses 47–49 use pictures to describe the possible reactions to Jesus' teaching, either obedience or disobedience. Obedience, he claims, gives life a firm foundation, while disobedience leads to ruin. It is interesting that both in Luke and in the parallel passage in Matt 7.24–27, the person who built his house on the rock is mentioned first, so that the collapse of the house built on the sand forms the end and the climax of the story. The effect of this is to challenge the hearers or readers to consider how they will react, and whether they are prepared to take the risk of disobedience. If the order were the other way round, the end and climax would come with the survival of the house built on the rock. The effect then would probably be to encourage complacency in the audience rather than to mount a challenge. In view of the close link of v. 46 both with what comes before it and with what follows, it is best not to have a section heading either before v. 46 or before v. 47.

Conclusion

The Sermon on the Plain is a carefully constructed discourse falling into three well-defined sections (6.20b–26; 6.27–38; 6.39–49). Their internal structure is shown in diagram form below. If section headings are used, they should reflect this structure, and the themes which it carries. Suitable headings may be "Reversing earthly values" at v. 20, "Reflecting heavenly values" at v. 27, and "Responding to the teacher" at v. 39. Additional section headings are more likely to hinder than to help the reader in understanding the sermon as a whole.

Structural Diagram of the Sermon on the Plain

(Quotations use the wording of RSV, sometimes with the word order adjusted to show the Greek word order more closely.)

The Sermon on the Plain

Section 1 (vv. 20b–26)

20b–26 Four blessings and four woes

20b–21 Three blessings, parallel with	24–25 Three woes
Blessed are you poor...	Woe to you that are rich...
Blessed are you that hunger now...	Woe to you that are full now...
Blessed are you that weep now	Woe to you that laugh now...
22–23 A fourth blessing	26 A fourth woe
Blessed are you when men hate you...	Woe to you when all men speak well of you...
Rejoice...for behold, your reward is great in heaven	(No parallel, but compare 6.35)
for so their fathers did to the prophets	for so their fathers did to the false prophets

Section 2 (vv. 27–38)

27–28 Four imperatives: unqualified commands
    Love...do good... bless... pray...

29–30 Four more imperatives: two pairs of illustrative commands
    To him who...offer...; and from him who... do not withhold...
    To everyone who...give...; and of him who... do not ask...

31 First summary
    As you wish that men would do to you, do so to them

32–34 Three conditional questions
    If you love those...what credit is that to you? For even sinners...
    If you do good to those... what credit is that to you? For even sinners...
    If you lend to those... what credit is that to you? Even sinners...

35 Second summary
    But love... do good... lend...
    and your reward will be great, and you will be sons of the Most High;
    for he is kind to the ungrateful and the selfish

36–38 Commands illustrating kindness like God's
36 One qualified general command:
>Be merciful, even as your Father is merciful

37–38a Two pairs of commands giving particular examples:
>Judge not...; condemn not...; forgive...; give...

38b Third summary
>For the measure you give will be the measure you get back

Section 3 (vv. 39b–49)

39b–40 Analogy and interpretation
39b Analogy
>Can a blind man lead a blind man? Will they not both fall into a pit?

40 Interpretation
>A disciple is not above his teacher...
>
>41–42 Aside – rebuke of teacher to disciple (2nd person singular):
>Why do you see...? How can you say...? Hypocrite, first take...

43–45a Analogy and Interpretation
43–44 Analogy
>No good tree bears bad fruit...figs are not gathered from thorns...

45a Interpretation
>The good man produces good... the evil man produces evil...

45b Summary
>For out of the abundance of the heart his mouth speaks

46–49 Challenge to obedience
46 Question
>Why do you call me 'Lord, Lord,' and not do what I tell you?

47–49 Double comparison
>Every one who hears my words and does them is like...
>he who hears and does not do them is like...

6

VOCATIVE DISPLACEMENT IN ACTS AND REVELATION

Introduction

In chapter four, I discussed the occurrences of vocatives in the Gospels.[1] In those books approximately 70% of all vocatives occur in initial position within their sentence. This was therefore regarded as the normal, or unmarked position, and the challenge was to account for the other 30% of cases where the vocative is displaced from initial position. I suggested a number of influential factors, and included the caveat that a study of the vocatives in the other narrative books of the NT, Acts and Revelation, might necessitate some modification of the analysis. There has now been opportunity to carry out a study of Acts and Revelation, and this article discusses the findings. The letters of the NT are not considered in this article: since they are of a different genre, it seems intrinsically likely that their patterns in the use of vocatives may be different from those in narrative texts.

Distribution of Vocatives

In the book of Acts, there is a total of 81 vocative occurrences, 9 of them containing more than one vocative (such as *archontes tou laou kai presbuteroi* in

---

[1] Previously published in *BT* 47, no. 3 (1996): 313–321.

4.8). Of these 81 occurrences, 47 are initial within the sentence, and 34 (or 42%) non-initial. This is a higher proportion than in Mark, Luke or John, (22%, 24% and 18% respectively) but slightly lower than in Matthew (44%). The percentage of non-initial, or displaced, vocatives in Acts is therefore within the same range as that found in the Gospels as a whole. In the book of Revelation on the other hand, out of a total of 17 vocative occurrences (10 of them containing more than one vocative, such as *hoi ouranoi kai hoi en autois skēnountes*), 16 are displaced. That is 94%, more than double the percentage in other narrative books. One might wish to argue that Revelation is a different genre of literature from the Gospels and Acts, but even so, the divergence is striking. This article will look first at the vocatives in Acts to see how well the explanatory categories proposed in the Gospels fit it, and will then move on to Revelation to discuss the significantly different distribution there.

Acts Compared with the Gospels

In the Gospels, it was found that factors leading to the displacement of vocatives from initial position within the sentence fell under two broad categories, termed lexico-syntactic and sociolinguistic. In the first category, one-word adverbial phrases, phrases based on fossilised imperatives, and certain interjections invariably preceded a vocative, and thus displaced it from sentence initial position. There are few examples of any of these in Acts, but those that there are do not break this pattern. The phrase *mēdamōs, kurie* (Acts 10.14; 11.8) is an example of a one word adverbial phrase, using an adverb which does not happen to have occurred in this position in the Gospels. Of fossilised imperatives, the only clear example is in Acts 9.10 *idou egō kurie*. It is just possible that in 13.41 *idete hoi kataphronētai* may be another such example, though the plural *idete* is not found in this use in the Gospels. This occurrence is in fact in a quotation from the Septuagint version of Hab 1.5, where it translates a Hebrew second person imperative verb, and not the interjection *hinnēh* normally rendered by *idou*, so it is unconvincing to regard *idete* as a fossilised imperative in Acts 13.41. (In fact in the Septuagint of the next verse, Hab 1.6, there is an instance of *idou egō* translating *hinēnî*.) There are no examples of interjections with vocatives in Acts. There are four occurrences of *ō* before a vocative (1.1; 13.10; 18.14; 27.21), but as in the Gospels, this is not regarded as an item which displaces vocatives.

It was further proposed in the Gospels that the occurrence of a personal pronoun increased the likelihood that a vocative would be displaced, though this was by no means an invariable conditioning factor. In those cases where a pronoun did occur in the material that preceded the vocative, it was often difficult to see whether it was the occurrence of the pronoun that caused the displacement, or a sociolinguistic factor. The only instances in Acts where the occurrence of a pronoun looks to be a possible factor in displacement are:

> *su kurie kardiognōsta pantōn...* (1.24); and
> *egō, andres adelphoi, ouden enantion poiēsas...* (28.17).

The sociolinguistic factors identified in the previous article were labelled "rebuke" and "superior to inferior," though the more generic expression "increased social distance between the interlocutors" was also used. Examples that might be included under the label of rebuke in Acts are:

> Paul to the man who ordered him to be struck *tuptein se mellei ho theos, toikhe kekoniamene* (23.3); and perhaps
> *edei men, ō andres* (27.21).

One could also claim that there is an element of rebuke in *mēdamōs, kurie* in Acts 10.14; 11.8 mentioned above. The category of superior to inferior, on the other hand, is more common in Acts. Among the examples are:

> the heavenly voice to Peter *anastas, Petre, thuson kai phage* (10.13; 11.7);
> Gallio to the complaining Jewish delegation *ei men ēn adikēma ti ē rhadiourgēma, ō Ioudaioi* (18.14);
> James and the elders to Paul *theōreis, adelphe, posoi...* (21.20);
> Festus to Paul *mainē, Paule* (26.24);
> and an angel to Paul *mē phobou, Paule* (27.24).

What is most interesting in Acts is that there are several examples where the vocative is displaced when the social relationship is very obviously the exact opposite of that above, namely, inferior to superior. Examples are:

> Tertullus to Felix *...kratiste Fēlix...* (24.3);
> Paul to Agrippa *peri pantōn hōn egkaloumai hupo Ioudaiōn, basileu*

Agrippa... (26.2);

Paul to Festus *ou mainomai, phēsin, kratiste Fēste...* (26.25); and perhaps

Paul to the other passengers on the ship *edei men, ō andres...* (27.21) and *dio euthumeite, andres...* (27.25).

Probably Paul's apologetic *ouk ēdein, adelphoi* before the council in 23.5 should also be included in this category. Indeed, the other example cited above of displacement possibly caused by the presence of a pronoun (1.24, *su kurie kardiognōsta pantōn*) could also be analysed as an example of inferior (the apostles) to superior (the Lord).

The recognition of inferior to superior as well as superior to inferior as a conditioning factor in the displacement of vocatives has two effects. First it allows a more generic, and therefore more powerful statement to be made about sociolinguistic factors in displacement, and second it helps to sharpen understanding of the personal interaction between participants in places where this is not always obvious. In terms of sociolinguistic influence on vocative displacement, it would be useful to return to the expression used in chapter four, "increased social distance between the interlocutors." This would embrace the previously identified factors "rebuke," and "superior to inferior," and also the new factor "inferior to superior." To use terms used in other linguistic studies, one could say that the unmarked order with the vocative in sentence initial position indicates an actual or desired solidarity between the participants, and the marked order with the vocative displaced indicates an actual or desired power relationship. This power relationship may be either condescending (higher to lower) or deferential (lower to higher). Under this categorisation, the label "rebuke" becomes redundant, because in a situation where one person rebukes another, there is always increased social distance, irrespective of whether the speaker is of higher or lower status.

The only place where the above observations do not seem to hold is in Acts 13.10. Despite a highly confrontational situation between Paul and Elymas, Paul's vocative is not displaced. Perhaps this is due to its length and complexity (*ō plērēs pantos dolou kai pasēs rhadourgias, huie diabolou, echthre pasēs dikaiosunēs*), and the fact that it is functioning as a covert predicate. The very meaning of the words makes the increased social distance obvious!

In the study of the Gospels, it was noted that when Luke uses a repeated vocative (Luke 10.41; 13.34; 22.31), the tone is always reproachful. The same feature is also found in Acts. The only repeated vocative is *Saoul Saoul*, which occurs not only in the editorial narrative of Saul's conversion (Acts 9.4), but also in the two retellings of this event by Saul/Paul himself (Acts 22.7 and 26.14).

One final note with regard to Acts is that where a noun (normally a masculine singular noun) has a vocative form which is different from the nominative, the vocative form is always used in a vocative construction. There is only one exception, and that is Acts 7.42, where Stephen is quoting from the Septuagint of Amos 5.25, and retains a nominative form, *oikos Israēl*, exactly as it occurs in the Septuagint.

Revelation

In the book of Revelation, there is only one vocative which is not displaced, that in 7.14 (*kurie mou, su oidas*). It is interesting to note that this is the only place in the main body of the book of Revelation where John, the author, speaks with a vocative. He is addressing one of the 24 elders, that is to say a human figure, albeit an honourable one. The author is presumably the speaker also at the end of the book in 22.20 where the vocative is displaced, but there are other possible factors in that verse, as discussed below.

There is one definite instance of a one word adverbial phrase displacing a vocative (*Nai kurie ho theos ho pantokratōr* in 16.7), and another possible one (*Amēn, erchou kurie Iēsou* in 22.20). The word *Amēn* has not co-occurred with a vocative in the other material studied, so it is not possible to determine how influential its presence here may be.

There are no fossilised imperatives in Revelation, but there are three examples of interjections preceding a vocative. These are all a repeated *ouai ouai hē polis hē megalē* in the laments in 18.10, 16 and 19. It might also be possible to consider the expression *Amēn, erchou kurie Iēsou* in 22.20 as an example of an interjection rather than an adverbial phrase preceding a vocative. There are no examples in Revelation of *ō* with a vocative.

Apart from the five cases already mentioned, all the remaining twelve examples of vocatives in Revelation are displaced. Five of them (11.17; three vocatives in 15.3–4; 18.4) might be accounted for on the basis of the occurrence of pronouns (*soi, sou, sou, tís,* and *mou* respectively), but the other seven (in 4.11; 6.10; 12.12; 16.5; 18.20; 19.5) cannot be explained on the basis of the categories proposed in my earlier article. However, it is striking that under the more generic category of "increased social distance," not only can all seven be accounted for, but also the five listed above where pronouns occur. In eight of these twelve examples, it is God who is being addressed, so deference is in order irrespective of who the speaker may be. In two instances (12.12 and 19.5) a heavenly voice is addressing the inhabitants of heaven, that is to say redeemed people. In one case (18.4) the voice is presumably the voice of God, since it addresses "my people" (*ho laos mou*). In all three cases a note of authority leading to the displacement of the vocative is appropriate. The remaining case is that in 18.20, where those who are bewailing the fate of Babylon address the inhabitants of heaven, and indeed God himself, if *ourane* is a euphemism. Again deference is to be expected.

This is true also of the two cases in Acts mentioned above where the presence of a pronoun might have been considered influential. In the first case (Acts 1.24) the disciples are addressing a request to God, and a deferential attitude is appropriate. In the second case (Acts 28.17) Paul is making a defensive speech to a group of Jewish leaders who are not personally known to him, so again, politeness would suggest the recognition of a degree of formality and social distance.

In Matt 15.22; 20.30, 31, it was noted that the true vocative form *kurie* was conjoined with the nominative phrase *huios David* in apposition. The same combination of a true vocative with a nominative occurs three times in Revelation (11.17; 15.3; 16.7). In each case the words are the same: *kurie ho theos ho pantokratōr*. In Revelation with its larger assortment of grammatical deviations such an oddity is less surprising. In contrast with Acts, where Luke is scrupulous to use correct vocative forms in the singular where they differ from nominative forms, in Revelation the occurrence of nominative singular forms in an indisputably vocative function is common. Examples are found in 4.11; 6.10; 15.3; 16.5 and 18.4. Apart from the vocative *kurie* (7.14; 11.17; 15.4; 22.20), the only true vocative singular is *ourane* in 18.20.

There is also one curious case in 12.12 where *ouai* is followed by an accusative in what appears to be a vocative function: *ouai tēn gēn kai tēn thalassan*. The regular pattern in Revelation is *ouai ouai* followed by a nominative (18.10, 16, 19). The anomaly in 12.12 is not counted as a vocative, even though it may need to be translated as a vocative in many languages. One may compare the occurrences of *ouai* with a dative in Luke 11.42, 43, 46, 52, which were also excluded from the count of vocatives in the article on the Gospels.

VOCATIVE DISPLACEMENT IN ACTS AND REVELATION

Summary of Acts and Revelation, and Implications

The investigation of vocatives in Acts and Revelation partly confirms and partly modifies the results of earlier work done on the Gospels. Nothing in either of these books contradicts the view that one word adverbial phrases, fossilised imperatives, and interjections all routinely precede a vocative, with no particular sociolinguistic overtones. However, there is no real evidence that the presence of a pronoun causes the displacement of a vocative. Even in the Gospels, the evidence for this was far from conclusive, though the possibility was accepted as a working hypothesis.

The major deduction from the study of these two books is that the formulation of sociolinguistic factors in the displacement of vocatives in the Gospels was skewed. Instead of speaking of "rebuke" and "superior to inferior" as separate factors, it is more comprehensive to speak of a single factor of "increased social distance." This formulation includes not only situations where one participant rebukes another, and situations where a superior addresses an inferior, but also the situations more prominent in Acts and especially Revelation than in the Gospels, where an inferior addresses a superior. Thus the initial (unmarked) position of a vocative in its sentence is sociolinguistically neutral and relatively egalitarian. A displaced vocative indicates a non-egalitarian relationship of increased social distance. Whether this is to be interpreted as superior to inferior or inferior to superior depends both on the denotative content of the sentence, and on the context in which it occurs.

A possibly important feature on which no comment was made in the Gospels is the position of the sentence including a vocative within the utterance in which it occurs. The majority of sentences containing vocatives are the first sentence of an utterance, but in Acts and Revelation, there are a number of instances where a multi-sentence utterance contains more than one vocative. These include Acts 2.14–36; 3.12–26; 4.24–30; 7.2–53; 11.5–17; 13.16–41; 22.3–21; 25.24–27; 26.2–23, 25–27; 27.21–26; Rev 18.19–20. These may be divided into two subsets. In the first, the addressee(s) change(s) in the course of the utterance, and the later vocative marks the change of addressee. In Acts 25.24–27, Festus begins by addressing *Agrippa basileu kai pantes hoi sumparontes hēmin andres*, then narrows down to one addressee, *basileu Agrippa*, in 25.26. In Acts 26.25–27, Paul begins by addressing a statement to *kratiste Fēste*, then in v. 27 changes to address a question to *basileu Agrippa*. In Rev 18.19–20, the matter is not quite so clear cut. The opening words of the utterance *ouai ouai, hē polis hē megalē*, are probably to be taken as a vocative addressed to Babylon on the basis of the identical expressions in 18.10, 16, the first of which is accompanied by a second person singular pronoun *sou*. Then in 18.20 the addressee changes to the multiple *ourane kai hoi hagioi kai hoi apostolai kai hoi prophētai*.

In the other subset, the repetition of a vocative seems to mark the start of a new paragraph directed to the same addressee(s). In Acts 2.14–36, Peter begins his address with the formal and general but not deferential *Andres Ioudaioi kai hoi katoikountes Ierousalēm pantes*. In 2.22 after a long quotation from Joel 2, he begins a new paragraph with *Andres Israēlitai*, then in 2.29, after another lengthy quotation, this time from Ps 16, he begins a third paragraph with *Andres adelphoi*. This series is interesting not only as showing where a new paragraph begins, but also as demonstrating by the choice of terms a progression of decreasing social distance as the speaker develops rapport with the audience. A similar phenomenon recurs in 3.12–26, where Peter begins with *Andres Israēlitai*, and changes in 3.17 to *adelphoi*. This time the greater solidarity of *adelphoi* is courteously balanced by its displacement. In 3.17, UBS[4] fails to recognise a new paragraph, though NA[27] has a new subparagraph. In 4.24–30, the prayer of the believers begins with the very formal vocative *Despota* (found elsewhere only in Luke 2.29) and moves on in 4.29 to the less formal *kurie*: the apparent decrease in formality is again offset by the fact that the second vocative, unlike the first, is displaced. It would be appropriate to begin a new paragraph at 4.29, though neither UBS[4] nor NA[27] does so. It is interesting to notice the similarity between the contexts of the second vocatives in these two speeches: *kai nun, adelphoi* in 3.17 and *kai ta nun, kurie* in 4.29. In both cases a new stage in the utterance is indicated, and a new paragraph is in order.

In the speech of Stephen in Acts 7.2–53, the situation is more complex. There are four vocatives in the course of the speech, but those in 7.26 and 7.42 are embedded in second degree quotations, and so do not form part of the interaction between Stephen and his audience. In a tense situation, Stephen begins with the formal (but not displaced) *Andres adelphoi kai pateres*, and ends with the provocative and even abrasive *Sklērotrachēloi kai aperitmētoi kardiais kai tois ōsin*, which is not even softened by displacement. In 13.16–41, the situation is somewhat parallel to that in the speeches of Peter in chs. 2 and 3. Paul begins in 13.16 with the formal *Andres Israēlitai kai hoi phoboumenoi ton theon*, then opens a new paragraph in 13.26 with the longwinded but slightly less formal *Andres adelphoi, huioi Abraam kai hoi en humin phoboumenoi ton theon*. Neither of these is displaced, but as Paul moves towards his climax in 13.38, he uses the less formal *andres adelphoi*, but softens it with displacement, just as Peter did in 3.17. The occurrence of the vocative in 13.38, especially since it is linked with *oun*, suggests that a new paragraph begins there, even though this is not recognised either in UBS[4] or in NA[27].

In Acts 26.2–23 there are no less than six vocatives, but the two in 26.14–15 are embedded in the account of Paul's conversion, and do not form part of Paul's interaction with his current audience. In this speech, Paul is addressing King Agrippa, and as we would by now expect, all the vocatives are displaced as a mark of deference. At the beginning in 26.2 and again near the end in 26.19, Paul uses the longer and presumably more formal *basileu Agrippa*, and in the intervening places the shorter *basileu*. In 26.13, the *basileu* occurs in what UBS[4] recognises as the first sentence of a new paragraph beginning in 26.12, but in 26.7, the *basileu* is displaced right to the end of a long sentence that began in 26.6, so it can hardly be the marker of a new paragraph there. If it has a function at discourse level, it is not clear what that function may be. Some kind of intermediate climax, perhaps? It is intriguing that the sentence in which this vocative occurs also began with *kai nun* (26.6, compare 3.17; 4.29). In 26.19, the vocative does again coincide with the beginning of a new paragraph in UBS[4]. (NA[27] recognises only new subparagraphs at 26.12 and 19.)

In Acts 27.21–26, there are three vocatives, of which the second, in 27.24, is embedded. The other two occur one at the beginning in 27.21 and the other at the hortatory peak of the address in 27.25. It is no surprise that both are displaced, as befits a mere prisoner addressing a group who would consider themselves his social superiors. Both times the vocative is *andres*, which does not suggest any special familiarity or solidarity. There is hardly a question of beginning a new paragraph in what is a fairly short utterance. But the occurrence of *dio* in 27.25 shows that a conclusion is about to be drawn from the preceding statements, and is accompanied by a change from indicative verbs to an imperative *euthumeite*. There is a parallel occurrence in Rev 12.12, where a vocative near the end of a speech extending from 12.10–12 is accompanied by *dia touto* and a change from indicative verbs to an imperative *euphrainesthe*. A less close parallel occurs in Acts 6.3, where a vocative *adelphoi* that is not in the first sentence of a paragraph is displaced after an imperative *episkepsasthe*. In each of these places, the displacement of the vocative may have the effect of softening the peremptoriness of the imperative verb.

In sum, then, the speeches in Acts where more than one vocative occurs show a consistent pattern that supports the conclusions reached from the more general study. There is a tendency for solidarity with an audience to increase in the course of an address, and there is a regular displacement of vocatives from sentence initial position to indicate deference.

The Gospels Revisited

First of all, it will be useful to look again at the items noted in the earlier article as possible residues. The first group of items was those where the vocative *oligopistoi* occurred in a displaced position, and though formally a vocative, functioned as a covert predicate. I mooted the possibility of setting up a category of covert predication, but did not pursue it because in all the places affected (Matt 6.30; 8.26; 16.8; Luke 12.28), pronouns preceded the vocative. The occurrence of a pronoun is no longer to be considered a conditioning feature, but the broader sociolinguistic factor of increased social distance will cover these four texts. In each case, Jesus is administering a rebuke, and therefore the social distance from his interlocutors is automatically increased, at least temporarily.

The case of *kratiste Theophile* in Luke 1.3 was regarded as a probable exception, despite the fact that it is preceded by several pronouns, on the grounds that the analogous *ō Theophile* in Acts 1.1 is displaced without the presence of any pronoun. Both these occurrences are covered by the category of increased social distance. In both, the writer is dedicating his book to a prestigious person, and therefore a displaced vocative showing a deferential attitude is what would be expected.

The remaining exceptions in John 8.11; 9.35–38 are also handled by the category of increased social distance. The adulterous woman in 8.11 could hardly be other than deferential to the *didaskalos* who had brought about the collapse of the case against her. Likewise the blind man in 9.35–38 would surely be polite to the person who had healed him, especially after suffering social ostracism from the Pharisees. Such a sociolinguistic analysis avoids the need to squeeze exegetically dubious theological juice from the two parallel occurrences of *kurie* in 9.36 and 38.

In the Gospels, it is also worth while to look again at the places where more than one vocative occurs in the same utterance. A little surprisingly, there are relatively few such places, and of those which do occur, the repeated vocatives are often embedded in second degree quotations, and thus do not reflect the relations of the speaker with the audience. Such instances are found in Matt 6.9; 7.21–23; 25.11–44; and Luke 13.25–27; 15.12–31; 16.24–30;

18.11–13; 19.16–22. There are however some examples of repeated vocatives which are not embedded, and these are worth looking at in more detail.

In Matthew 11.21, the utterance of Jesus begins *ouai soi, Chorazin, ouai soi Bēthsaida*, and in 11.23 the next vocative *kai su, Kapharnaoum* simply changes the addressee. In the next utterance (11.25–30), the second vocative *nai ho patēr* in 11.26 appears simply to reinforce the first *pater* in 11.25. In 11.28 the third vocative, *Deute pros me pantes hoi kopiōntes kai pephortismenoi* changes the addressees. In Matt 23, there is a whole chain of vocatives (23.13, [14,] 15, 16, 17, 19, 23, 24, 25, 26, 27, 29, 33, 37), and several vocative functions seem to be identifiable. The vocative *ouai humin grammateis kai Pharisaoi hupokritai* occurs in 23.13, [14], 15, 23, 25, 27 and 29, and in each of these places marks the beginning of a new paragraph. In 23.16 the *ouai humin* formula occurs, but with a different noun phrase, *hodēgoi tuphloi hoi legontes*.... On the whole it seems likely that this also marks a new paragraph. The vocative occurrences in 23.17, 19, 24, 26 and 33 do not have the *ouai humin* formula, and seem to reinforce the paragraph initial occurrences, maintaining the vehemence of the whole utterance. Interestingly none of them is displaced, so this vehemence is in no way softened. With the exception of 23.33, these occurrences all contain adjectives, and it could be proposed that they thereby function as covert predicates. The last and longest vocative in the series, *Ierousalēm Ierousalēm, hē apokteinousa tous prophētas kai lithobolousa tous apestalmenous pros autēn* in 23.37, has a different and well-recognised function, that of changing the addressee.

There are no repeated vocatives in Mark, but Luke offers some examples. Those in Luke 10.13, 15 are identical with those in Matt 11.21, 23, and those in Luke 10.21a and 21b are identical with those in Matthew 11.25, 26: neither need further comment. Luke 11.39–44 shows both similarities and differences from the partial parallel in Matt 23. It is not clear whether the opening words of the utterance (11.39) *Nun humeis hoi Pharisaioi to exōthen tou potēriou kai tou pinakos katharizete...* are a vocative or not. The absence of a comma after *Pharisaioi* in both UBS[4] and NA[27] indicates that their editors did not perceive a vocative here, and this text was not counted as a vocative in my earlier article. However, *aphrones* in Luke 11.40 seems to function very much like the adjectival vocatives in Matt 23.17, 19, that is to say reinforcing an earlier assertion, so perhaps the punctuation in 11.39 should be altered to treat *Nun humeis hoi Pharisaioi* as a vocative. The *ouai humin* formulae in Luke 11.42, 43, 44 were not treated as vocatives because they are followed by a dative. The whole utterance (11.39b–44) is too short for them all to be treated as marking new paragraphs, but perhaps the first one in 11.42 could be taken as a new paragraph marker since it alone is preceded by *alla*. A somewhat similar situation is found in the next utterance of Jesus in Luke 11.46–52; the occurrence of *ouai* in 11.46, 47 and 52 is again accompanied by datives, and the utterance is too short for each occurrence to be regarded as a new paragraph marker.

Within the utterance Luke 12.22–40, there is no initial vocative, but two medial ones. The first, *oligopistoi* in 12.28 is closely parallel to the identical term in Matt 6.30, and seems to function more at sentence level as a covert predicate than at paragraph level. The second, *to mikron poimnion* in 12.32, has no parallel, and functions either to change addressees, or to switch focus to a different aspect of the relationship between the speaker and the hearers.

The remaining Gospel example of multiple vocatives within an utterance is in John 17.1–26. This opens with the sentence initial vocative *pater*, and continues with a displaced *pater* in 17.5, a sentence initial *pater hagie* in 17.11, a displaced *pater* in 17.21, and two sentence initial vocatives, *pater* in 17.24 and *pater dikaie* in 17.25. With the probable exception of the last, these vocatives can be plausibly interpreted as marking new paragraphs. In 17.5 the vocative may be displaced to soften the imperative which it accompanies. The fact that its sentence begins with the words *kai nun* (compare Acts 3.17; 4.29; 26.6) suggests too that the new paragraph should begin at 17.5 rather than at 17.6 as in UBS^4 and NA^{27}. The vocative in 17.21 may also be displaced for a similar reason to that in 17.5. Although there is no imperative in its sentence, the construction *erōtō... hina* functions pragmatically as a surrogate imperative. At *pater hagie* in 17.11, neither NA^{27} nor UBS^4 has a new paragraph, though UBS^4 begins the sentence with a capital letter, indicating a medium rather than a major break. On the other hand, a new paragraph at 17.24 is recognised by NA^{27} but not by UBS^4. It is extremely difficult to determine what were the linguistic principles on which either version chose the location of new paragraphs (or indeed whether there were any). If any of the vocatives in this speech are to be interpreted as not indicating a new paragraph, it would probably be those in 17.11 and 17.25. This would be on the analogy of the adjectival vocatives in Matt 23.17, 19, 24 and 26, as discussed above.

There remains one small textual point to mention. In the light of Luke's meticulousness in using correct vocative forms both in Acts and in the Gospel, it seems very odd that in Luke 8.48 both UBS^4 and NA^{27} prefer the nominative form *thugatēr* over the true vocative form *thugater* in a vocative function, despite strong manuscript evidence in favour of the true vocative. Surely this is a place where pressure of Lucan usage should weigh heavily, especially since the meaning is not in any way affected.

Conclusion

The study of vocatives in the narrative books of the NT has proved more interesting than I expected when I began it. The normal, or unmarked position for a vocative is sentence initial. In some restricted situations (in combination with certain one word adverbial phrases, fossilised imperatives, and interjections), the vocative is automatically displaced from initial position in the sentence without any sociolinguistic implications. Displacement in other settings, however, does indicate an increased social distance between the participants in the dialogue. Whether this is to be interpreted as deference or the assertion of authority depends on the context.

Finally, it must be emphasised once more that translators should not simply copy the patterns of vocative displacement found in NT Greek. They should examine the patterns of vocative usage in their own language to determine whether variation in the position of a vocative is permissible, and if so, what implications may be carried by the different possible positions. They should then try to match the sociolinguistic functions of the Greek vocatives with the functions in the receptor language. This may sometimes result in quite different patterns of vocative placement from those in the Greek, both within the sentence and within the paragraph. It may sometimes lead also to the omission of Greek vocatives from the translation in the receptor language (for instance in John 2.4 in some English versions), or to the insertion of vocatives where the Greek does not have them. This last situation occurs in languages where the absence of a vocative would imply a rudeness and/or social distance which the source language does not intend.

7

DISCOURSE STRUCTURE IN TITUS

Background

This article arises from lectures prepared for a seminar in Russia on the Discourse Analysis of Titus. Since it inevitably contains a lot of detail, a summary of the results of the analysis is presented at the beginning as an indication of the destination to which the discussion will lead.

My presupposition is that the letter is a coherent literary unit, put purposefully by an author or redactor into the form in which we have it today. It is thus likely to be basically well structured, but not necessarily perfectly structured. Even if the present form of the text incorporates citations from other sources (explicitly so in 1.12), translators have to deal with the letter as it now stands, and so this article does not touch on questions of unity or authorship. I shall refer to the author as "Paul" in order to avoid clumsy periphrases. The Greek text cited is UBS[4], with punctuation slightly adjusted to reflect the discourse structure. My basic criteria of analysis are syntactic (especially the occurrence of imperative verbs), with close attention also paid to lexical recursions and other rhetorical features. Alternative possible analyses are discussed at some points.

Glosses of the Greek words are taken as much as possible from the RSV, but where it uses different English words to translate the same Greek word, I have chosen to use one of its variants consistently in order to show the repetition in the Greek. I have also changed the RSV word order and made such other alterations as seemed necessary to let the glosses reflect the Greek structure more closely, or where I disagree with the RSV rendering and propose an alternative. The result is neither elegant nor natural, but fits the purposes of this article.

Rather than trying to interact with a wide range of modern scholars, I will restrict myself to making occasional comparisons with the Translator's Handbook on *Paul's Letters to Timothy and to Titus* and with the magisterial commentary on *The Pastoral Epistles* by I. Howard Marshall.[1] I have followed Marshall in glossing ἐπισκοπος as "overseer" and do not discuss the question of its fuller meaning.

Structural Outline

In summary form this is as follows:

Introduction	1.1–4
Section A	1.5–13a
Section B	1.13b–3.8a
Section C	3.8b–11
Conclusion	3.12–15

The analysis will now be shown in more detail:
 Introduction 1.1–4 Greetings and theological presuppositions
  Introduction of several key terms: πιστις, εὐσεβεια, ἐλπις ζωης αἰωνιου, φανερουν, σωτηρ (faith, godliness, hope of eternal life, appear, saviour)
 Section A 1.5–13a Reminder of Titus' aims in Crete
  Key terms, all in 1.9: παρακαλειν, διδασκαλια ὑγιαινουσα, ἐλεγχειν (to encourage, sound doctrine, to rebuke)
 Section B 1.13b–3.8a Three principal commands, carried by imperative verbs: ἐλεγχε, λαλει or παρακαλει, ὑπομιμνησκε (rebuke, speak or encourage, remind)
   B1 1.13b–16 ἐλεγχε (rebuke)
    Key terms: ὑγιαινωσιν ἐν τῃ πιστει (be sound in the faith)
   B2(a) 2.1–10 λαλει... παρακαλει (speak... encourage) four clas-

---

[1] Daniel C. Arichea and Howard A. Hatton, *A Handbook on Paul's Letters to Timothy and to Titus* (United Bible Societies, 1995); I. Howard Marshall, *The Pastoral Epistles*, ICC (T&T Clark, 1999).

ses of people
Key terms: ὑγιαινουσα διδασκαλια, πιστις, καλα ἐργα (sound teaching, faith, good deeds)

B2(b) 2.11–14 ἐπεφανη γαρ (appeared): theological undergirding
Key terms: ἐπεφανη, εὐσεβως, ἐλπις, σωτηρ, καλα ἐργα (appeared, godly, hope, saviour, good deeds)

B2(c) 2.15 λαλει και παρακαλει και ἐλεγχε (speak and encourage and rebuke)

B3(a) 3.1–2 ὑπομιμνησκε (remind)
Key terms: ἐργον ἀγαθον (good work)

B3(b) 3.3–8a ἡμεν γαρ ποτε... ὁτε δε...: theological reinforcement (for we were once... but when...)
Key terms: ἐπεφανη, σωτηρ, ἐλπις ζωης αἰωνιου (appeared, saviour, hope of eternal life)

Section C 3.8b–11 Three subsidiary pastoral commands: διαβεβαιουσθαι, περιϊστασο, παραιτου (insist, avoid, have nothing to do with)
Key term: καλα ἐργα (good deeds)

Conclusion 3.12–15 Three subsidiary practical commands: σπουδασον, προπεμψον, ἀσπασαι (do your best, speed on their way, greet)
Key term: καλα ἐργα (good deeds)

Introduction 1.1–4

There is no dispute over the boundaries of this section, as it follows the normal epistolary conventions. The basic structure of the section is

1 Παυλος... 4 Τιτῳ ... χαρις και εἰρηνη... (Paul... to Titus... grace and peace)

The complexity lies in the large amount of information added in apposition to Παυλος in 1.1b–3. Since this stands outside the formulaic (and therefore more predictable) part of the introduction, it is in fact where the semantic focus lies. This is the first of the three heavily theological passages in Titus, the others being 2.11–14 and 3.4–7. It is noteworthy that all three are in syntactically subordinate positions. In order to retain their semantic prominence in translation, it will often be necessary to avoid syntactic subordination. These verses can be set out as follows (the use of indentation to indicate items at the same syntactic level is fairly consistent, but for practical reasons of page width may contain occasional anomalies):

1 Παυλος
δουλος θεου,
ἀποστολος δε Ἰησου Χριστου
    κατα πιστιν ἐκλεκτων θεου
    και ἐπιγνωσιν ἀληθειας
        της κατ᾿εὐσεβειαν
        2 ἐπ᾿ ἐλπιδι ζωης αἰωνιου
            ἡν ἐπηγγειλατο ὁ ἀψευδης θεος προ χρονων αἰωνιων
            3 ἐφανερωσεν δε καιροις ἰδιοις τον λογον αὐτου ἐν κηρυγματι
                ὁ ἐπιστευθην ἐγω κατ᾿ἐπιταγην του σωτηρος ἡμων θεου
4 Τιτῳ γνησιῳ τεκνῳ κατα κοινην πιστιν
χαρις και εἰρηνη ἀπο θεου πατρος
                και Χριστου Ἰησου του σωτηρος ἡμων.

1 Paul
a servant of God
an apostle of Jesus Christ
    according to faith of God's elect
    and knowledge of truth
        according to godliness
        2 in hope of eternal life
            which the never-lying God promised before eternal ages
            3 and manifested at the right time [in] his word through preaching
                [with] which I have been entrusted by order of our saviour God
4 to Titus, true child according to common faith
grace and peace from God [our] Father
                and Christ Jesus our saviour.

There are a number of exegetical problems in this section:

1. What is the meaning of the first occurrence of κατα? The common meaning "according to" which fits its other two occurrences in 1.2–3 fits the first less readily. RSV renders as "to further" and TEV "to help," and these seem plausible interpretations. Another possibility (based on a structural overview of the whole of 1.1–4) may be to take κατα πιστιν ἐκλεκτων θεου in 1.1 as parallel with κατα κοινην πιστιν in 1.4. The effect would then be "Paul... who holds the faith that God's people hold and knows the truth... to Titus, who is a true son in this shared faith..."

2. Is ἐπ' ἐλπιδι ζωης αἰωνιου (in hope of eternal life) subordinate to της κατεὐσεβειαν (according to godliness) or co-ordinate with it? The fact that other items are paired (two nouns describing Paul, two noun phrases governed by κατα, two verbs following ἡν) suggests that co-ordination is more probable, and that is what is shown above. Marshall reaches a similar conclusion by a different route.[2]

3. What is the precise antecedent of ἡν ἐπηγγειλατο (which [God] promised)? There are no less than six preceding feminine nouns, but only the last two ἐλπιδι and ζωης (hope and life) are semantically credible as possibilities. Probably the link of ζωη (life) with ἐπαγγελια (promise) in 2 Tim 1.1 tips the scales in favour of taking ζωης αἰωνιου (eternal life) as the antecedent of ἡν ἐπηγγειλατο (which [God] promised) here.

4. Is there a chiasmus involved in the four nominal phrases following the first κατα? This possibility would resolve the question raised under 2 above. Marshall does not mention such a possibility, but that is hardly decisive: the Translator's Handbook gives several options for interpretation, but admits that none is compelling.[3] If there is a chiasmus, the phrases could be set out as

κατα πιστιν ἐκλεκτων θεου
και ἐπιγνωσιν ἀληθειας
της κατεὐσεβειαν
ἐπ' ἐλπιδι ζωης αἰωνιου

Since there is a lot more descriptive material qualifying the last phrase, any translation based on a chiastic interpretation would do well to keep the phrase "eternal life" till the end as the link with what follows. A possible translation model is: "...to encourage God's chosen people to know the truth that leads them to godly living, and to hold the faith that gives them hope of eternal life." Translators could then do as TEV has done and begin a new sentence to translate the description of this eternal life.

5. The Greek construction is rather awkward with ἡν (which) as direct object of ἐπηγγειλατο (promised), and τον λογον (the word) as direct object of ἐφανερωσεν (manifested). This is an example of less than perfect structure. In translation, beginning a new sentence with ἡν as in TEV can reduce this awkwardness.

---

[2] Marshall, *Pastoral Epistles*, 123–124.
[3] Arichea and Hatton, *Handbook*, 261–263.

New Testament Discourse

Section A 1.5–13a

Though this section is longer, its structure is less complex, with much obvious co-ordination. The basic structure is

5 τουτου χαριν ἀπελιπον σε... ἱνα... ἐπιδιορθωσῃ και καταστησῃς...
7 δει γαρ τον ἐπισκοπον... εἰναι... 9 ἱνα δυνατος ᾖ...
10 εἰσιν γαρ πολλοι... 11 οὑς δει ἐπιστομιζειν...

5 for this cause I left you... so that... you might amend and appoint...
7 for it is necessary for an overseer to be... 9 so that he can...
10 for there are many... 11 whom it is necessary to silence...

Verses 12 and 13a are essentially parenthetic to the basic structure, probably adding a touch of wry humour. This section may be set out as follows:

5 τουτου χαριν ἀπελιπον σε ἐν Κρητῃ
   ἱνα τα λειποντα ἐπιδιορθωσῃ
   και καταστησῃς κατα πολιν πρεσβυτερους
      ὡς ἐγω σοι διεταξαμην
    6 εἰ τις ἐστιν ἀνεγκλητος
      μιας γυναικος ἀνηρ
      τεκνα ἐχων πιστα
         μη ἐν κατηγοριᾳ ἀσωτιας
         ἢ ἀνυποτακτα.
   7 δει γαρ τον ἐπισκοπον ἀνεγκλητον εἰναι ὡς θεου οἰκονομον
    μη αὐθαδη
        μη ὀργιλον
        μη παροινον
        μη πληκτην
        μη αἰσχροκερδη
     8 ἀλλα φιλοξενον
    φιλαγαθον
        σωφρονα
        δικαιον
        ὁσιον
        ἐγκρατη
   9 ἀντεχομενον του κατα την διδαχην πιστου λογου

ἵνα δυνατος ᾖ και παρακαλειν ἐν τῃ διδασκαλιᾳ τῃ ὑγιαινουσῃ
    και τους ἀντιλεγοντας ἐλεγχειν.
10 εἰσιν γαρ πολλοι [και] ἀνυποτακτοι
      ματαιολογοι
      και φρεναπαται
        μαλιστα οἱ ἐκ της περιτομης
    11 οὕς δει ἐπιστομιζειν
    οἵτινες ὁλους οἰκους ἀνατρεπουσιν
    διδασκοντες ἁ μη δει αἰσχρου κερδους χαριν.
12 εἰπεν τις ἐξ αὐτων
    ἰδιος αὐτων προφητης
      Κρητες ἀει ψευσται
      κακα θηρια
      γαστερες ἀργαι.
13a ἡ μαρτυρια αὑτη ἐστιν ἀληθης.

5 For this cause I left you in Crete
  so that what was defective you might amend
  and appoint in every town elders
    as I directed you
6 if any man is blameless
      husband of one wife
      having children who believe
          not open to accusation of profligacy
          nor insubordinate.
7 For it is necessary for an overseer to be blameless as God's steward
          not arrogant
          not quick-tempered
          not drunken
          not violent
          not greedy for gain
        8 but hospitable
        loving goodness
        prudent
        upright
        holy
        self-controlled
  9 holding the sure word according to the doctrine

so that he can both encourage in sound teaching
and rebuke those who contradict it.
10 For there are many insubordinate
empty talkers
and deceivers
especially those of the circumcision
11 whom it is necessary to silence
who upset whole families
teaching what they ought not for the sake of gain.
12 Said one of them
a prophet of their own
"Cretans are always liars
evil beasts
lazy gluttons."
13a This testimony is true.

Τουτου (this) in 1.5 is clearly cataphoric, and αὐτη (this) in 1.13a is clearly anaphoric, and this sets a semantic boundary to the unit. This is reinforced by the occurrence of ἀνυποτακτος (insubordinate) in both 1.6 and 1.10, and by the occurrence of χαριν (cause/sake) in both 1.5 and 1.11. The fact that 1.12–13a come after the closure of the unit marked by χαριν, and are asyndetic, suggests their analysis as an aside. It is notable that the semantic climax comes in the subordinate purpose clause introduced by ἱνα in 1.9. This clause introduces the two verbs παρακαλειν (encourage) and ἐλεγχειν (rebuke) around which 1.13b–2.15 are structured. Chiastically, the command to rebuke is enlarged on first in 1.13b–16, and the command to encourage second in 2.1–14. It is no accident that these two verbs are repeated in reverse sequence in 2.15, the verse which sums up 2.1–14, thus forming a chiastic inclusio. This verse (1.9) also introduces the phrase διδασκαλια... ὑγιαινουσα (sound teaching) which constitutes the theme of the subsection covered by 2.1–10. The presence of γαρ (for) in 1.10 serves to link this verse to what precedes, and argues against the widely held view that a major break occurs at the beginning of 1.10. Compare the use of γαρ in 1.7; 2.11; 3.3, 9, 12. The affirmation in 1.13a serves as a closure marker for the section (compare 3.8a).

The repetition of ἀνεγκλητος (blameless) from 1.6 in 1.7 is to be seen as resumptive rather than contrastive. Both occurrences are generic, introducing lists of specific qualities required first in family life (1.6), then in personal character (1.7–9).

I am inclined to see humour in v. 13a. Since a statement by a Cretan that Cretans are liars might logically be itself untrue, perhaps the implication of 13a is "This testimony at any rate is true!"

Section B 1.13b–3.8a

This is the main body of the letter, and is structured around second person singular imperative verbs, ἔλεγχε (rebuke, in 1.13b, picking up the same verb in 1.9), λάλει (speak, in 2.1) and its resumptive and more specific near-synonym παρακάλει (encourage, in 2.6, also repeated from 1.9), and ὑπομίμνῃσκε (remind, in 3.1). On the basis of these imperatives, the section can be conveniently subdivided into three parts, B1, 1.13b–16; B2, 2.1–15; and B3, 3.1–8a. Each part will be displayed separately. Although this structure is clearly marked both lexically and syntactically, it has been almost entirely ignored by translators and, as a chart by Marshall shows, also by commentators.[4] The only version available to me that begins a new paragraph at 1.13b is the New American Bible, and even it does not put a section heading at this point.

Section B1 1.13b–16

The basic structure is simply

13 ἔλεγχε αὐτούς... ἵνα ὑγιαίνωσιν ἐν τῇ πίστει...
16 θεὸν ὁμολογοῦσιν εἰδέναι, τοῖς δὲ ἔργοις ἀρνοῦνται...
13 rebuke them... so that they may be sound in the faith...
16 They claim to know God, but by [their] deeds they deny him...

The separate sentence in 1.16 is semantically subordinate to what precedes it. The words δι' ἣν αἰτίαν (for which reason) in v. 13 are clearly anaphoric, and form the link between sections A and B. The fact that the new section begins somewhat unusually with a relative phrase seems to have prevented translators and commentators from recognising the structural importance of the imperative that follows it. This section may be set out as below:

---

[4] Marshall, *Pastoral Epistles*, 19.

13b δι' ἣν αἰτιαν ἐλεγχε αὐτους ἀποτομως
    ἱνα ὑγιαινωσιν ἐν τῃ πιστει
14 μη προσεχοντες Ἰουδαϊκοις μυθοις
      και ἐντολαις ἀνθρωπων ἀποστρεφομενων την ἀληθειαν,
        15 παντα καθαρα τοις καθαροις
          τοις δε μεμιαμμενοις
            και ἀπιστοις οὐδεν καθαρον
   ἀλλα μεμιανται αὐτων και ὁ νους
      και ἡ συνειδησις.
16 θεον ὁμολογουσιν εἰδεναι,
τοις δε ἐργοις ἀρνουνται
    βδελυκτοι ὀντες
    και ἀπειθεις
    και προς παν ἐργον ἀγαθον ἀδοκιμοι.

13b On which ground rebuke them sharply
    so that they may be sound in the faith
14 not giving attention to Jewish myths
      and to commands of people who reject the truth,
        15 [saying] "All things [are] pure to those [who are] pure
          but to the defiled
            and unbelieving nothing is pure."
    But what is defiled is both *their* mind
        and [their] conscience!
16 They claim to know God
but by their deeds they deny [him]
    being detestable
    and disobedient
    and for all good deeds unfit.

    The main exegetical problem in this section is the status of the asyndetic παντα καθαρα τοις καθαροις (all things [are] pure to those [who are] pure). Some commentators seem uncomfortable with this statement as an opinion of Paul's, and indeed it does not fit into the context at all easily when taken in this way. The similar phrase παντα μεν καθαρα in Romans 14.20 refers specifically to food taboos, but (notwithstanding the views of Arichea & Hatton, and Marshall) there is nothing in the immediate context of Titus 1 to suggest a similar topic here.

In this discourse analysis, the asyndeton is seen as a pointer towards a different way of punctuating and construing the first clause of 1.15, namely to drop the full stop after 1.14, and take 1.15a as a quotation by Paul from the false teachers he is in process of describing. Some scholars have viewed the clause as a proverb, but I have not found any who take it as a citation of the false teachers. If it is taken this way, the question then arises how far the quotation of the opponents' words extends. The options are to include only παντα καθαρα τοις καθαροις, or to include also τοις δε μεμιαμμενοις και απιστοις οὐδεν καθαρον (but to the defiled and unbelieving nothing is pure). In the analogous passages in 1 Cor 6.12 and 10.23, the rejection of the opinion stated in the four citations consistently begins with ἀλλα (but). When I discussed the present passage with Prof. John Karavidopoulos, he was firmly of the opinion that if this is a citation, it also must go as far as ἀλλα. I am more than ready to accept the opinion of a scholar who is not only an editor of UBS[4], but also a native speaker of Greek!

Though I have not been able to find this view proposed elsewhere, it has two virtues. First, it removes the difficulty of trying to understand as an apostolic opinion a clause readily capable of ethical misuse. Second, it treats this clause in a manner analogous to the similar expressions παντα (μοι) ἐξεστιν (all things are lawful [for me]) in 1 Cor 6.12; 10.23, which are widely recognised as quotations from opponents. If this interpretation is accepted, the clause would stand in apposition to ἐντολαις (commands) giving an example of a pernicious command of the false teachers. The citation forms a neat aphoristic chiasmus. Paul's riposte to this opinion then begins with ἀλλα, as four times in 1 Cor 6.12; 10.23.

On this analysis a translation model for vv. 14–15 is "...not paying attention to Jewish myths, and the commandments of people who reject the truth, with their 'All things are pure to those who are pure, but to those who are defiled and unbelieving, nothing is pure.' On the contrary it is *their* minds and consciences that are defiled." This interpretation takes account of the emphatic position of αὐτων (their), marked by front-shifting within its phrase.

It is worth mentioning briefly the meaning of καθαρα/καθαροις (pure). Arichea & Hatton observe that this root can refer both to ritual and to moral purity, and Marshall agrees.[5] If 1.15a is taken as an opinion of the writer, then the fuller meaning is "All things are ritually pure to those who are morally

---

[5] Arichea and Hatton, *Handbook*, 279; Marshall, *Pastoral Epistles*, 208–209.

pure." On the other hand if 1.15a is taken as a citation of the false teachers, then the focus is reversed, and the meaning is "All things are morally pure to those who are ritually pure," that is, to people who follow the commands of those who reject the truth (1.14). This is surely an opinion that the writer would reject, as indeed he does very vigorously in 1.15b–16.

Section B2 2.1–15

This section is structurally the centre of the letter, and it appears to be the semantic core also. The structure is broadly similar to that in Section A, but because it is longer and more complex, it will be convenient to subdivide it into three sub-units as detailed below. The basic structure is

1 συ δε λαλει... 2 πρεσβυτας νηφαλιους ειναι...
       3 πρεσβυτιδας ὡσαυτως...
            4 ἱνα σωφρονιζωσιν τας νεας...
  5 ἱνα μη...
      6 τους νεωτερους ὡσαυτως παρακαλει σωφρονειν...
         7 σεαυτον παρεχομενος τυπον... 8 ἱνα...
    9 δουλους ιδιοις δεσποταις ὑποτασσεσθαι...
       10 ἱνα...
11 ἐπεφανη γαρ ἡ χαρις του θεου... 12 ἱνα... ζησωμεν...
15 ταυτα λαλει και παρακαλει και ἐλεγχε...

1 But [as for] you, speak... 2 [for] older men to be temperate...
      3 [for] older women likewise...
          4 in order that they may train the young women...
  5 in order that... not...
      6 the younger men likewise encourage to be self-controlled...
        7 showing yourself a model... 8 in order that...
      9 slaves [encourage] to be submissive to their own masters...
        10 in order that...
11 For the grace of God has appeared... 12 in order that... we should live...
15 These things speak and encourage and rebuke...

Whereas in Section A the outline was fairly simple:

Indicative verb... ἵνα...
Indicative verb + γαρ... ἵνα...
Indicative verb + γαρ...

here there is an outline which is more highly developed:

1 Generic imperative verb + object 1...
3 Implicit repetition of imperative verb + object 2... ἵνα... + object 3... ἵνα μη...
6 Resumption of (more specific) imperative verb + object 4... + object 5... ἵνα...
9 Implicit repetition of specific verb + object 6... ἵνα...
11 Indicative verb + γαρ... ἵνα... (with considerable further subordination)
15 Three imperative verbs repeated from earlier occurrences.

Because of this greater complexity, three sub-units are established as follows.

Section B2a 2.1–10

This sub-unit provides the essential ethical attitudes which Titus is to inculcate in his congregations. It opens with the emphatic συ δε (But [as for] you) contrasting Titus with the false teachers of the previous paragraph, and deals with six categories of people. Semantically these six are probably co-ordinate, though syntactically the younger women are subordinate to the older women, and Titus himself is subordinate to the younger men. One may speculate whether there is any sociolinguistic significance in this. Probably it is just that younger women are a subset of women, and Titus is a subset of younger men. One must also ask why the change from λαλει (speak) in 2.1 to παρακαλει (encourage) in 2.6. As noted above this is a narrowing from a more generic verb to a more specific one. Perhaps the reason may be that Paul considered παρακαλει too strong a term to use for a younger man's words to older people, though suitable for words to his own age group. Such a factor could be influential in many cultures, and translators may wish to take it into account in choosing their terms.

The section may be set out as follows:

1 συ δε λαλει ά πρεπει τη ύγιαινουσῃ διδασκαλιᾳ.
2 πρεσβυτας νηφαλιους εἰναι
    σεμνους
    σωφρονας
    ὑγιαινοντας τῃ πιστει
        τῃ ἀγαπῃ
        τῃ ὑπομονῃ
3 πρεσβυτιδας ὡσαυτως ἐν καταστηματι ἱεροπρεπεις
    μη διαβολους
    μη οἰνῳ πολλῳ δεδουλωμενας
    καλοδιδασκαλους
4 ἱνα σωφρονιζωσιν τας νεας φιλανδρους εἰναι
    φιλοτεκνους
    5 σωφρονας
    ἀγνας
    οἰκουργους ἀγαθας
    ὑποτασσομενας τοις ἰδιοις ἀνδρασιν
ἱνα μη ὁ λογος του θεου βλασφημηται.
6 τους νεωτερους ὡσαυτως παρακαλει σωφρονειν 7 περι παντα
    σεαυτον παρεχομενος τυπον καλων ἐργων
        ἐν τῃ διδασκαλιᾳ ἀφθοριαν
        σεμνοτητα
    8 λογον ὑγιη ἀκαταγνωστον
    ἱνα ὁ ἐξ ἐναντιας ἐντραπῃ
        μηδεν ἐχων λεγειν περι ἡμων φαυλον.
9 δουλους ἰδιοις δεσποταις ὑποτασσεσθαι ἐν πασιν
    εὐαρεστους εἰναι
    μη ἀντιλεγοντας
    10 μη νοσφιζομενους
    ἀλλα πασαν πιστιν ἐνδεικνυμενους ἀγαθην
    ἱνα την διδασκαλιαν την του σωτηρος ἡμων θεου κοσμωσιν ἐν πασιν.

1 But [as for] you, speak what befits sound teaching
2 [for] older men to be temperate
      serious
      sensible
      sound in faith
         in love
         in steadfastness;
3 [for] older women likewise [to be] reverent in behaviour
      not slanderers
      not slaves to heavy drinking
      teaching what is good
4 in order that they may train the young women to love their husbands
            to love their children
            5 to be sensible
            chaste
            good housekeepers
            submissive to their own husbands
in order that the word of God may not be discredited;
6 the younger men likewise encourage to be self-controlled 7 in all respects
      showing yourself a model of good deeds
         [showing] integrity in your teaching
         gravity
         8 speech sound beyond reproach
     in order that an opponent may be shamed
         having nothing evil to say of us;
9 slaves [encourage] to be submissive to their own masters in all things
      to be well-pleasing
      not contradicting
      10 not pilfering
      but showing all good faith
in order that they may adorn the teaching of God our saviour in all things.

Within this sub-unit some comments are necessary. First of all, παρακαλει (encourage) in v. 6 is taken to be a lexically more specific but functionally more or less synonymous repetition of λαλει (speak) in v. 1 (compare Marshall).[6] The formal justification for this lies in the repetition of ὡσαυτως in vv.

---

[6] Marshall, *Pastoral Epistles*, 253.

3 and 6. The first occurrence in v. 3 clearly implies that λαλει is to be understood as repeated from v. 1, making vv. 3–5 in some sense parallel with vv. 1–2, so it seems reasonable to take the second occurrence in v. 6 as continuing the link and the conceptual parallelism. The gap after v. 1 is now rather long, so in v. 6 Paul makes the imperative verb explicit, but this time chooses a term which is not just a bland verb of speaking, but one which includes an attitudinal component of meaning, namely παρακαλει. This is no random choice, but picks up the use of the same verb in 1.9, just as ελεγχε (rebuke) in 1.13 did. Although the verb is not repeated in 2.9, there is no doubt that it is presupposed there, as is shown by the continued accusative and infinitive construction.[7]

In 2.3, the syntax implies the repetition of ειναι (to be) from 2.2. In 2.7, the words περι παντα (in all respects) may be understood as going either with what precedes or with what follows.[8] In favour of the former it may be noted that in each group mentioned, the people are identified as the first item in the clause, so it seems likely that in the case of Titus, σεαυτον (yourself) is the first item in the clause. This suggests that περι παντα goes with what precedes it, just like εν πασιν (in all things) twice in 2.9–10. This is the punctuation of UBS[4] and NA[27], and is a low-level decision with no major structural ramifications. Also in 2.7–8, we may note that the nouns αφθοριαν, σεμνοτητα, and λογον (integrity, gravity, and speech) are, like σεαυτον (yourself) and τυπον (model) formally objects of the participle παρεχομενος (showing). Even if the style is not the smoothest, the meaning is not obscured.

Other noteworthy points in this unit are the recurrence of the words τη υγιαινουση διδασκαλια (sound teaching) in 2.1 from 1.9, where they occurred in the opposite sequence, thus forming a low profile chiasmus. Other repeated items are υγιαινειν (εν) τη πιστει (sound in the faith, 1.13 and 2.2), though no chiasmus is involved there; the root σωφρον- (glossed in several different ways) first occurring in 1.8, and repeated in 2.2, 4, 5, 6, and again in 2.12 below; and the phrase του σωτηρος ημων θεου (God our saviour) in 2.10, echoed from 1.3. This unit also includes the first occurrence of καλα εργα (good deeds) in 2.7, to be repeated in 2.14; 3.8; 3.14. It is hard to see any distinction of meaning between καλα εργα in these places and εργον αγαθον in 1.16 and 3.1.[9]

Finally, we may note that each of the sub-units ends with a purpose

---

[7] So Marshall, *Pastoral Epistles*, 259.

[8] Precedes: Marshall, *Pastoral Epistles*, 253. Follows: Arichea and Hatton, *Handbook*, 286.

[9] Compare Marshall, *Pastoral Epistles*, Excursus 6, pp. 227–229.

clause with ἵνα that expresses the spiritual goal behind the ethical instructions: ἵνα μη ὁ λογος του θεου βλασφημηται (in order that the word of God may not be discredited) in 2.5, ἵνα ὁ ἐξ ἐναντιας ἐντραπῃ (in order that an opponent may be shamed) in 2.8, and ἵνα την διδασκαλιαν την του σωτηρος ἡμων θεου κοσμωσιν ἐν πασιν (in order that they may adorn the teaching of God our saviour in everything) in 2.10. The last of these clearly qualifies only the behaviour of the slaves,[10] but with the first two, the range of their reference is less obvious. The second could refer to the behaviour of both Titus and other younger men (2.6–8a), but given the prominence of Titus in the congregation, it seems more likely that it refers primarily if not exclusively to him. The most problematic is the first. It could refer back only to the younger women in 2.4–5,[11] but the structure of the whole sentence makes it seem more likely that its range includes the older women in 2.3, and possibly also the older men in 2.2.

Section B2b 2.11–14

This sub-unit is at the formal syntactic level somewhat parallel with the sub-unit beginning δει γαρ (for it is necessary) in 1.7, but at the semantic level, it has more in common with 1.1–3, since it provides a strongly theological rationale for the preceding ethical exhortations. The section may be set out as follows:

```
11 ἐπεφανη γαρ ἡ χαρις του θεου σωτηριος πασιν ἀνθρωποις
            12 παιδευουσα ἡμας
        ἵνα ἀρνησαμενοι την ἀσεβειαν
                    και τας κοσμικας ἐπιθυμιας
            σωφρονως
            και δικαιως
            και εὐσεβως ζησωμεν ἐν τῳ νυν αἰωνι
        13 προσδεχομενοι την μακαριαν ἐλπιδα
                και ἐπιφανειαν της δοξης του μεγαλου θεου
                            και σωτηρος ἡμων Ἰησου Χριστου
            14 ὁς ἐδωκεν ἑαυτον ὑπερ ἡμων
                ἵνα λυτρωσηται ἡμας ἀπο πασης ἀνομιας
```

---

[10] Compare Arichea and Hatton, *Handbook*, 289.
[11] So Arichea and Hatton, *Handbook*, 285; Marshall, *Pastoral Epistles*, 250.

                              και καθαριση εαυτω λαον περιουσιον
                                         ζηλωτην καλων ἐργων.

11 For the grace of God has appeared salvific for all people
    12 training us
  in order that denying irreligion
                     and worldly passions
        soberly
        and uprightly
        and piously we should live in the present world
    13 awaiting the blessed hope
            and appearing of the glory of our great God
                    and saviour Jesus Christ
      14 who gave himself for us
          in order that to redeem us from all iniquity
          and to purify for himself a people of his own
                    zealous for good deeds.

    The section, though simple in outline, is complex in detail, with the first purpose clause with ἵνα containing a pair of participles, both having a pair of direct objects; the last of these direct objects is qualified by a pair of possessives, the second followed by a relative clause leading to a second ἵνα clause which contains a pair of verbs. The recurrence with even greater frequency of the pairing noted in 1.1–4 is striking, and has a climactic rhetorical effect. In this way, that which is syntactically deeply subordinate is made semantically prominent.

    Exegetically there are two main questions that relate to the structure. The first is whether in v. 11 πασιν ἀνθρωποις (to all people) is to be linked with σωτηριος (salvific) or with ἐπεφανη (has appeared). This is one of the mercifully rare places where theology may influence exegesis. Against RSV and TEV, and also against Arichea & Hatton and Marshall,[12] but with KJV, NIV, the German Luther Revision of 1984, and the German and Italian Common language versions, this analysis proposes to take it with ἐπεφανη. If one argues structurally rather than theologically, taking it with ἐπεφανη produces a neat chiasmus which is fully in keeping with the rhetorically elaborated nature of the passage.

---

[12] Arichea and Hatton, *Handbook*, 291; Marshall, *Pastoral Epistles*, 268.

```
A ἐπεφανη γαρ
  B ἡ χαρις
    C του θεου
  B σωτηριος
A πασιν ἀνθρωποις
```

The words ἐπεφανη... πασιν ἀνθρωποις (has appeared... to all people) refer to the incarnation of Jesus Christ, and are balanced by the later reference to his second ἐπιφανεια (appearing) in v. 13.

The second question is whether in v. 13 θεου (God) and σωτηρος (saviour) refer to the same person (as for instance TEV text) or to different persons (as TEV margin). The absence of the definite article before σωτηρος is a strong argument in favour of the first view, as both Arichea & Hatton and Marshall note.[13] It is strengthened by the further consideration that within the same clause, την μακαριαν ἐλπιδα και ἐπιφανειαν (the blessed hope and appearing) is clearly a hendiadys, as RSV, NIV, and Marshall[14] recognize: it is therefore rhetorically balanced and appropriate to take θεου και σωτηρος as another hendiadys. More pairing!

It may also be noted that in 2.13, the phrase σωτηρος ἡμων Ἰησου Χριστου (our saviour Jesus Christ) repeats the words of 1.4, but in a different order; contrast 3.6, where the order is different again. Is there any significance in this variation? In the present case, it may be due to no more than the minor syntactic advantage of having the proper name immediately before the relative pronoun ὁς which follows.

Section B2c 2.15

This short sub-unit functions as a summary of section B2, repeating the key imperative verbs λαλει (speak, from 2.1), παρακαλει (encourage, from 2.6), and ἐλεγχε (rebuke, from 1.13b). The latter two verbs also occurred in the infinitive in 1.9. The final clause μηδεις σου περιφρονειτω (let no one disregard you) would probably be better punctuated as a separate sentence (against UBS[4] and NA[27]). With its third person imperative it is in a sense the semantic obverse of the instruction in the previous clause, and adds nothing radically new. Another third person imperative occurs in 3.14. The section can be set

---

[13] Arichea and Hatton, *Handbook*, 293; Marshall, *Pastoral Epistles*, 277–282.
[14] Ibid., 275.

out as follows:

15 ταυτα λαλει
    και παρακαλει
    και ελεγχε μετα πασης επιταγης.
μηδεις σου περιφρονειτω.

15 These things speak
    and encourage
    and rebuke with all authority.
Let no one disregard you.

The first word ταυτα (these things) is anaphoric, and refers back to the whole of 1.13b–2.14. One could claim support for the view that λαλει (speak) and παρακαλει (encourage) are structurally near-synonyms from the word order here. The verbs come in a partially chiastic order in that ελεγχε (rebuke) came first in section B1 (1.13) but last here, whereas λαλει and παρακαλει come here in the same order as they occurred in section B2 (2.1, 6), suggesting that they represent in some sense a single concept in the mind of the writer. The chiastic structure would then be seen as ABBA, with each B unit being composite, and having two parts. A more subtle variety of pairing, perhaps?

A ελεγχε (rebuke, 1.13)
    B1 λαλει (speak, 2.1)
        B2 παρακαλει (encourage, 2.6)
    B1 λαλει (speak, 2.15)
        B2 παρακαλει (encourage, 2.15)
A ελεγχε (rebuke, 2.15)

It can be also noted that επιταγη occurred already in 1.3 where it referred to the divine authority with which Paul was invested. Is Paul covertly hinting that Titus shared his own divine authority? Finally, from the translation point of view, it may need to be made clear that the third person imperative (Let no one disregard you) is surely an instruction for other members of the church in Crete, as is the similar third person imperative in 3.14. It is surely not, as it may appear from the English, an instruction to Titus himself, as

Marshall takes it.[15] It should thus be rendered with the sense "Other people must not disregard you" rather than the sense "Don't let other people disregard you." How could Titus stop them if they were determined enough?

Sections B3a and B3b 3.1–8a

Section B3a opens with the third distinct imperative verb ὑπομιμνῃσκε (remind). The section is outside the lexically close-knit B1 and B2 sections where the key imperatives are foreshadowed in 1.9, but it could be claimed to echo 1.5 at the conceptual (though not the lexical) level. In 1.5 Paul reminds Titus why he had left him in Crete, and in 3.1, he explicitly instructs Titus to remind his congregations of their primary responsibilities in social ethics. The basic structure of this section is

1 ὑπομιμνῃσκε αὐτους...
3 ἠμεν γαρ ποτε και ἡμεις...
4 ὁτε δε... ἐπεφανη... 5 ἐσωσεν ἡμας...
    7 ἱνα... κληρονομοι γενηθωμεν...

1 Remind them...
3 for we ourselves were once...
4 but when... appeared... 5 he saved us...
    7 in order that... we might become heirs...

Verses 4–7 (or perhaps 3–7, notwithstanding the punctuation in UBS[4] and NA[27]) form a single sentence with considerable subordination. It is the third theological statement, and again syntactic subordination is no mark of semantic prominence.

In the outline at the beginning of this paper, this section was divided into two, B3a (3.1–2) and B3b (3.3–8a). In structural terms such an analysis shows the parallelism with B2a and B2b, with one or more imperatives justified by an explanation introduced by γαρ (for). Since B3 in total is rather short, it could also be regarded as a single unit. Such an analysis would offer a better balance with B1, and provide more of a chiastic structure within section B as a whole. Sections B3a and B3b may be set out as follows:

---

[15] Ibid., 297–298.

1 ὑπομιμνῃσκε αὐτους ἀρχαις ἐξουσιαις ὑποτασσεσθαι
                πειθαρχειν
                προς παν ἐργον ἀγαθον ἑτοιμους εἰναι
                2 μηδενα βλασφημειν
                ἀμαχους εἰναι
                ἐπιεικεις
                πασαν ἐνδεικνυμενους πραϋτητα >>>
                προς παντας ἀνθρωπους.
3 ἠμεν γαρ ποτε και ἡμεις ἀνοητοι
            ἀπειθεις
            πλανωμενοι
            δουλευοντες ἐπιθυμιαις και ἡδοναις ποικιλαις
            ἐν κακιᾳ και φθονῳ διαγοντες
            στυγητοι
            μισουντες ἀλληλους.
4 ὁτε δε ἡ χρηστοτης
            και ἡ φιλανθρωπια ἐπεφανη του σωτηρος ἡμων θεου
5 οὐκ ἐξ ἐργων των ἐν δικαιοσυνῃ
        ἁ ἐποιησαμεν ἡμεις
ἀλλα κατα το αὐτου ἐλεος ἐσωσεν ἡμας >>>
            δια λυτρου παλιγγενεσιας
            και ἀνακαινωσεως πνευματος ἁγιου
                  6 οὑ ἐξεχεεν ἐφ'ἡμας πλουσιως δια Ἰησου Χριστου >>>
                  του σωτηρος ἡμων
            7 ἱνα δικαιωθεντες τῃ ἐκεινου χαριτι κληρονομοι γενηθωμεν >>>
                κατ'ἐλπιδα ζωης αἰωνιου.
8 πιστος ὁ λογος.

1 Remind them to be submissive to rulers and authorities
            to be obedient
            to be ready for any good work
            2 to speak evil of no one
            not to be quarrelsome
            [to be] gentle
            showing all gentleness to all people.
3 For we ourselves were once foolish
            disobedient
            deceived

>   enslaved to various passions and pleasures
>   in malice and envy passing our days
>   hated
>   hating one another
> 4 but when the goodness
>   and kindness of God our saviour appeared
> 5 not by deeds in righteousness
>   which we ourselves had done
> but according to his own mercy he saved us >>>
>   through the washing of regeneration
>   and renewal of the Holy Spirit
>   6 whom he poured out on us richly through >>>
>   Jesus Christ our saviour
> 7 in order that being justified by his grace we might become heirs >>>
>   according to hope of eternal life.
> 8 Sure [is] the saying.

The use of the pronoun αὐτους (them) rather than any noun(s) at the beginning supports the link of 3.1–8a with 1.13b–2.15. The antecedents of the pronoun are formally the nouns πρεσβυτας (older men) in 2.2, πρεσβυτιδας (older women) in 2.3, νεωτερους (younger men) in 2.6, and δουλους (slaves) in 2.9.

There are no serious exegetical problems in these verses, though the period at the end of 3.3 in UBS[4] is questionable and a period after 3.8a seems essential. It is notable that there is a marked switch from frequent coordination in vv. 1–3 to complex subordination in vv. 4–7. It is also interesting to see that the syntactic units in vv. 4–7 are longer than in any previous part of the letter: for the first time it has become impossible to accommodate the whole of a unit on one line. The symbol >>> is used above to indicate that the line which follows should be a continuation of the line on which the symbol occurs, but for reasons of space rather than syntax the unit has had to be divided.

Pairing is again a prominent feature: ἀρχαις (rulers) and ἐξουσιαις (authorities) in v. 1, ἐπιθυμιαις και ἡδοναις (passions and pleasures) and κακια και φθονῳ (malice and envy) in v. 3, ἡ χρηστοτης και ἡ φιλανθρωπια (goodness and kindness) in v. 4, the contrastive οὐκ ἐξ ἐργων... ἀλλα κατα... ἐλεος (not by deeds... but according to... mercy) in v. 5, and also in v. 5 the possibly chiastic δια λυτρου παλιγγενεσιας και ἀνακαινωσεως πνευματος ἁγιου (through the washing of regeneration and renewal of the Holy Spirit). For a detailed discussion of the meaning of these last two phrases, see Arichea & Hatton and especially Marshall.[16] There are also significant lexical recursions: ὑποτασσεσθαι (to be submissive) in v. 1, echoing 2.4, 9 (contrast ἀνυποτακτ- [insubordinate] in 1.6, 10); ἐπεφανη (appeared) in v. 4 echoing 2.11, 13 and probably 1.3; τοῦ σωτηρος ἡμων θεου (God our saviour) in v. 4, echoing 1.3 and 2.10; Ἰησου Χριστου του σωτηρος ἡμων (Jesus Christ our saviour) in v. 6 echoing (with variations in word order) 1.4 and 2.13; and κατ ἐλπιδα ζωης αἰωνιου (according to hope of eternal life) in v. 7 echoing (with a different preposition) 1.2.

The affirmation in 3.8a is clearly anaphoric like the one in 1.13a, and functions as a closure marker for the section. Many modern versions begin a new paragraph at 3.8b, and a few including NAB, JB, NJB and REB correctly recognise a major break at this point, inserting a section heading.

Section C 3.8b–11

This section, like section A, has a looser and less complex basic structure:

8 ... βουλομαι σε διαβεβαιουσθαι, ἱνα φροντιζωσιν... οἱ πεπιστευκοτες θεῳ
9 μωρας δε ζητησεις... περιϊστασο...
εἰσιν γαρ...
10 αἱρετικον ανθρωπον... παραιτου...

8 ...I want you to insist, in order that those may be careful... >>>
                                      who have believed in God
9 Stupid controversies... avoid...
for there are...
10 A factious person... have nothing to do with...

It is interesting to observe that just as section B was structured around three imperative ideas, so is section C. Formally there are only the two imperatives περιϊστασο (avoid) and παραιτου (have nothing to do with), but the expression βουλομαι σε διαβεβαιουσθαι (I want you to insist) is semantically also an imperative, even though it is couched in a surrogate form. The same verb βουλομαι is used in 1 Tim 2.8; 5.14 with similar effect. Here it is "tanta-

---

[16] Arichea and Hatton, *Handbook*, 302–303; Marshall, *Pastoral Epistles*, 316–322.

mount to a command" according to Marshall, though he does not seem to realise the structural significance of this observation.[17] This section however differs from section B in that the imperatives occur later in their clauses rather than at the beginning. Sociolinguistically, is this perhaps a way of toning down the authoritarian aspect of a command? Perhaps Paul is addressing Titus less peremptorily than he expects Titus to address the Cretan congregation. The section may be set out as follows:

8 και περι τουτων βουλομαι σε διαβεβαιουσθαι
    ἱνα φροντιζωσιν καλων ἐργων προϊστασθαι οἱ πεπιστευκοτες θεῳ
        ταυτα ἐστιν καλα
            και ὠφελιμα τοις ἀνθρωποις.
9 μωρας δε ζητησεις
        και γενεαλογιας
        και ἐρεις
        και μαχας νομικας περιΐστασο
εἰσιν γαρ ἀνωφελεις
        και ματαιοι.
10 αἱρετικον ἀνθρωπον μετα μιαν και δευτεραν νουθεσιαν παραιτου
    11 εἰδως ὁτι ἐξεστραπται ὁ τοιουτος
        και ἁμαρτανει ὠν αὐτοκατακριτος.

8 About these things I want you to insist
   in order that those may be careful to apply themselves to good deeds >>>
                             who have believed in God;
      these are good
          and profitable to people.
9 But stupid controversies
      and genealogies
      and dissensions
      and quarrels over the law avoid
for they are unprofitable
      and futile.
10 [As for] a factious person after a first and second admonition >>>
      have nothing to do with him,
        11 knowing that such a person is perverted
            and sins, being self-condemned.

---

[17] Ibid., *Pastoral Epistles*, 330.

There are no significant exegetical problems in this section, though we may ask exactly what the anaphoric τουτων in 3.8 refers back to. Since it is quickly linked with good deeds, which have not been mentioned in the previous paragraph, it seems likely that it refers back at least to the whole of 2.1–3.8a, and probably the whole of 1.13b–3.8a. In Marshall's view, "probably it includes all that is included in the previous section of the letter" and not just 3.1–7.[18] The last clause of 3.8 would be better punctuated as a separate sentence. Again, it is not certain exactly what ταυτα (these) refers back to, but in this case, the decision does not seem to be structurally important. There is a possible chiasmus in v. 9, where the structure is as follows:

Adjective + Noun   μωρας δε ζητησεις (stupid controversies)
Noun   και γενεαλογιας (and genealogies)
Noun   και ερεις (and dissensions)
Noun + Adjective   και μαχας νομικας (and quarrels over the law)

Could the "stupid controversies" be equated with the "quarrels over the law"? If so, could the intervening "genealogies and dissensions" be a hendiadys (quarrels about genealogies)? Another possible interpretation (also chiastic, but pairing the constituents in a different way) would be "stupid controversies about genealogies" and "dissensions over legal disputes" (presumably different interpretations of the Jewish law). It is hard to see any conclusive evidence. However, other pairs are unquestionably present in καλα και ωφελιμα (good and profitable, 3.8) and ανωφελεις και ματαιοι (unprofitable and futile, 3.9). One may also note the recurrence of καλων εργων (good deeds, 3.8), echoing 2.7, 2.14, and foreshadowing 3.14.

Conclusion 3.12–15

The basic structure of this section is simple, being little more than a series of juxtaposed sentences, as laid out on the following page:

---

[18] Ibid., 330.

12 ὅταν πεμψω... σπουδασον ἐλθειν...
        ἐκει γαρ...
13 Ζηναν... προπεμψον,
        ἱνα μηδεν...

14 μανθανετωσαν... οἱ ἡμετεροι...

    ἱνα μη...
15 ἀσπαζονται σε...
ἀσπασαι τους φιλουντας...

12 When I send... do your best...
        for there...
13 Zenas... speed on their way,
        in order that nothing...

14 *Let our people... learn...*

    in order that... they should not...
15 ...greet you
Greet those...

In full this may be set out as follows:

12 ὅταν πεμψω Ἀρτεμαν προς σε
        ἠ Τυχικον
σπουδασον ἐλθειν προς με εἰς Νικοπολιν
        ἐκει γαρ κεκρικα παραχειμασαι.
13 Ζηναν τον νομικον
και Ἀπολλων σπουδαιως προπεμψον
        ἱνα μηδεν αὐτοις λειπῃ.
14 μανθανετωσαν δε και οἱ ἡμετεροι καλων ἐργων προϊστασθαι >>>
        εἰς τας ἀναγκαιας χρειας
    ἱνα μη ὠσιν ἀκαρποι.
15 ἀσπαζονται σε οἱ μετ᾽ ἐμου παντες.
ἀσπασαι τους φιλουντας ἡμας ἐν πιστει.
ἡ χαρις μετα παντων ὑμων.

12 When I send Artemas to you
    or Tychicus
do your best to come to me at Nicopolis
    for there I have decided to spend the winter.
13 Zenas the lawyer
and Apollos speed on their way
    in order that nothing be lacking for them.
14 Let our people also learn to apply themselves to good deeds>>>
                                      to meet urgent needs
    in order that they should not be unfruitful.
15 All those with me greet you.
Greet those who love us in [the] faith.
Grace [be] with you all.

Even though there is no complex structure, it is interesting to note that once again the section contains three second person singular imperatives, σπουδασον (do your best), προπεμψον (speed on the[ir] way) and ἀσπασαι (greet). This gives a balance to the conclusion that matches the balance of sections B and C. The balance is somewhat diminished, however, by the addition of the third person imperative μανθανετωσαν (let them learn, compare 2.15). There are also two further examples of pairing: Ἀρτεμαν... ἢ Τυχικον (Artemas... or Tychicus) and Ζηναν... και Ἀπολλων (Zenas... and Apollos).

Summary

In this article we have analysed the discourse of Titus in detail, and discovered structural reasons for making breaks at certain points and not at other points. In particular, we have seen that major breaks occur at 1.13b and 3.8b, the first of which has hardly ever been recognised by translators. Greater clarity on the placement of major breaks must be of practical help to translators in deciding where to put section headings, and consequently what the content of the section headings should be. We have also seen that at various places (especially 1.14–15) a consideration of structural features can point to one exegesis being preferable to another. We have also noted that at least in this letter, deeper syntactic subordination is a mark of deeper theological content. In a letter with a primarily pastoral and ethical aim, it appears that the more profound theological insights are presented syntactically almost as throw-away lines.

8

A DISCOURSE ANALYSIS OF JUDE

Methodology

This chapter will propose an analysis of the letter of Jude based primarily on the syntax of the Greek sentences, especially the changes in the person of verb forms, and paying close attention also to lexical recursions and other rhetorical features, not least markers which have proved significant in the discourse analysis of other biblical books. The presupposition of this analysis is that this letter is a coherent literary unit, put purposefully by an author or redactor into the form in which we have it today. It is thus likely to be basically well structured, but not necessarily perfectly structured. Even though the present form of the text incorporates citations from or allusions to other sources, scholars have to deal with the letter as it now stands, and so questions relating to sources or authorship will not be discussed. The Greek text cited is that of NA[27] with punctuation adjusted (very significantly adjusted in some places) to reflect the discourse analysis. The issue is also raised whether discourse analysis may have a contribution to make in the field of textual studies.

Glosses of the Greek words are taken as much as possible from the RSV, but where it uses different English words to translate the same Greek word, one of its variants will be used consistently in order to show the repetition in the Greek. The RSV word order may be changed, together with other alterations as deemed necessary to let the glosses reflect the Greek structure more closely. The result is neither elegant nor natural, but fits the purposes of this analysis.

Sample analyses of the letter's structure by several earlier scholars are recorded, but they all appear to be impressionistic in nature and do not offer any principles of analysis. The present analysis differs from all of them, and is based on explicitly linguistic criteria. Some more recent analyses are also considered, but again, the one presented here differs from all of them.[1]

Macrostructural Outline

Since the analysis inevitably contains a lot of detail, a summary of the results is presented at the beginning as an indication of the destination to which the discussion will lead. The subsequent discussion will show the reasoning behind the decisions made. In summary form the outline is as follows:

A. 1–2 Greetings
B. 3–23 Main body
    B1. 3–6 1st person main verbs
        B1a. 3–4
        B1b. 5–6
    B2. 7–16 3rd person main verbs
        B2a. 7–8
        B2b. 9–10
        B2c. 11–13
        B2d. 14–16
    B3. 17–23 2nd person main verbs
        B3a. 17–19
        B3b. 20–23
C. 24–25 Doxology

Figure 8.1: The Macrostructure of Jude

Macrostructural Markers

There is no problem at all in delimiting the opening and closing greetings, vv. 1–2 and 24–25 respectively. All scholars are in agreement that these short

---

[1] This essay incorporates the results first presented in my paper in "Discourse Structure in Jude," *BT* 55, no. 1 (2004), 125–137, used by kind permission of the current editor, Dr. Stephen Pattemore.

passages fall within the expectations of the ancient Christian letter form. When these greetings are isolated, vv. 3–23 are left as the body of the letter.[2] There is much less agreement about how these verses are structured, so this is where the main interest of the present analysis lies. Earlier analyses appear to be based on intuitive evaluations of the content rather than on formal criteria, so the challenge is to see if there are objective structural markers that point to one analysis rather than another.

Below are given four fairly random examples of analysis.[3] The differences are displayed in chart form below.

James	Guthrie	Leahy	Arichea & Hatton
1–2	1–2	1–2	1–2
3	3–4	3–4	3–23: 3–4
4			
5–7	5–7	5–16: 5–7	5–7
8–11	8–19: 8–10	8–16	8–16
	11		
12–13	12–13		
14–16	14–16		
17–19	17–19	17–23: 17–19	17–23
20–23	20–23	20–23	
24–25	24–25	24–25	24–25

Figure 8.2: Four Analyses of the Structure of Jude

James splits vv. 3–23 into eight short paragraphs, beginning at vv. 3, 4, 5, 8, 12, 14, 17 and 20. Guthrie has four paragraphs, beginning at vv. 3, 5, 8, and 20, though he subdivides vv. 8–19 into five shorter units, beginning at vv. 8, 11, 12, 14, and 17. Leahy has only three paragraphs, beginning at vv. 3, 5 and 17, though he subdivides the latter two into two smaller units each, beginning at vv. 5, 8, 17 and 20. Arichea & Hatton keep vv. 3–23 together, but subdivide into four shorter units beginning at vv. 3, 5, 8 and 17. There is thus fairly broad agreement about where the divisions fall, but surprising diversity

---

[2] This terminology is borrowed from Daniel C. Arichea and Howard A. Hatton, *Handbook on the Letter from Jude and the Second Letter from Peter* (United Bible Societies, 1993).

[3] Montague Rhodes James, *The Second Epistle General of Peter and the General Epistle of Jude* (Cambridge University Press, 1912); Donald Guthrie, *New Testament Introduction: Hebrews to Revelation* (Tyndale, 1962); Thomas W. Leahy SJ, *The Epistle of Jude*, JBC (Prentice Hall, 1968), 2:378–380; Arichea and Hatton, *Handbook*.

about the relative importance assigned to them.

In the analysis of other Biblical books, a vocative has proved to be a common marker of a new unit, and there are several occurrences of the vocative ἀγαπητοί (beloved) in Jude, at vv. 3, 17, and 20, so it is reasonable to suppose that a new unit or sub-unit is likely to begin in each of these verses. Even so, that still leaves vv. 3–16 to be analysed, nearly sixty percent of the whole letter.

Another potential marker of a new (sub-)unit is the interjection οὐαί, which serves this function elsewhere, most notably in Matt 23:13–36.[4] So it seems likely that the same interjection in v. 11 will also be an opening marker at some level, but even if this is accepted, it still leaves vv. 3–10 to be analysed.

Microstructural Markers

NA[27], UBS[4], all four analyses mentioned above, all available English versions, and almost all versions available in fifteen other languages begin a new paragraph or other unit at v. 8, and it is easy to start by assuming that this must be a correct division. However, v. 7 begins with ὡς (as) and v. 8 with Ὁμοίως (so), a combination which rings mental bells. In some OT texts, there are places where a lengthy comparison is built around the terms כַּאֲשֶׁר (ka'äsher, "as") and כֵּן (kên, "so"), for instance Zec 8:12–13, 14–15.[5] So could this not be a similar example here in Jude? Although written in Greek and not Hebrew, the letter of Jude is heavily influenced by OT writings, and the present passage is actually dealing with an OT example, that of Sodom and Gomorrah. The Greek does not offer any compelling reason why v. 7 has to be linked with v. 6, so why should it not be linked with v. 8 instead? This has the effect of making an explicit comparison of the false teachers who "defile the flesh" with the people of Sodom and Gomorrah, who "indulged in unnatural lust" and now "serve as an example" of punishment.

If this view of the structure is accepted, it entails an adjustment of the punctuation in NA[27] and UBS[4], so as to place a full stop at the end of v. 6 and a comma at the end of v. 7, rather than the other way round as at present. It is not at all obvious on what principles the editors of NA[27] and UBS[4] have

---

[4] See chapter 3, "Discourse Structure in Matthew's Gospel," in this volume.
[5] See David J. Clark, "Discourse Structure in Zechariah 7.1–8.23," *BT* 36, no. 3 (1985): 328–335.

decided where and what kind of punctuation marks to place in their texts. Although the two editions are claimed to be identical in terms of their wording, they are by no means identical in their punctuation, their identification of citations, and even their paragraphing, but neither states clearly how they have arrived at their decisions in such matters, so they must be open to question.

For examples of punctuation differences in Jude, we can note the following:

1. In vv. 9, 10 and 12, NA²⁷ begins the sentences with a capital letter, whereas UBS⁴ does not.
2. In v. 9, NA²⁷ has a colon after εἶπεν (said), and by using italics identifies the following three words as a citation, whereas UBS⁴ has a comma and does not identify any citation.
3. In v. 14, NA²⁷ has a colon after λέγων (saying), and begins the following direct speech with a small letter, whereas UBS⁴ has a comma after λέγων and begins the direct speech with a capital letter.
4. In v. 18, NA²⁷ has a colon after ὑμῖν (to you), and begins the (presumably indirect) quotation with a small letter, whereas UBS⁴ has no colon and begins the (presumably direct) quotation with a capital.
5. In v. 20, NA²⁷ begins a new paragraph, whereas UBS⁴ does not.
6. In vv. 10, 12, 16 and 22, NA²⁷ indicates by the use of a larger space what we might call new sub-paragraphs whereas UBS⁴ begins a new sentence at each of these places, but only in v. 16 does the new sentence begin with a capital letter.

This amounts to over a dozen differences in a mere 25 verses. If there is any rationale for these variations it remains opaque. Such examples are multiplied vastly in the entire NT, and they do have discourse implications that affect both exegesis and translation. The conclusion that seems unavoidable is that decisions on these matters have been made on a largely impressionistic basis, and this was confirmed in a personal communication from Prof. Bruce Metzger, one of the editors of both NA²⁷ and UBS⁴. Although this is in one way rather alarming, it does give the discourse analyst more confidence in proposing a change in the punctuation that is based on some objective evidence.

Let us now come back to the question of whether ὡς (as) and Ὁμοίως (so) can be credibly treated as a pair like כַּאֲשֶׁר (ka'äsher, "as") and כֵּן (kên, "so").

Rather surprisingly, there appears to be no other example exactly like this in the NT. The regular pair of adverbs used in comparisons is καθὼς... οὕτως... (Luke 11:30; 17:26; John 3:14; 12:50; 14:31; 15:4; 2 Cor 1:5; 8:6; 10:7; Col 3:13; Heb 5:3). In the LXX there seems to be only a single example of ὡς... ὁμοίως..., in Prov 1:27, and one example of the very similar οὕτως... ὁμοίως ..., in Esther 1:18. But even one clear example is sufficient to prove that the combination, though unusual, is possible. In a personal communication, Prof. Johannes Louw considered that the analysis of Jude 7-8 as a single sentence balanced around the combination ὡς... Ὁμοίως ... is quite acceptable. It may also be noted that the verses are further linked by the occurrence of σάρξ in both.

Further Discourse Factors

The Precise Meaning of Ὁμοίως Μέντοι

A further question arises about the adverb μέντοι (RSV yet) that follows Ὁμοίως in Jude 8. Lust, Eynikel & Hauspie show only five occurrences of this word in the LXX, all in Proverbs (5:4; 16:25, 26; 22:9a; 26:12), and state that the meaning is "mostly adversative."[6] All these examples are indeed clearly adversative. Louw & Nida treat μέντοι together with πλὴν as "markers of contrast" (89.130), and this fits well with five of the eight occurrences of μέντοι in the NT (John 4:27; 7:13; 20:5; 21:4; 2 Tim 2:19).[7] They treat the occurrence in James 2:8 as more affirmative (§89.136), and that in John 12:42 as "a marker of an implied clause of concession" (§89.75). It is noteworthy that in this one context the whole phrase is ὅμως μέντοι, rather similar to Ὁμοίως μέντοι in Jude 8 (which Louw & Nida do not mention). Moulton & Milligan note that Hort also argued that μέντοι in James 2:8 "retains its original force of a strong affirmation."[8] Liddell & Scott (under μέν B.II.4.b) give numerous classical examples of μέντοι carrying the sense of "eager or positive assent."[9] There seems to be no reason why it could not have this sense in Jude, reinforcing ὁμοίως with the meaning "in the same way indeed."

---

[6] J. Lust, E. Eynikel, and K. Hauspie, *Greek-English Lexicon of the Septuagint* (Deutsche Bibelgesellschaft, 1996), s.v. ὁμοίως.

[7] Louw-Nida, §89.130.

[8] James Hope Mouton and George Milligan, *The Vocabulary of the Greek Testament* (Hodder and Stoughton, 1957), 397.

[9] Henry George Liddell and Robert Scott, *A Greek-English Lexicon* (Clarendon Press, 1953), s.v. μέν B.II.4.b.

Arndt & Gingrich state that μέντοι is "mostly adversative" and give the same five NT verses as Louw & Nida as exemplifying this sense.[10] They give the meaning in James 2:8 as *really, actually,*" and say a little curiously that in Jude 8, the meaning is "weakened to *but*," though they adduce no supporting evidence. For the combination ὅμως μέντοι in John 12:42, they offer *yet, despite that*. However, when they deal with ὅμως, they cite all the three NT examples (John 12:42; 1 Cor 14:7; Gal 3:15), and after offering the meaning *all the same, nevertheless, yet*, they go on to argue that the two Pauline examples should perhaps better be linked with the older form ὁμῶς, with different accentuation, and taken to mean *equally, likewise* (compare Liddell & Scott). If two of the three occurrences of this word are taken that way, why not the third, especially in combination with μέντοι taken as affirmative? It thus seems at least arguable that the sense of ὅμως μέντοι in John 12:42 may be affirmative like that in James 2:8, with the meaning "likewise indeed." This would imply that the statement in John 12:42 refers back only to 12:41 rather than to 12:37–40. The paragraph would then be understood to be saying that although the majority of people did not believe in Jesus, a few saw his glory "in the same way, indeed" as Isaiah did, and so believed. Does not such an understanding give more point to the next comment in 12:42b–43 that these people did not make a public confession of their faith because "they loved the glory of men more than the glory of God"?

Lust, Eynikel & Hauspie give five occurrences of ὅμως in the LXX (2 Macc 2:27; 14:18; 15:5; 4 Macc 13:27; 15:11) and state the meaning as *yet, nevertheless*. This seems very clear in four of the five cases, but in 2 Macc 14:18, one might perhaps make a case for reading ὁμῶς and taking the sense as affirmative. However the uncertainty over the meaning of the previous verse makes the situation indecisive.

The end result of this digression is that while there is only a small amount of evidence to support the analysis of ὡς ... Ὁμοίως ... in Jude 7–8 as a single sentence, there is no evidence against it, and this analysis therefore adopts it. Among recent versions in European languages, the French *Traduction Œcuménique* and the Russian Cassian have the whole of vv. 5–15/5–16 in a single paragraph, thus supporting a closer link between vv. 7 and 8 than is usual, and the Italian Common Language version *Parola del Signore* actually begins a new paragraph at v. 7, thus separating it from v. 6 more sharply than is usu-

---

[10] William F. Arndt and F. Wilbur Gingrich, *A Greek-English Lexicon of the New Testament and Other Early Christian Literature* (University of Chicago Press, 1952), s.v. μέντοι.

al. However *Parola del Signore* also begins a new paragraph at v. 8, and does not link vv. 7 and 8 closely.

Further Considerations

Thus far, then, the following divisions appear: vv. 1–2, 3–6, 7–10, 11–16, 17–19, 20–23, and 24–25. The next question is whether there are any other breaks that should be recognised, and finally what relative importance should be attached to the various breaks. In examining the first question, it can be observed that after the initial introduction of the false teachers as τινες ἄνθρωποι (certain people) in v. 4, they are thereafter referred to only as οὗτοι (these, in vv. 8, 10, 12, 16, 19) with no noun, which is probably rather disparaging. In each of these occurrences, οὗτοι begins the second half of a comparison or contrast. A recognition of this repeated rhetorical balance leads to the identification of other breaks at vv. 9 and 14. The occurrence of οὗτοι in v. 8 supports the view that this verse is the second half of a unit, and should be joined with v. 7 rather than with v. 9. Furthermore it can be noted that two units now end with the words ζόφος (nether gloom) and τετήρηκεν/τετήρηται (kept, vv. 6 and 13). While two occurrences of a collocation hardly amount to a formula, it is encouraging to see that the collocations do occur at similar places in their paragraphs, as this lends some *a posteriori* support to the paragraph divisions.

When attention is turned to the verbs, it become clear that through the letter there is a movement in the dominant verbs in the various sections from first person in vv. 3–6 to third person in vv. 7–16 to second person in vv. 17–23. The expression "dominant verbs" is used because it is not the case that every finite verb in each of the three sections is in the same person. But in vv. 3–6 παρεισέδυσαν γάρ (for they slipped in) in v. 4 is clearly dependent on the first person clause ἀνάγκην ἔσχον γράψαι (I found it necessary to write) in v. 3, and the verbs ἀπώλεσεν (destroyed) and τετήρηκεν (kept) in vv. 5 and 6 are in a subordinate clause. In vv. 7–16 all the finite verbs are third person. In v. 18 the third person verbs ἔλεγον (they said) and ἔσονται (there will be) are in subordinate clauses. The only real exception to the pattern is εἰσιν (are) in v. 19, and this is probably to be explained by its link with οὗτοι (these) as part of the repeated contrasts noted above. It is also significant that taking v. 7 with v. 8 instead of v. 6 strengthens rather than weakens the pattern of change in the person of the dominant verbs.

Detailed Display

In any language, the verb forms are likely to hold the most vital keys to discourse structure, and so in assessing the relative importance of the different breaks, the changes of person are to be given greater weight than other factors. Taking the highest level break as that between the opening and closing greetings and the body of the letter, the change of person will then mark the second level breaks, and other factors will mark third level breaks. The outline is displayed more fully as follows:

```
============ indicates a major break
=-=-=-=-=-=-= indicates a medium break
--------------------- indicates a minor break
```

A. 1–2 Greetings Ἰούδας... τοῖς... ἠγαπημένοις... ἔλεος ὑμῖν...
                    Jude... to those loved...mercy... to you...

==

B1. First main paragraph, with two sub-paragraphs
        3–6   Vocative +1st person main verbs
        B1a   3–4   ἀγαπητοί... ἀνάγκην ἔσχον γράψαι...
                            Beloved... I found it necessary to write...
                              παρεισέδυσαν γάρ τινες ἄνθρωποι...
                              for certain people have slipped in...

        B1b   5–6   ὑπομνῆσαι δὲ ὑμᾶς βούλομαι...
                              I want to remind you...

=-=

B2. Second main paragraph, with four sub-paragraphs
        7–16   3rd person main verbs
        B2a   7–8   ὡς Σόδομα καὶ Γόμορρα... ὁμοίως μέντοι καὶ οὗτοι...
                              Just as Sodom and Gomorrah... so indeed these
                              [people]...

        B2b   9–10   ὁ δὲ Μιχαήλ... οὗτοι δὲ...
                              Michael... but these [people]...

        B2c   11–13 οὐαὶ αὐτοῖς... οὗτοί εἰσιν... οἷς...
                              Woe to them... These [people] are... for whom...

B2d	14–16	προεφήτευσεν δὲ... οὗτοί εἰσιν...
		[Enoch] prophesied... These [people] are

=-

B3. Third main paragraph, with two sub-paragraphs
    17–23   Vocatives, with 2nd person main verbs
    B3a   17–19   ὑμεῖς δέ, ἀγαπητοί, μνήσθητε... οὗτοί εἰσιν...
                                  But you, beloved, remember... These [people] are...

    B3b   20–23   ὑμεῖς δέ, ἀγαπητοί... ἑαυτοὺς... τηρήσατε...
                                  But you, beloved,... keep yourselves...
                                  καὶ οὓς μὲν ἐλεᾶτε... οὓς δὲ σῴζετε... οὓς δὲ ἐλεᾶτε...
                                  have mercy on some... save others... have mercy on others...

===

C. 24–25 Doxology   τῷ δὲ δυναμένῳ... μόνῳ θεῷ σωτῆρι... δόξα...
                                  To him who is able... to the only God our saviour... glory...

Figure 8.3: Detailed Display of Jude's Structure

This display incorporates one third level break not previously identified, namely that between vv. 4 and 5. There is no overpowering reason to propose this break. The new first person verb phrase Ὑπομνῆσαι δὲ ὑμᾶς βούλομαι (I want to remind you) in v. 5 suggests a change of topic from vv. 3–4, though this is a rather subjective judgement. However the results of making this break are aesthetically gratifying. Not only do sections B1 and B3 now have two sub-paragraphs each, but there is a lexical echo from Ὑπομνῆσαι (remind) in B1b to μνήσθητε (remember) in B3a. There is also an eschatological note in both these sections. Moreover sections B1a and B3b both contain references to faith, which is not mentioned elsewhere in the letter. There is thus a low key chiastic link between sections B1 and B3. Overall this ends with a 2-4-2 pattern in section B, with all the four sub-paragraphs in B2 showing the οὗτοι (these) in their second half. The other οὗτοι in B3 (v. 19) balances τινες ἄνθρωποι (certain people) in B1 (v. 4).

A Discourse Analysis of Jude

Comparisons and Contrasts

Three other studies of Jude deserve comparison. The first is by Lauri Thurén.[11] While this analysis is not without interest, it does bring its own set of presuppositions and often undefined rhetorical categories. Moreover, it reaches no clear conclusions, and thus can offer no real help to exegetes or translators. Ideally an analysis of the type attempted above, one that looks in detail at the text and its formal structure should precede efforts to apply more subjective categories. Such analysis could offer some relatively objective limits to the application of rhetorical categories, and if it proposes results that conflict with those arising from other approaches, then there is the prospect of further dialogue as to why this should be, and what the differences imply for future methodology.

The second study is a much more positive one by Ernst R. Wendland.[12] Wendland gives a brief summary of the rise and fall of Rhetorical Criticism (RC) under the initial influence of Classical Rhetoric (CR). He is well aware of "the imprecise (hence often debatable) use of the detailed technical categories and terminology, the frequent lack of any alternative perspective on the overall organisation of a given discourse, and an often undiscriminating application of the classical rhetoric framework..."[13] He goes on to examine in some detail the analysis of Jude along CR lines by Duane F. Watson.[14] In comparison with the four outlines given above, Watson's analysis is closest to that of James, the main difference being that Watson links v. 11 with vv. 12–13 rather than with vv. 8–10. While Wendland recognises that it can be helpful to analyse Jude on these CR principles, he insists that the conclusions "do not tell the whole story" and he particularly objects to Watson's view that the text must be interpreted *only* by CR methodology.[15]

Wendland goes on to study the analysis of Richard J. Bauckham along RC rather than CR lines, though Bauckham himself does not use this terminolo-

---

[11] Lauri Thurén "Hey Jude! Asking for the Original Situation and Message of a Catholic Epistle," *NTS* 43 (1997): 451–465.

[12] Ernst Wendland, "A Comparative Study of 'Rhetorical Criticism', Ancient and Modern – with Special Reference to the Larger Structure and Function of the Epistle of Jude," *Neotestamentica* 28, no. 1 (1994): 193–228.

[13] Ibid., 203.

[14] Duane F. Watson, *Invention, Arrangement, and Style: Rhetorical Criticism of Jude and 2 Peter*, SBLDS 104 (Scholars Press, 1988).

[15] Wendland, "Comparative Study," 206.

gy.¹⁶ In comparison with the outlines given above, Bauckham's is closest to that of Guthrie, though more detailed in that he separates v. 16 from vv. 14–15, and v. 19 from vv. 17–18. Wendland then explains why he prefers the conclusions of Bauckham at all the major points where they differ from those of Watson, namely on "the organisation and function of vv. 3–4, 17–19, and 20–23."¹⁷

Wendland next offers his own analysis of the text in the form of "an extended chiasm, or 'introversion,' that spans the entire text. This is not viewed as... displacing the consecutively organised patterns presented above, but rather as constituting another – a complementary – level of rhetorically shaped discourse organisation."¹⁸ Since a chiasmus is better displayed than described, its outline is reproduced below.

A Epistolary introduction (v. 1)
  B Salutation (v. 2)
    C Purpose introduced (v. 3)
      D Motivation (v. 4)
        E Reminder (vv. 5–7)
          F Description -- heretics (v. 8)
            G Extracanonical example (v. 9)
              H Description -- heretics (v. 10)
                I Woe oracle (v. 11)
              H' Description -- heretics (vv. 12–13)
            G' Extracanonical prediction (vv. 14–15)
          F' Description -- heretics (v. 16)
        E' Reminder (vv. 17–18)
      D' Motivation (v. 19)
    C' Purpose elaborated (vv. 20–21)
  B' Commission (vv. 22–23)
A' Epistolary conclusion (vv. 24–25)

Wendland's chiastic pattern focusses on the semantic content more than the syntactic form which is the focus of the present study, but the two are by no means incompatible. If Wendland were to accept the proposal to link v. 7 with v. 8 rather than v. 6, it would actually strengthen the balance of his chi-

---

[16] Richard Bauckham, *Jude, 2 Peter*, WBC 50 (Word Books, 1983).
[17] Wendland, "Comparative Study," 207.
[18] Ibid., 210.

astic pattern by removing the only place where it has to put three verses into one unit. Verse 7 in fact fits his label for unit F (Description) better than it does his label for unit E (Reminder).

Wendland concludes his article with a section on the contemporary relevance of the study of biblical rhetoric, and draws on his experience at a Translation Consultant in Central Africa to show its relevance for Bible translation. Though that is not a topic for the present volume, it is certainly one that deserves to be explored and developed in much greater detail with respect to all biblical books. As Wendland says, "No single method of investigation is sufficient unto itself to satisfactorily accomplish such a multifaceted task."[19] What has been attempted here is perhaps a small part of a prolegomenon to that task.

The third work is by Charles Landon.[20] This assesses the Greek text of Jude from the perspective of thoroughgoing eclecticism, and on that basis constructs a text differing from that of UBS^4/NA^{27} at 21 points. It is worth asking whether discourse analysis has any contribution to bring to the field of textual decisions. It is after all one of the various factors that must come into play in a holistic view of the text, and an eclectic approach more than any other should theoretically be willing to take account of such additional evidence. In the case of Jude, there are some considerations arising from the analysis presented above that may be germane to textual issues, but there are few places where they would lead to direct opposition to the recommendations of Landon. Even if his recommendations were accepted *in toto*, it would make no difference to the major features of the present analysis.

The following comments are limited to two categories of text: (1) those places where Landon differs from the text of NA^{27}/UBS^4 and on which discourse analysis may make a contribution to the debate; and (2) those places where Landon's comments may find either support or opposition from discourse considerations. The comments below mark with an asterisk (as Landon does) those places where he differs from UBS^4, and using his numerical notation for referring to each place.

*5.3 For the omission of [ὁ] before κύριος, Landon's arguments by analogy with the anarthrous κύριος in vv. 9 and 14 look sound, but his adducing of κύριος in v. 4 as anarthrous seems highly questionable, since it is there part of a compound nominal phrase τὸν μόνον δεσπότην καὶ κύριον ἡμῶν Ἰησοῦν

---

[19] Ibid., 225.
[20] Charles Landon, *A Text-Critical Study of the Epistle of Jude*, JSNTSS 135 (Sheffield Academic Press, 1996).

Χριστόν.

*6.1 Landon prefers δέ to the τε in UBS⁴. He cites the occurrences of δέ in vv. 1, 14, and 24 in support, claiming that "In places where τε or δέ would be optional, Jude always prefers δέ" (p. 78). However, he overlooks the fact that in Jude, δέ does not come twice in one sentence unless it is part of a balanced pair or triplet, as in vv. 8 and 23. If δέ is read in v. 6, this would be its second occurrence in the sentence that began in v. 5, and it would not be part of a balanced pair or triplet. This is an argument in favour of retaining τε, especially if a full stop is placed at the end of v. 6. This makes the example of the angels in v. 6 co-ordinate with the example of the people rescued from Egypt in v. 5, which is surely more appropriate than implying a contrast, however mild. It is noteworthy that Landon nowhere discusses punctuation. Even though there is little of it in the manuscripts, the consideration of where it is best placed in printed editions of the NT should surely form part of textual discussions. The placement of punctuation can have a significant impact on the overall perception of textual structure, and this should not be excluded as a factor in an eclectic approach.

*6.6 A Greek text that depends on a retroversion from a quotation of a Latin father is surely weakened when it changes the word order of the Latin original (*sanctorum angelorum sub tenebras* > ὑπὸ ζόφον ἁγίων ἀγγέλων). Moreover the anarthrous collocation ἁγίων ἀγγέλων is unparalleled in the NT. At Luke 9:26, there is the phrase τῶν ἁγίων ἀγγέλων, but this is not anarthrous. The anarthrous phrase ἐνώπιον ἀγγέλων ἁγίων is found in Rev 14:10, but in this case the word order is different. We must judge that in this instance, by not looking at the wider implications of his proposal, Landon has failed to make his case. Indeed his very proposal of a conjectural emendation goes against the principle of Elliott that he cites with approval in fn 253 on p. 132. Furthermore, there are discourse arguments against this conjectural reading. The introduction of ἁγίων ἀγγέλων into v. 6 creates a gratuitous ambiguity, since the sentence already contains ἀγγέλους. Landon himself admits that this would have caused confusion (p. 84). And in v. 9, Michael is introduced with an article as ὁ ἀρχάγγελος, which very probably marks him as a new participant. This would hardly have been necessary if he had already been referred to implicitly in v. 6 as one of the ἁγίων ἀγγέλων.

7.1 The proposal in the present analysis to begin a new sentence at the beginning of v. 7, balancing ὡς here with ὁμοίως in v. 8 supports the reading of a single occurrence of ὡς.

7.2 The view that τούτοις refers forward to οὗτοι in v. 8 is surely not necessary if Landon's proposal 6.6 is rejected. Arguments cited by Landon in favour of this view would be weakened if the proposal of a full stop at the end of v. 6 is accepted.

8.1 The existence of the A variant ὅμως for ὁμοίως is interesting, and perhaps offers some support for the present suggestion to link v. 7 with v. 8 rather than v. 6. However, as argued above, it would be preferable to accentuate the A variant as ὁμῶς, understood in the sense of "likewise."

8.5 If, as Landon argues, the antecedent of δόξας here is the ἁγίων ἀγγέλων that he wants to read in v. 6, then surely one would expect an article with δόξας since this would then no longer be new information. Is this not a further argument against reading ἁγίων ἀγγέλων in v. 6?

*15.1 Against Landon's preference for "a stylistically polished formula," one could argue that introducing the root ἀσεβ- a fourth time into one sentence is hardly conducive to stylistic polish! But this, like most stylistic arguments, is rather subjective.

*17.1 A purely discourse argument against a present imperative here is that an aorist is needed to balance the corresponding aorist imperative τηρήσατε in v. 21. If this were recognised by copyists, it is hardly incredible that it should have been recognised by the original writer.

*19.1 Landon wants to include the reflexive pronoun ἑαυτοὺς after ἀποδιορίζοντες. Part of his argument in favour of this reading is that there is an "antithetical parallel between v. 19 and v. 20, to which ἑαυτοὺς in v. 19 is essential" (p. 126). From a discourse perspective the real parallel is between vv. 20–21 and v. 17, so that this part of Landon's case cannot be given much weight. Moreover, Liddell & Scott offer only one other occurrence of this verb, in Aristotle's *Politics* 1290b26. There is no reflexive in the Aristotle passage, as is hinted at by the fact that in citing Jude 19 they add "(sc. ἑαυτοὺς)." So it appears that there is no example of this verb with a reflexive pronoun in the whole of Greek literature. If so, the case for adding the reflexive here is surely weakened.

*22–23.1 In favour of the NA^{27} reading with the three clauses, one could argue that it produces an A-B-A pattern with the imperative verbs. Since such a pattern is not central in the structure of the letter as a whole, this is not a strong argument.

*24.1 Landon's proposed reading would introduce another NT *hapax legomenon* into the text of Jude with ἀγνευομενους (not, as he prints it on p. 150, ἀγνευομενους). Linking a participle with two adjectives and claiming that the result "is a striking example of triadic illustration" (p. 135) seems to be going beyond the evidence. Moreover Liddell & Scott do not cite any examples of this verb being used in the passive, though some references they print but do not cite.

*24.3 The proposal to omit ἀμώμους here is necessitated by the decision taken at 24.1 to include it there. The weakness of the reasoning there militates against accepting Landon's recommendation here.

*25.1 The inclusion of σοφῷ here is not strictly comparable with the phrase in Rom 16:27 because in that place there is no additional noun following θεῷ. The phrase μόνῳ σοφῷ θεῷ σωτῆρι ἡμῶν sounds distinctly overloaded.

*25.3 The addition of αὐτῷ is certainly no improvement to a book that is supposed to be in good style, neither is the repetition of δόξα and κράτος.

Conclusion

Finally the entire NA[27] text of Jude, laid out in accordance with the above analysis, is printed below. The sign + indicates that the following line is a continuation line.

1 Ἰούδας Ἰησοῦ Χριστοῦ δοῦλος, ἀδελφὸς δὲ Ἰακώβου,
   τοῖς ἐν θεῷ πατρὶ ἠγαπημένοις
   καὶ Ἰησοῦ Χριστῷ τετηρημένοις κλητοῖς·
2 ἔλεος ὑμῖν καὶ εἰρήνη καὶ ἀγάπη πληθυνθείη.
==
3 ἀγαπητοί, πᾶσαν σπουδὴν ποιούμενος γράφειν ὑμῖν +
                περὶ τῆς κοινῆς ἡμῶν σωτηρίας
  ἀνάγκην ἔσχον γράψαι ὑμῖν
      παρακαλῶν ἐπαγωνίζεσθαι τῇ ἅπαξ παραδοθείσῃ τοῖς ἁγίοις πίστει.
4 παρεισέδυσαν γάρ τινες ἄνθρωποι,
     οἱ πάλαι προγεγραμμένοι εἰς τοῦτο τὸ κρίμα,
     ἀσεβεῖς,
     τὴν τοῦ θεοῦ ἡμῶν χάριτα μετατιθέντες εἰς ἀσέλγειαν
     καὶ τὸν μόνον δεσπότην καὶ κύριον ἡμῶν Ἰησοῦν Χριστὸν +
     ἀρνούμενοι.
----
5 ὑπομνῆσαι δὲ ὑμᾶς βούλομαι
    εἰδότας ὑμᾶς πάντα
    ὅτι [ὁ] κύριος ἅπαξ λαὸν ἐκ γῆς Αἰγύπτου σώσας
    τὸ δεύτερον τοὺς μὴ πιστεύσαντας ἀπώλεσεν,

6 ἀγγέλους τε τοὺς μὴ τηρήσαντας τὴν ἑαυτῶν ἀρχὴν
    ἀλλὰ ἀπολιπόντας τὸ ἴδιον οἰκητήριον +
    εἰς κρίσιν μεγάλης ἡμέρας δεσμοῖς ἀϊδίοις ὑπὸ ζόφον τετήρηκεν.

=-

7 ὡς Σόδομα καὶ Γόμορρα καὶ αἱ περὶ αὐτὰς πόλεις +
    τὸν ὅμοιον τρόπον τούτοις ἐκπορνεύσασαι [τούτοις = angels in 6]
    καὶ ἀπελθοῦσαι ὀπίσω σαρκὸς ἑτέρας,
πρόκεινται δεῖγμα,
    πυρὸς αἰωνίου δίκην ὑπέχουσαι,
8 ὁμοίως μέντοι καὶ οὗτοι ἐνυπνιαζόμενοι σάρκα μὲν μιαίνουσιν,   [οὗτοι = men in 4]
    κυριότητα δὲ ἀθετοῦσιν,
    δόξας δὲ βλασφημοῦσιν.

---

9 ὁ δὲ Μιχαὴλ ὁ ἀρχάγγελος,
    ὅτε τῷ διαβόλῳ διακρινόμενος διελέγετο περὶ τοῦ Μωϋσέως σώματος,
οὐκ ἐτόλμησεν κρίσιν ἐπενεγκεῖν βλασφημίας
ἀλλὰ εἶπεν, Ἐπιτιμήσαι σοι κύριος.
10 οὗτοι δὲ
    ὅσα μὲν οὐκ οἴδασιν
βλασφημοῦσιν
    ὅσα δὲ φυσικῶς ὡς τὰ ἄλογα ζῷα ἐπίστανται,
ἐν τούτοις φθείρονται.

---

11 οὐαὶ αὐτοῖς,
    ὅτι τῇ ὁδῷ τοῦ Κάϊν ἐπορεύθησαν
        καὶ τῇ πλάνῃ τοῦ Βαλαὰμ μισθοῦ ἐξεχύθησαν
        καὶ τῇ ἀντιλογίᾳ τοῦ Κόρε ἀπώλοντο.
12 οὗτοί εἰσιν οἱ ἐν ταῖς ἀγάπαις ὑμῶν σπιλάδες συνευωχούμενοι ἀφόβως,
    ἑαυτοὺς ποιμαίνοντες,
    νεφέλαι ἄνυδροι ὑπὸ ἀνέμων παραφερόμεναι,
    δένδρα φθινοπωρινὰ ἄκαρπα δὶς ἀποθανόντα,
    ἐκριζωθέντα,
    13 κύματα ἄγρια θαλάσσης ἐπαφρίζοντα τὰς ἑαυτῶν αἰσχύνας,
    ἀστέρες πλανῆται
    οἷς ὁ ζόφος τοῦ σκότους εἰς αἰῶνα τετήρηται.

---

14 προεφήτευσεν δὲ καὶ τούτοις ἕβδομος ἀπὸ Ἀδὰμ Ἐνὼχ λέγων,
    Ἰδοὺ ἦλθεν κύριος ἐν ἁγίαις μυριάσιν αὐτοῦ

15 ποιῆσαι κρίσιν κατὰ πάντων
    καὶ ἐλέγξαι πᾶσαν ψυχὴν περὶ πάντων τῶν ἔργων ἀσεβείας αὐτῶν
        ὧν ἠσέβησαν
    καὶ περὶ πάντων τῶν σκληρῶν
        ὧν ἐλάλησαν κατ' αὐτοῦ ἁμαρτωλοὶ ἀσεβεῖς.
16 οὗτοί εἰσιν γογγυσταί μεμψίμοιροι κατὰ τὰς ἐπιθυμίας ἑαυτῶν πορευόμενοι,
   καὶ τὸ στόμα αὐτῶν λαλεῖ ὑπέρογκα,
      θαυμάζοντες πρόσωπα ὠφελείας χάριν.

=-

17 ὑμεῖς δέ, ἀγαπητοί, μνήσθητε τῶν ῥημάτων τῶν προειρημένων +
      ὑπὸ τῶν ἀποστόλων τοῦ κυρίου ἡμῶν Ἰησοῦ Χριστοῦ
   18 ὅτι ἔλεγον ὑμῖν·
     [ὅτι] Ἐπ' ἐσχάτου [τοῦ] χρόνου ἔσονται ἐμπαῖκται
        κατὰ τὰς ἑαυτῶν ἐπιθυμίας πορευόμενοι τῶν ἀσεβειῶν.
19 οὗτοί εἰσιν οἱ ἀποδιορίζοντες,
    ψυχικοί,
    πνεῦμα μὴ ἔχοντες.

---

20 ὑμεῖς δέ, ἀγαπητοί, ἐποικοδομοῦντες ἑαυτοὺς τῇ ἁγιωτάτῃ ὑμῶν πίστει,
    ἐν πνεύματι ἁγίῳ προσευχόμενοι,
21 ἑαυτοὺς ἐν ἀγάπῃ θεοῦ τηρήσατε
    προσδεχόμενοι τὸ ἔλεος τοῦ κυρίου ἡμῶν Ἰησοῦ Χριστοῦ +
        εἰς ζωὴν αἰώνιον.
22 καὶ οὓς μὲν ἐλεᾶτε διακρινομένους,
23 οὓς δὲ σῴζετε ἐκ πυρὸς ἁρπάζοντες,
  οὓς δὲ ἐλεᾶτε ἐν φόβῳ μισοῦντες καὶ τὸν ἀπὸ τῆς σαρκὸς ἐσπιλωμένον χιτῶνα.

===

24 τῷ δὲ δυναμένῳ φυλάξαι ὑμᾶς ἀπταίστους
     καὶ στῆσαι κατενώπιον τῆς δόξης αὐτοῦ ἀμώμους ἐν ἀγαλλιάσει,
25 μόνῳ θεῷ σωτῆρι ἡμῶν διὰ Ἰησοῦ Χριστοῦ τοῦ κυρίου ἡμῶν
  δόξα
  μεγαλωσύνη
  κράτος
  καὶ ἐξουσία
    πρὸ παντὸς τοῦ αἰῶνος
    καὶ νῦν
    καὶ εἰς πάντας τοὺς αἰῶνας, ἀμήν.

9

A DISCOURSE MARKER IN THE SYNOPTIC GOSPELS:
ἀμὴν λέγω ὑμῖν/σοι

Introduction

This article presents the findings of an investigation into the way the formula ἀμὴν λέγω ὑμῖν/σοι ("truly I say to you") is used in the synoptic gospels. This formula obviously occurs only in direct speech, and is always spoken by Jesus. It is particularly characteristic of the Gospel of Matthew, where it occurs 24 times with the plural indirect object ἀμὴν λέγω ὑμῖν, and once more where the word ἀμήν ("truly") is textually doubtful. There are two further instances of ἀμὴν λέγω σοι ("truly I say to you [singular]") and four of ἀμὴν γὰρ λέγω ὑμῖν ("for truly I say to you [plural]").

In the Gospel of Mark, ἀμὴν λέγω ὑμῖν occurs eleven times, with one further occurrence of ἀμὴν λέγω σοι and one of ἀμὴν δὲ λέγω ὑμῖν ("but truly I say to you [plural]"). In the Gospel of Luke ἀμὴν λέγω ὑμῖν occurs only five times, with one further occurrence (using a different word order) of ἀμὴν σοι λέγω ("truly to you [singular] I say").

The total number of occurrences of the phrase unquestionably including ἀμήν is therefore 30 for Matthew, 13 for Mark, and 6 for Luke. Since over 60% of all the occurrences in the synoptic gospels are in Matthew, the following presentation is based on that gospel, with the other gospels used for comparison. It is assumed that it makes no difference to any discourse function whether the indirect object "you" is singular or plural. This choice is dictated by the context. It is worth noting that John uses the similar expressions ἀμὴν ἀμὴν λέγω ὑμῖν/σοι 25 times, but that evidence is the subject of a separate study.

The Distribution of ἀμὴν (γάρ) λέγω ὑμῖν/σοι in Matthew

Initially the occurrences of the formula ἀμὴν λέγω ὑμῖν/σοι in Matthew may be divided into five categories, the first two associated with the end of a unit or sub-unit within the utterance, the next two associated with the beginning of the utterance, and the last comprising functionally uncertain cases. In this essay, I deliberately use the neutral terms "unit" and "sub-unit" to refer to stretches of text that are usually more than one sentence. It seems better to reserve the more specific terms "paragraph" and "sub-paragraph" for a fuller discourse analysis of the gospels to define. That task is beyond the scope of this article, in which those terms are used only to refer to the layout of printed editions of the Greek text.

(1) There are twelve places where the formula marks the final sentence of a unit (5.26; 6.2, 5, 16; 10.15, 23, 42; 16.28; 23.36; 24.34, 47; 26.13).

(2) There are two places (17.20; 26.34) where the formula seems to indicate closure of the episode of which the speech is part rather than just the speech itself.

(3) There are six places (8.10; 18.3; 19.23, 28; 21.21, 31) where the formula occurs in the first sentence of a longer speech and so is readily understood as an opening marker for a larger unit.

(4) There is one other place (26.21) where the utterance with the formula consists of only one sentence, so it is hard to claim any specifically discourse function in the narrower context. In such a situation however, it seems plausible to think of the formula as connected with the opening of the speech, and perhaps as putting the following statement under strong emphasis.

(5) There are ten further places (including the textually doubtful one) where the status of the formula is more complex, and requires discussion before assignment to any group. These are 5.18; 11.11; 13.17; 18.13, 18, 19; 24.2; 25.12, 40, 45.

We shall examine each group in turn, keeping the same order as above.

A Discourse Marker in the Synoptic Gospels

Ἀμὴν (γὰρ) λέγω ὑμῖν/σοι in the Final Sentence of a Unit

Group (1) has twelve members. In the first instance, 5.26, the singular pronoun σοι makes it formally clear that this sentence relates to what has preceded rather than what follows, since the second person forms change to plural in the next verse. The content of the statement introduced by the formula reinforces this and thus the formula must come at the end of a unit.

The three instances in 6.2, 5 and 16 are identical in form and parallel with each other in location. In each case the formula functions as a closure marker preceding a contrast opened by a second person singular pronoun, but since in each case the complete unit (6.2–4, 5–6 and 16–18) comprises paired negative and positive commands, it seems more realistic here to see the formula as closing a sub-unit rather than a full unit. In chapter 10 there are also three occurrences of the formula which are parallel in function. The third (10.42) is in the last sentence of the long speech covering 10.5–42, and so any discourse function it has can be only as a closure marker. This makes it very probable that the other occurrences in the same discourse in 10.15 and 23 also function in the same way and mark the end of intermediate units. The occurrence of γάρ in 10.23 strengthens its link with what has preceded. This analysis of the function of the formula affects the understanding of the whole speech, especially vv. 24–33, as argued in chapter three, §3.1.

In 16.28, the formula comes in the final sentence of a speech covering vv. 24b–28, and is readily recognised as associated with closure. In 23.36 the formula marks the end of the series of "woes" before the lament over Jerusalem in vv. 37–39. A formal indication of this is the fact that the second person plural pronoun form in 23.36 changes to singular in 23.37.

In 24.34, the formula is linked with the end of a unit, though in this case it occurs not in the final but in the penultimate sentence of that unit. The final sentence in 24.35 contains an echo of 5.18, which we shall discuss below. That a new unit begins in 24.36 is clearly shown by its opening phrase περὶ δὲ ("now concerning..."), a regular opening marker for a new unit (compare for instance 1 Cor 7.1, 25; 8.1; 12.1; 16.1, 12; 1 Thess 4.9; 5.1). In 24.47 the situation is similar to that in 6.2, 5 and 16 in that the formula closes the first half of a parable preceding a contrast described in the second half. It therefore closes a sub-unit rather than a full unit. In 26.13, the formula introduces the final sentence of Jesus' speech in vv. 10b–13 and thus clearly functions as a closure marker.

We next examine the members of group (2), first ἀμὴν γὰρ λέγω ὑμῖν in

17.20. The formula begins the second sentence of a two-sentence utterance. The first sentence is an elliptical response to a question asked by the disciples, and the second is a spontaneous additional remark by Jesus. In view of the brevity of the utterance, it seems too much to claim that the formula introduces the closure of the speech, yet at the same time it does not occur at the beginning. The hypothesis suggests itself that the formula does have a closing function, but that it is exercised not within the speech itself, but within the larger unit 17.14–20, of which the speech is a small part. If this is the case, the formula, while occurring in the direct speech, actually has its primary discourse function beyond the limits of that speech. The γάρ then links the statement not so much with the immediately preceding answer to the question as with the whole preceding incident. An analogy taken from morphology and syntax would be that of a verbal affix in an agglutinative language which occurs within the structure of a verb, and has to be described as part of that structure, but which functions not to affect the tense, aspect, or person of the verb, but rather to indicate at clause level that the clause is conditional. The hypothesis that the formula may have such a function will become stronger if further examples are found.

In 26.34, Jesus contradicts Peter's vehement assertion of loyalty with a speech opened by the formula (this time, as befits the context, with a singular pronoun). The occurrence of the formula at that particular point in its unit (26.31–35) strongly suggests that like 17.20 it has a discourse function beyond the speech itself, and marks the climax of the unit.

ἀμὴν (γάρ) λέγω ὑμῖν/σοι in the Opening Sentence of a Unit

We now turn to group (3) with six members. In 8.10, the situation is complex. The centurion has expressed his faith in 8.9, but instead of replying immediately to him, Jesus addresses the people around him in 8.10b–12 before speaking to the centurion in 8.13. So the remark in 8.10 is a comment on the previous utterance rather than a reply to it. We may note that the situation indicates a reversal of expectation, as indicated by the first verb in the verse ἐθαύμασεν ("he was amazed").

In 18.3 the formula introduces the verbal response to a question from the disciples in 18.1. It follows the acted response of setting a child in the middle of the group in 18.2. The speech that begins in 18.3b continues until 18.20, so the formula introduces a long unit, or more probably series of units. There is again a reversal of expectation in 18.3, but in this case the expectation is not that of the speaker but that of the hearers.

In 19.23 the formula opens a comment on the reaction of the rich young man in the previous verse. In this case the speech is fairly short (19.23b–24 only), but again there is a reversal of expectation, this time in the content of what follows the formula. That Jesus' words contradicted commonly held views is shown by the extreme astonishment of the disciples in 19.25 on hearing them. The conversation with the disciples continues, and two turns later in 19.28 Jesus again opens his speech with ἀμὴν λέγω ὑμῖν in response to Peter's question "What's in it for us?" The formula may well imply another reversal of expectation. If so, then what follows is not simply a list of rewards, but carries the idea of "You'll get far more than you could possibly imagine." At the very least there is an element of surprise involved.

In 21.21 the formula introduces a short speech punctuated in UBS[4]/NA[27] as a single sentence, though it could equally well be taken as two sentences. The context again includes the idea of reversal of expectation, though this has already happened before Jesus starts to speak, in the disciples' amazement at the withering of the fig tree. The use of the formula here probably reinforces the thrust of what follows: "You haven't seen anything yet!" In 21.31 Jesus is explaining the force of the parable he has just told about the two sons, which the audience of priests and elders (21.23) had correctly understood. Here as in 18.3, this reverses the expectations of the hearers.

We now examine the sole member of group (4). In 26.21, the formula opens the first turn in a complex conversation that covers most of the unit 26.20–25. In the midst of a Passover meal that celebrated redemption and joint membership of the people of God, Jesus speaks of betrayal, so it seems that once more the formula occurs in a context where reversal of expectation is involved.

Doubtful Cases

Finally we come to the ten members of group (5). In 5.18 the formula (with γάρ) occurs in the second sentence of the unit that spans 5.17–20. In v. 17 Jesus rebuts any notion that he sought to undermine the authority of the Law by asserting that he came to give it a deeper fulfilment. This is an implied reversal of expectation. The formula is then used to introduce the assertion that the Law will last as long as heaven and earth. Probably this example has more in common with group (3) than with any other group, and so should be reallocated to that group.

In 11.11 the formula is used in the middle of a speech covering vv. 7b–19. Within this speech, units are opened with rhetorical questions in vv. 7 and 16. It is perfectly possible that the formula in v. 11 indicates that a further unit begins there. There is no γάρ to suggest a very close link with the preceding OT quotation. The function of the formula here may be to give a surprisingly strong reinforcement of a controversial view already stated: John the Baptist was not merely more than a prophet (v. 9), but was the greatest man born up to that time. Probably this example should also be allotted to group (3).

In 13.17 the formula, which here includes γάρ, comes in the middle of a speech that extends from vv. 11b–23. Verse 18 begins with an emphatic pronoun and an imperative verb, marking the beginning of the interpretation of the parable of the sower. The γάρ links v. 17 closely with the preceding statement in v. 16. There is little doubt therefore that v. 17 is the end of a (sub)unit, and that the formula indicates this. This example is therefore reassigned to group (1).

In 18.13, the formula closes the brief parable in vv. 12–13. The following verse relates to what preceded the parable and indeed to the whole of vv. 1–13. It seems therefore that the occurrence of the formula in the parable at this point may indicate a function in marking the end of the whole unit 18.3b–14, and we therefore reassign it to group (2).

In 18.18 the formula occurs in a speech that extends from 18.3b–20. The train of thought through this monologue is not at all easy to follow, though it is fairly widely agreed that vv. 15–20 form a separate sub-unit. If the analysis suggested in chapter three, §3.5 is accepted, vv. 15–20 are related to the question about greatness posed by the disciples in 18.1 as dealing with greatness in the handling of discord in personal relationships. UBS[4] starts a new paragraph with our formula ἀμὴν λέγω ὑμῖν at v. 18, but NA[27] begins only a sub-paragraph at v. 18, and other editions of the Greek NT such as that of Souter (*Novum Testamentum Graece, Editio Altera*) make no break at all. It seems to make better sense to treat v. 18 as the end of a unit covering vv. 15–18 rather than the beginning of a unit covering vv. 18–20. The decisions made by the believing community (18.17) have in some mysterious way a binding force that is more than merely earthly (18.18). Thus this verse, contrary to the paragraphing in UBS[4], should be added to group (1) as an example of the formula functioning as a closure marker. At any rate there is no convincing reason to link v. 18 with vv. 19–20.

In the next verse, 18.19, we come to the one place where the word ἀμήν is textually doubtful and is placed in square brackets in UBS[4]/NA[27] (πάλιν [ἀμὴν] λέγω ὑμῖν "again [truly] I say to you"). Indeed it was not included in the first two editions of the UBS text, but Metzger's Textual Commentary does not indicate why the editorial committee changed their minds in the third edition. There is no example in any of the gospels where the adverb πάλιν ("again") co-occurs with ἀμὴν λέγω ὑμῖν, and thus pressure of usage not only in Matthew but also in the other synoptics supports its omission here. If ἀμήν is retained here, it creates a further anomaly in that there is no synoptic example of ἀμὴν λέγω ὑμῖν being used twice in successive verses. (Compare the comments on Luke 4.24–5 below.) On the other hand if the text here is read as πάλιν λέγω ὑμῖν, there is a parallel in 19.23–24, where ἀμὴν λέγω ὑμῖν in 19.23 is followed in the next verse by πάλιν δὲ λέγω ὑμῖν. I therefore believe that in this verse ἀμήν should probably not be included, and for the purposes of the present investigation the verse should be disregarded.

The next verse to consider is 24.2. It has some similarity with 17.20 in that the formula occurs in the second sentence of the utterance: the difference is that in 17.20 the first sentence was the answer to a question, whereas here the first sentence is itself a (rhetorical) question. The utterance consists of only two sentences, so there is no debate as to whether the formula opens or closes a unit. The utterance itself is near the beginning of a unit and is not in a parable, so there is no possibility of the formula marking a climax. The simplest analysis is to take the formula as the beginning of the real content of the utterance, and, like several members of group (3), as indicating a reversal of the expectations of the hearers. They saw the Temple buildings as a symbol of magnificence and stability, and Jesus foretells their total destruction. This example can be reallocated to group (3).

Although the last three examples (25.12, 40, 45) are all spoken by Jesus, he puts them into the mouths of characters in parables. In the first case, the second-degree quotation constitutes the last sentence of the parable about the ten girls, and forms the climax of the parable. The following verse represents Jesus' comment on the parable, taking up the theme of watchfulness already introduced in 24.42–43. So it appears that here as in 17.20 the formula has a discourse function not so much within the speech of which it is a part, as in the whole parable covering 25.1–12. The other examples in 25.40 and 45 are linked in that they both come in second-degree quotations that form the climax of the two contrasting halves of the parable. Jesus' final comment in 25.46 is a brief summary of the results of the events narrated in each half of the parable. So again it becomes evident that the formula has a discourse function within a unit larger than the speech in which it occurs. These three places, then, lend support to the analysis of 17.20 above, and can be reassigned to group (2).

Summary of Matthew

If the reallocations proposed in the above discussion are accepted, we end with 30 examples, divided into four groups rather than five. Group (1) now contains fourteen examples, group (2) six examples, group (3) nine examples, and group (4) one example. Thus in two thirds of the examples in Matthew in groups (1) and (2), the formula is associated with the closure of a unit or sub-unit, and in one third in groups (3) and (4), it is associated with the opening of a unit or sub-unit. In these latter cases there is usually some element of surprise or reversal of expectation involved.

Comparison with Mark and Luke

As noted above there are 30 examples of ἀμὴν (γὰρ) λέγω ὑμῖν/σοι in Matthew, thirteen examples of ἀμὴν (δὲ) λέγω ὑμῖν/σοι in Mark and six examples of ἀμὴν λέγω ὑμῖν/σοι λέγω in Luke. All three synoptic writers have places where they alone use the formula, but Matthew alone uses it much more often than Mark alone or Luke alone. There are only two places where all three writers use the formula in parallel passages, six where Matthew and Mark use it, and only one where Mark and Luke use it but Matthew does not. These figures bring out clearly how very characteristic the formula is of Matthew. This information is shown in chart form below. The actual occurrences are displayed in a second chart at the end of the essay.

Matthew, Mark & Luke	2	Matthew only	22
Matthew & Mark	6	Mark only	4
Matthew & Luke	None	Luke only	3
Mark & Luke	1		
Figure 9.1: Comparison with Mark and Luke			

The Distribution of ἀμὴν (δὲ) λέγω ὑμῖν/σοι in Mark

The categories that were observed in Matthew turn out to be broadly applicable to Mark also. In group (1) there are four examples (10.15; 13.30; 14.9, 25), and two (8.12; 14.30) in group (2). In group (3) there are two examples (10.29; 12.43), and in group (4) one (14.18). In group (5) there are four places where the status is less clear (3.28; 9.1, 41; 11.23). We shall examine each group in turn.

In group (1) there is at 10.15 a clear parallel with Luke 18.17, but it is not certain whether there is a real parallel in Matthew or not. The *Synopsis Quattuor Evangeliorum* is inconsistent: when dealing with Mark 10.13–15, it shows Matt 18.3 as a parallel, but when dealing with Matt 18.1–5, it does not show Mark 10.15 as a parallel although there is ample space to do so. The words in the two places are similar but not closely parallel, and the context is significantly different, so it seems fairer not to consider this a true parallel. In contrast with Matthew, the formula in Mark comes in the final sentence of the short speech, and in the wider context there is an element of reversal of expectation for the hearers.

In 13.30 there is a clear parallel both with Matt 24.34 and with Luke 21.32. As in Matthew, the formula occurs in the penultimate sentence of the unit, and the beginning of the following unit is marked by the phrase περὶ δέ ("now concerning..."). In 14.9 as in Matt 26.13, our formula clearly marks the end of a unit, with some reversal of expectation for the hearers. The addition of δέ to the formula may help to sharpen the contrast between what Jesus is about to say and the attitude of the disciples, but as it is unique, it may be no more than one of Mark's stylistic infelicities. In 14.25, although the general context is close to Matt 26.29, the word ἀμήν is not present in Matthew so for our purposes there is no true parallel. The formula in Mark is in the final sentence of a short speech and can be seen as an indicator of closure.

In group (2) the first example comes at 8.12. The utterance has a broad parallel in Luke 11.29 and two broad parallels in Matt 12.39 and 16.4. However, only Mark uses the formula. It opens the second and final sentence of an utterance after a rhetorical question, and appears to carry a wider function, providing a forceful closure not just to the speech, but to the short unit as a whole. In 14.30 there is a close parallel with Matt 26.34, and the comments made above on that verse also apply here. There is a broad parallel with Luke 22.34, but Luke uses the vocative Πέτρε ("Peter") instead of ἀμήν. There is also a parallel with John 13.38, which has ἀμήν twice.

In group (3) both cases are marked by reversal of expectation, or at least surprise. Mark 10.29 is parallel with both Matt 19.28 and Luke 18.29, all three having the formula at the beginning of the utterance. In 12.43 the formula again begins the utterance, and there is a broad parallel only with Luke 21.3, but since Luke has ἀληθῶς ("truly") instead of ἀμήν, the parallel is not exact.

In group (4) the formula in 14.18 is at the beginning of the utterance as in Matt 26.21, and reversal of expectation is implied. There is also a fairly close parallel at John 13.21, though as is his custom John has ἀμήν twice.

In group (5) the example at 3.28 is somewhat anomalous. The formula occurs at the beginning of the last sentence in a speech covering vv. 23b–29. It is however a long sentence, and could equally well be punctuated as two sentences. Thus it is not certain whether the formula marks the closure of the speech as a whole, or opens a new sub-unit within the speech. There is a broad parallel to the speech as a whole in Matt 12.25–32, but in 12.31, the verse equivalent to Mark 3.28, Matthew has διὰ τοῦτο λέγω ὑμῖν ("Because of this I say to you"). The rest of the speech in Matthew is significantly longer than in Mark, so perhaps Matthew avoided our formula because the end of the speech was not near enough to use a closure marker. On the whole it seems better to reckon that in Mark 3.28 ἀμὴν λέγω ὑμῖν is intended to be a closure marker. So this example can be reassigned to group (1).

The example at 9.1 has broad parallels both in Matt 16.28 and Luke 9.27. However neither is an exact parallel. Though both have very closely similar wording in the quoted utterance, Luke again substitutes ἀληθῶς for ἀμήν, and both Matthew and Luke lack the quotative clause καὶ ἔλεγεν αὐτοῖς ("and he said to them") that comes at the beginning of Mark 9.1. The effect of this is that whereas the formula occurs in Matthew at the close of a lengthy speech and is in group (1), in Mark it is at the beginning of a separate speech that consists of a single sentence. Thus in Mark the utterance seems to be intended to mark closure for the whole unit that began in 8.34 or possibly earlier. It is therefore placed in group (2).

To 9.41 there is a broad parallel in Matt 10.42, but the parallel extends only to this one verse, which is set in a very different context in Matthew and so is not very relevant. In Mark the speech covers vv. 39b–50, and the formula is at neither the beginning nor the end. The most plausible analysis is that the formula indicates the closure of the first sub-unit within the speech. If this is so, this example can be reassigned to group (1).

In 11.23, the formula occurs at the beginning of the second sentence of a speech covering vv. 22b–25. It comes after a brief command at the beginning of the speech. There is a broad parallel in Matt 21.21, but there the formula is at the beginning of the utterance, and what is a command in Mark 11.22 takes the form of a conditional clause after the formula. It seems likely that here as there the formula is best regarded as an opening marker. This example could therefore be reallocated to group (3). As often in group (3), there is some element of reversal of expectation.

Summary of Mark

If the reallocations proposed above are accepted, the five groups are again reduced to four. Group (1) now has six members, group (2) three members, group (3) three members and group (4) one member. Thus in Mark the balance between the uses of the formula as an opening marker and a closing marker is similar to that in Matthew, with nine examples as a closing marker in groups (1) and (2), and four as an opening marker in groups (3) and (4). The latter are again associated with reversal of expectation.

The Distribution of ἀμὴν λέγω ὑμῖν/σοι λέγω in Luke

The categories we have used in Matthew and Mark will serve us again. In group (1) there are two examples (18.17 and 21.32), and in group (2) one (23.43). Group (3) has two examples (4.24 and 18.29) but group (4) none. Group (5) also has a single example (12.37). We shall again examine each group in turn.

In group (1) 18.17 is identical with Mark 10.15 both in wording and in location within the final sentence of the speech. Luke 21.32 is one of only two places where all three synoptics display our formula in their parallel passages (Matt 24.34 and Mark 13.30). As in Matthew and Mark, the formula occurs in the penultimate sentence of the speech.

In group (2) we have just the one example in 23.43, unique to Luke. There is a strong element of both surprise and reversal of expectation in the context. Jesus has ignored the words of the abusive thief, which are rebuked by the second thief. That Jesus should welcome this man to paradise is unexpected enough, but the surprise is reinforced by the unique word order ἀμὴν σοι λέγω. There are only four other places in the synoptics where the indirect object σοι precedes the verb without the presence of an emphatic subject pronoun ἐγώ ("I"). In Mark 2.11 and its parallel Luke 5.24 Jesus is addressing the paralysed man after speaking to the scribes, and the front-shifting of σοι marks a change of addressee. In Mark 5.41 and Luke 7.14 Jesus is addressing a corpse, and the front-shifting seems to emphasise the oddity of the situation: nobody is expected to address corpses! In the present case the front-shifting of σοι seems to underline that Jesus is responding to someone who unexpectedly shows a repentant attitude, as well as introducing a remark of astonishing content.

In group (3) 4.24 is another of the three places where Luke alone uses the formula. There are rough parallels in Matt 13.57 and Mark 6.4, but they are set in very different contexts, and both lack the formula or any equivalent to it. It is interesting to observe that although the previous verse is also the direct speech of Jesus, Luke inserts a fresh quotative formula at the beginning of v. 24. Perhaps he felt that the formula was stylistically inappropriate in the middle of a speech, and deliberately chose to start a new speech for that reason. This theory gains some support from the following verse, which opens with ἐπ' ἀληθείας δὲ λέγω ὑμῖν ("in truth I say to you"). The meaning is hardly distinguishable from that of our formula, but Luke apparently wanted to avoid putting the formula in the middle of a speech, and perhaps also to avoid repeating the formula twice in successive sentences. (Compare the comments on Matt 18.19 above.) As in many other places where our formula occurs at the beginning of an utterance, there is an element of reversal of expectation in the context.

In 18.29 we find the other place where all three synoptics have the formula (Matt 19.28; Mark 10.29), in all cases as the opening words of the utterance. There is also an element of reversal of expectation, or at least surprise, inherent in the statement that follows.

In group (5) there is only 12.37, again unique to Luke. This place appears to fit in none of the categories recognised above, though it is associated with surprise or reversal of expectation. Unlike any other example, the formula comes in the middle of a paragraph that is part of a long speech covering 12.22b–40, and there is no convincing way of changing the paragraph divisions that would help. The nearest examples with any similarity are Matt 6.2, 5, 16 and perhaps Matt 24.47; 25.40, 45 and Mark 9.41. In all these places the formula occurs at the end of a sub-unit, and one might try to maintain that this is the situation here also. However there is no obvious reason why the following verse should be regarded as the beginning of a new sub-unit. It seems safest to list this occurrence of our formula as anomalous, and not try to reallocate it. So the group membership remains unchanged from what was proposed at the beginning of this section.

There are then three examples where the formula is associated with the end of a unit, and two where it is associated with the beginning, a balance comparable with that in Matthew and Mark.

A Discourse Marker in the Synoptic Gospels

General Summary, and Implications for Translators

When we put together the analyses of the three synoptics, we find that group (1) has 22 members, group (2) ten, group (3) fourteen and group (4) two. Thus in 32 cases our formula is linked with the closure of a unit and in 16 with the opening. That is to say roughly two thirds of all the examples are linked with closure and one third with opening. Only one example out of a total of 49 does not fit into this pattern.

What are the implications of this study for translators? First of all it is clear that the familiar formula ἀμὴν λέγω ὑμῖν and its variants do not occur randomly in discourse. In every case except one, it is an indication either of the beginning of a unit or sub-unit, or else of the end. This should influence the recognition of paragraph breaks in the Greek text, and consequently in the translation. The formula is frequently found in a context where surprise or reversal of expectation is a prominent element, especially when it opens a (sub-)unit.

These observations suggest that it may be advisable not to use identical wording in the translation in every occurrence. There may be in the receptor language particles or verbal inflections that are linked with the beginning or end of a unit, and if so these should be selected appropriately. There may also be particles or other grammatical devices that indicate surprise or reversal of expectation, and if so these too should be used as befits each context. Such features may be small adjustments in the synoptics as a whole, but they can be significant in giving the translation a natural flavour for the readers, and so influence its overall acceptability.

Finally we add Figure 9.2 showing all the occurrences of our formula, with the group membership assigned to each. The entries follow the canonical order of Matthew and the parallels in the other gospels are in canonical order as far as possible. The figure shows # where one or more gospels has a parallel passage but lacks any equivalent to the formula. It also shows where Luke has a parallel passage but uses some variant expression as an equivalent of ἀμὴν λέγω ὑμῖν. This situation does not arise in Mark. Luke three times substitutes ἀληθῶς ("truly") for ἀμήν in Matthew and/or Mark, which surely indicates how he understood the meaning of ἀμήν. Once he substitutes ναί ("yes") for ἀμήν, once οὗ χάριν ("wherefore"), and on six occasions he simply omits ἀμήν.

Matthew	Mark	Luke
13.57 #	6.4 #	4.24 ἀμὴν λέγω ὑμῖν 3
5.18 ἀμὴν γὰρ λέγω ὑμῖν 3		
5.26 ἀμὴν λέγω σοι 1		12.59 λέγω σοι
6.2 ἀμὴν λέγω ὑμῖν 1		
6.5 ἀμὴν λέγω ὑμῖν 1		
6.16 ἀμὴν λέγω ὑμῖν 1		
8.10 ἀμὴν λέγω ὑμῖν 3		7.9 λέγω ὑμῖν
10.15 ἀμὴν λέγω ὑμῖν 1		10.12 λέγω ὑμῖν
10.23 ἀμὴν γὰρ λέγω ὑμῖν 1		
10.42 ἀμὴν λέγω ὑμῖν 1	9.41 ἀμὴν λέγω ὑμῖν 1	
11.11 ἀμὴν λέγω ὑμῖν 3		7.28 λέγω ὑμῖν
12.31 διὰ τοῦτο λέγω ὑμῖν	3.28 ἀμὴν λέγω ὑμῖν 1	
13.17 ἀμὴν γὰρ λέγω ὑμῖν 1		10.24 λέγω γὰρ ὑμῖν
12.39 # and 16.4 #	8.12 ἀμὴν λέγω ὑμῖν 2	11.29 #
16.28 ἀμὴν λέγω ὑμῖν 1	9.1 ἀμὴν λέγω ὑμῖν 2	9.27 λέγω δὲ ὑμῖν ἀληθῶς
17.20 ἀμὴν γὰρ λέγω ὑμῖν 2		17.6 #
18.3 ἀμὴν λέγω ὑμῖν 3	Cf. 10.15	Cf. 18.17
18.13 ἀμὴν λέγω ὑμῖν 2		
18.18 ἀμὴν λέγω ὑμῖν 1		
		12.37 ἀμὴν λέγω ὑμῖν 5
Cf. 18.3	10.15 ἀμὴν λέγω ὑμῖν 1	18.17 ἀμὴν λέγω ὑμῖν 1
19.23 ἀμὴν λέγω ὑμῖν 3	10.23 #	
19.28 ἀμὴν λέγω ὑμῖν 3	10.29 ἀμὴν λέγω ὑμῖν 3	18.29 ἀμὴν λέγω ὑμῖν 3
21.21 ἀμὴν λέγω ὑμῖν 3	11.23 ἀμὴν λέγω ὑμῖν 3	
21.31 ἀμὴν λέγω ὑμῖν 3		
23.36 ἀμὴν λέγω ὑμῖν 1		11.51 ναί λέγω ὑμῖν
	12.43 ἀμὴν λέγω ὑμῖν 3	21.3 ἀληθῶς λέγω ὑμῖν
24.2 ἀμὴν λέγω ὑμῖν 3	13.2 #	21.6 #
24.34 ἀμὴν λέγω ὑμῖν 1	13.30 ἀμὴν λέγω ὑμῖν 1	21.32 ἀμὴν λέγω ὑμῖν 1
24.47 ἀμὴν λέγω ὑμῖν 1		12.44 ἀληθῶς λέγω ὑμῖν
25.12 ἀμὴν λέγω ὑμῖν 2		
25.40 ἀμὴν λέγω ὑμῖν 2		
25.45 ἀμὴν λέγω ὑμῖν 2		
26.13 ἀμὴν λέγω ὑμῖν 1	14.9 ἀμὴν δὲ λέγω ὑμῖν 1	7.47 οὗ χάριν λέγω σοι
26.21 ἀμὴν λέγω ὑμῖν 4	14.18 ἀμὴν λέγω ὑμῖν 4	[cf. John 13.21]
26.29 λέγω δὲ ὑμῖν	14.25 ἀμὴν λέγω ὑμῖν 1	

26.34 ἀμὴν λέγω σοι 2	14.30 ἀμὴν λέγω σοι 2 [cf. John 13.38]	22.34 λέγω σοι, Πέτρε
		23.43 ἀμὴν σοι λέγω 2

Figure 9.2: All Occurrences of ἀμὴν λέγω ὑμῖν in the Synoptics

10

DISCOURSE STRUCTURE IN 3 JOHN

Introduction

The third letter of John is a fascinating text. It is short enough for the reader to take in the whole discourse, and it is clearly structured in that the major breaks in the discourse are easily identified. Yet there remain tantalising problems in assessing the relative importance of these breaks, and thus in discerning the main purpose of the letter. This essay presents an analysis of the letter depending on structural criteria.[1] The essay arises from using 3 John as a class assignment in master's degree courses both at Trinity Theological College, Singapore in October 2002, and in the University of Birmingham, England in December 2002. In both cases the class members provided stimulating and provocative observations, and deserve warm thanks.

Where Greek words are glossed in English, the wording of the RSV is followed as far as possible. Other glosses are sometimes used in order to reflect the Greek more literally, and are the author's own.

---

[1] For an alternative approach to this letter that considers also its information structure and rhetorical strategy, see Sebastiaan Floor, "A Discourse Analysis of 3 John" in *Notes on Translation* 4, no. 4 (1990): 1–17.

Criteria for the Division of the Discourse

Verses 1 and 15 separate themselves off almost automatically as the opening and closing of the letter. They fall within the bounds of the conventional format for letters of the period, with each introduced by a verbless clause. From a structural perspective, they are not of major interest.

Within the rest of the letter (vv. 2–14) the most striking structural feature is the repetition of the vocative Ἀγαπητέ, "beloved," in vv. 2, 5, and 11 (the last one reinforced by an imperative verb). Vocatives often mark the beginning of a new unit, and there is no reason why they should not be understood to do so here also. The occurrence of the connectives γάρ ("for," vv. 3 and 7) and οὖν ("so," v. 8), and the anaphoric τούτων ("these things," v. 4) support this analysis, and strongly suggest that vv. 2–4 and 5–8 form clearly marked units, which we may label paragraphs. Such an analysis is reinforced by the observation that the dominant main verbs in vv. 2–4 are first person singular (εὔχομαί, ἐχάρην, ἔχω, "I pray," "I rejoiced," and "I have"), whereas those in vv. 5–8 are second person singular (ποιεῖς, ἐργάσῃ, ποιήσεις, "you do," "you render," and "you will do").

A second notable structural feature is the asyndeton, or lack of any connective particle, at the beginning of vv. 9, 12, and 13. This may support the identification of new units of the discourse, but other criteria are also required before new units can be posited with confidence. With respect to v. 9, one such criterion is the change back from the second person singular dominant verbs in vv. 5–8 to first person in vv. 9–10 (Ἔγραψά, ἔλθω, ὑπομνήσω, "I wrote," "I may come," "I will remind"). Since v. 11 has already been identified as the beginning of a new unit because of the vocative that occurs there, it seems a fair conclusion that vv. 9–10 can be regarded as another, separate paragraph. The subject matter in these verses is significantly different from that in vv. 5–8 and 11, though "subject matter" is not a structural criterion, and is more open to arbitrary evaluation.

Similar arguments can be applied in vv. 13–14. The asyndeton is followed by verbs in the first person singular (εἶχον, οὐ θέλω, ἐλπίζω, "I had," "I do not want," and "I hope"), so these two verses may also be treated as a distinct unit that can be labelled a paragraph. Again the subject matter shows a marked change from the preceding verses.

The most difficult and interesting place is v. 12. Since in the two previous cases, the asyndeton is supported by other criteria, it seems reasonable to start by supposing that in this case also it marks the onset of a new unit. But this time the argument from the person forms of the verbs is inconclusive. In v. 11 the dominant main verb is the second person singular imperative (μὴ μιμοῦ, "do not imitate"), but in v. 12 the three main verbs are all in different persons: third person singular (μεμαρτύρηται, "is testified"), first person plural (μαρτυροῦμεν, "we testify"), and second person singular (οἶδας, "you know"). Likewise it is not obvious whether there is a change of subject matter or not. To arrive at a decision on this, other criteria must be found, and so it is necessary to turn to higher level considerations.

What are the implications for the overall analysis of the letter if we (a) analyse v. 12 as a unit separate from v. 11, and (b) link it with v. 11 into one unit? The options can be displayed as follows, with blank lines showing major divisions, and indentations indicating possible balancing units:

Option (a)		Option (b)	
1 Opening greetings		1 Opening greetings	
2–4 Prayer (+vocative)	1 sg	2–4 Prayer (+vocative)	1 sg
5–8 Commendation of Gaius (+voc)	2 sg	5–8 Commendation of Gaius (+voc)	2 sg
9–10 Condemnation of Diotrephes	1 sg	9–10 Condemnation of Diotrephes	1 sg
11 Instruction to Gaius (+voc+impt)	2 sg	11–12 Instructions to Gaius (+voc+impt)	2 sg
12 Commendation of Demetrius	mixed		
		13–14 Personal remarks	1 sg
13–14 Personal remarks	1 sg		
15 Closing greetings		15 Closing greetings	

Figure 10.1: Two Options for 3 John 12

Arguments for Each Possibility

Under both options, the opening and closing greetings (vv. 1 and 15) balance each other, as do the prayer (vv. 2–4) and the personal remarks (vv. 13–14). The difference lies in the main body of the letter (vv. 5–12). Under option (a) the commendations of Gaius (vv. 5–8) and Demetrius (v. 12) balance each other, but the pattern of alternation in the person of the dominant main verbs breaks down in v. 12, and the distribution of the vocatives is unbalanced and asymmetrical. The condemnation of Diotrephes and the instruction to Gaius are seen as joint items at the centre of the pattern, and could be construed as contrastive units together constituting the main purpose of the letter.

Under option (b) the commendation of and instructions to Gaius (vv. 5–8 and 11–12 respectively) balance each other, and the condemnation of Diotrephes is left as the sole unit in the centre of the pattern, thus probably forming the main purpose of the letter. The fact that v. 10 contains the longest and syntactically most complex sentence in the whole letter may point towards the same conclusion. Moreover by this analysis the pattern of alternation in the person of the dominant main verbs is preserved, and regarded as a significant structural factor. The linking of vv. 11 and 12 can be defended on the grounds that if these verses are regarded as a single unit, then they both begin and end with second person singular dominant main verbs (μὴ μιμοῦ in v. 11 and οἶδας in v. 12). This inclusion is thus taken as more significant than the variation in person of the other verbs in v. 12. Such an approach respects the pattern of person alternation, which is balanced and symmetrical.

How then is the asyndeton in v. 12 to be explained? Not as evidence for disjunction, as in vv. 9 and 13, but rather as juxtaposition with and further exemplification of the instruction in v. 11. The negative injunction to Gaius not to imitate evil is surely an anaphoric reference to the conduct of Diotrephes in vv. 9–10. The second injunction (with the imperative verb implicitly repeated as a positive command), to imitate good is supported by the following statement about Demetrius, which is added to provide an example of the good which Gaius is to imitate. The occurrence of the name (Δημητρίῳ) in a marked position at the beginning of the sentence reinforces this view. In all likelihood Demetrius was the bearer of the letter, and this may explain why there is no further description of him. He may have been one of the itinerant preachers mentioned in vv. 5–8, but for the writer's purpose it is sufficient to say that he is an approved colleague. As befits the bearer of the letter, he exemplifies its values, and so sets an example worth following.

It remains to note that v. 11 begins not only with a vocative, but with a vocative and imperative combination. Such a combination tends to mark a more important break in a discourse than a vocative on its own, and this too would support the analysis in option (b) above rather than that in option (a).

A further feature of note is the repetition of key lexical roots throughout the letter. Indeed every single verse participates in at least one such repetition, from ἀγαπητῷ-ἀγαπῶ ("love") in v. 1 to ἀσπάζονταί-ἀσπάζου ("greet") in v. 15. These repetitions seem to be of varying significance from a structural perspective. The most striking example is in vv. 9–10 where there is the chiastic repetition of ἐκκλησίᾳ - ἐπιδέχεται - ἐπιδέχεται - ἐκκλησίας ("church – receive – receive - church"). Does this not lend support to the view that these verses are the peak of the entire letter, and reveal the author's main purpose in writing it? In v. 11 there is another example almost as perfect with κακὸν - ἀγαθόν - ἀγαθοποιῶν - κακοποιῶν ("evil – good - doing good - doing evil"). At the other extreme is the repetition between vv. 7 and 15 of ὀνόματος-ὄνομα ("name"). There is no other connection between these verses, and in fact the word points to different referents in the two places, Christ in the first and the friends of Gaius in the second. There is almost certainly no structural importance in this particular repetition. The same is probably true of the repetition between vv. 1 and 6 of ἀγαπῶ-ἀγάπῃ ("I love-love") and that between vv. 9 and 13 of Ἔγραψά-γράψαι ("wrote-to write").

Other repetitions that may be of local cohesive significance within their own unit include εὐοδοῦσθαι-εὐοδοῦταί ("be well") in v. 2; ἐχάρην-χαράν and περιπατεῖς-περιπατοῦντα ("rejoiced-joy" and "you walk-walking") in vv. 3–4; ποιεῖς-ποιήσεις ("do-will do") in vv. 5–6, γράψαι-γράφειν ("to write") in v. 13; and στόμα ("mouth") in v. 14.

The most complex and puzzling set of repetitions is that involving the roots μαρτυρ- and ἀληθ- ("witness" and "true"). The first occurs in vv. 3, 6, and three times in 12; the second in vv. 1, 3, 4, 8, and twice in 12. Thus it may be plausibly be claimed that v. 12 has links both with the unit 2–4 and the unit 5–8. Both the analytical options outlined above would see more significance in the link with unit 5–8 than that with unit 2–4, despite the fact that the links with unit 2–4 are slightly more numerous (three as against two).

The Peak from a Structural Perspective

Under pattern (a) above, the condemnation of Diotrephes and the instruction to Gaius appear as joint items at the centre of the pattern, and could be construed as contrastive units together constituting the main purpose of the letter. The contrast however is unbalanced, and thus unconvincing.

Under the preferred option (b) vv. 5–8 and 11–12 balance each other, and the condemnation of Diotrephes in vv. 9–10 is left as the sole unit in the centre of the pattern and so probably forms the main purpose of the letter. As noted above, the fact that v. 10 contains the longest and syntactically most complex sentence in the whole letter may support this conclusion. If this is so, then it suggests that in v. 11, it is indeed appropriate to take τὸ κακὸν ("the evil") as anaphoric and its opposite τὸ ἀγαθόν ("the good") as cataphoric, pointing onward to the example of Demetrius in v. 12.

If vv. 9–10 are identified as the peak of the letter, then its main purpose is seen as administering a rebuke to Diotrephes. Since this man has already refused to acknowledge the authority of the author ("the elder" of v. 1) there would be little point in writing to him directly. By sending the rebuke via a trusted and esteemed third person, Gaius, the writer ensured that his message would both reach Diotrephes, and in the process become known to other members of the church. This would surely help to undermine Diotrephes' pretensions to leadership, and would also have the added advantage of politeness since it avoided a direct confrontation.

The above method of analysing the text demonstrates the actual structures, beginning with smaller units and working up to larger ones. It concludes that the peak of the letter is in vv. 9 and 10, and that the real purpose of the letter is therefore to puncture the pretensions of Diotrephes. The advantage of this empirical type of analysis is that it is relatively objective, and its claims are readily available for checking. For translators, such an analysis of the text is extremely helpful, not only in preparation for the actual translation, but also in evaluating the diverse analyses given in commentaries. These are often based on a relatively subjective response to the content, and do not always look rigorously at the over-arching syntactic patterns. If translators are to find appropriate structures in their own language, they must first have a firm grasp of the macro-structure in the source language.

First Person Plural Forms

One question that is not of direct importance to a structural analysis, but which will pose questions for many translators is whether the first person plural forms in this letter should be translated as inclusive or exclusive. The first of these occurs in v. 8. Up to this point all the first person forms (in vv. 1–4) have been singular and the writer has clearly been speaking of himself. The first person plural forms in v. 8 (ὀφείλομεν "we ought" and γινώμεθα "we may be") appear to be genuine plurals, not just "editorial" plurals used as a literary convention to refer to the author. The writer is saying that people like Gaius and himself should welcome the kind of itinerant preachers he has been talking about, and the plural is therefore inclusive.

In vv. 9–10 the picture is less clear. The verbs are in the first person singular but the pronoun references (ἡμᾶς "us") are in the plural. These plurals may perhaps still include Gaius, though this seems unlikely especially in v. 9. But they could also be taken as editorial, since in vv. 9–10 the writer is speaking about the rejection of a letter he himself had written (compare RSV "my... me..."). Such an interpretation does not sit comfortably with the singular verbs, however, and presupposes fluctuation between singular and plural that is apparently unmotivated. More likely the author intends to imply that Diotrephes rejects not only himself, but also those who support or represent him, perhaps "the brothers" of v. 5. In that case the first person plural form would be rendered as exclusive.

In v. 12 the first person plurals (ἡμεῖς δὲ μαρτυροῦμεν... ἡ μαρτυρία ἡμῶν "we testify... our testimony") may again be editorial, referring only to the author, and are taken this way by RSV, which renders as "I testify... my testimony..." However, since personal comments to Gaius are consistently in the first person singular (vv. 1–4, 13–14), it seems more likely that here the plural is referring to the author together with like-minded people at his location, perhaps οἱ φίλοι ("the friends") of v. 15. So it would be safer to translate as first person plural. The immediate context in which Gaius is identified as the recipient of the author's testimony makes it clear that if a plural is used, it should be exclusive.

In v. 14, the context makes it clear that the author is including Gaius, so the first person plural (λαλήσομεν "we will talk") should definitely be inclusive.

Display of the Text

In the following display of the Greek text, double lines (=======) are used to indicate breaks between major sections, and single lines (-------) to indicate breaks between smaller sections. The display follows the analysis given in option (b) above. Indentation shows approximately the degree of subordination, and items which are parallel with each other within a section are placed at the same degree of indentation as far as possible.

1 ὁ πρεσβύτερος Γαΐῳ τῷ ἀγαπητῷ,
          ὃν ἐγὼ ἀγαπῶ ἐν ἀληθείᾳ.

===

2 ἀγαπητέ, περὶ πάντων εὔχομαί σε εὐοδοῦσθαι
          καὶ ὑγιαίνειν,
               καθὼς εὐοδοῦταί σου ἡ ψυχή.
  3 ἐχάρην γὰρ λίαν ἐρχομένων ἀδελφῶν
          καὶ μαρτυρούντων σου τῇ ἀληθείᾳ,
               καθὼς σὺ ἐν ἀληθείᾳ περιπατεῖς.
  4 μειζοτέραν τούτων οὐκ ἔχω χαράν,
          ἵνα ἀκούω τὰ ἐμὰ τέκνα ἐν τῇ ἀληθείᾳ περιπατοῦντα.

===

5 ἀγαπητέ, πιστὸν ποιεῖς ὃ ἐὰν ἐργάσῃ εἰς τοὺς ἀδελφοὺς
          καὶ τοῦτο ξένους,
  6 οἳ ἐμαρτύρησάν σου τῇ ἀγάπῃ ἐνώπιον ἐκκλησίας,
     οὓς καλῶς ποιήσεις προπέμψας ἀξίως τοῦ θεοῦ·
     7 ὑπὲρ γὰρ τοῦ ὀνόματος ἐξῆλθον
          μηδὲν λαμβάνοντες ἀπὸ τῶν ἐθνικῶν.
  8 ἡμεῖς οὖν ὀφείλομεν ὑπολαμβάνειν τοὺς τοιούτους,
     ἵνα συνεργοὶ γινώμεθα τῇ ἀληθείᾳ.

---

9 ἔγραψά τι τῇ ἐκκλησίᾳ·
ἀλλ' ὁ φιλοπρωτεύων αὐτῶν Διοτρέφης οὐκ ἐπιδέχεται ἡμᾶς.
  10 διὰ τοῦτο,
     ἐὰν ἔλθω,
     ὑπομνήσω αὐτοῦ τὰ ἔργα
          ἃ ποιεῖ
               λόγοις πονηροῖς φλυαρῶν ἡμᾶς,
                    καὶ μὴ ἀρκούμενος ἐπὶ τούτοις
                    οὔτε αὐτὸς ἐπιδέχεται τοὺς ἀδελφοὺς
                    καὶ τοὺς βουλομένους κωλύει
                    καὶ ἐκ τῆς ἐκκλησίας ἐκβάλλει.

---

11 ἀγαπητέ, μὴ μιμοῦ τὸ κακὸν
          ἀλλὰ τὸ ἀγαθόν.
               ὁ ἀγαθοποιῶν ἐκ τοῦ θεοῦ ἐστιν·
               ὁ κακοποιῶν οὐχ ἑώρακεν τὸν θεόν.
12 Δημητρίῳ μεμαρτύρηται ὑπὸ πάντων

   καὶ ὑπὸ αὐτῆς τῆς ἀληθείας·
καὶ ἡμεῖς δὲ μαρτυροῦμεν,
καὶ οἶδας
 ὅτι ἡ μαρτυρία ἡμῶν ἀληθής ἐστιν.

===

13 πολλὰ εἶχον γράψαι σοι
 ἀλλ'οὐ θέλω διὰ μέλανος καὶ καλάμου σοι γράφειν·
14 ἐλπίζω δὲ εὐθέως σε ἰδεῖν,
καὶ στόμα πρὸς στόμα λαλήσομεν.

===

15 εἰρήνη σοι.
ἀσπάζονταί σε οἱ φίλοι.
ἀσπάζου τοὺς φίλους κατ' ὄνομα.

11

VOCATIVES IN THE EPISTLES

Introduction

In chapters four and six, I discussed the occurrences of vocatives in the narrative books of the NT.[1] In the Gospels and Acts more than two thirds of all vocatives occur in initial position within their sentence, and in narrative material this was taken as the normal, or unmarked, position. Various suggestions were put forward to account for the cases where the vocative was displaced to another position within its sentence. In brief, these were of two main categories. The first was one-word adverbial phrases, fossilised imperatives, and interjections, all of which routinely precede a vocative, with no sociolinguistic implications. The second was increased social distance between the interlocutors. These two categories sufficed to account not only for the displaced vocatives in the Gospels and Acts, but also for those in Revelation, where all the vocatives except one are displaced.

The opportunity has now arisen to examine the vocatives in the NT epistles, and this article presents the results.[2] In order to speed the investigation, two colleagues (Dr. Kees de Blois and Dr. Stefano Cotrozzi) independently produced for me lists of vocatives in the epistles, generated by different computer programmes. I was surprised to see that the two lists were by no

---

[1] Previously published in *BT* 47, no. 3 (1996): 313–321; *BT* 50, no. 1 (1999): 101–110.

[2] I am very grateful to Dr. Paul Ellingworth and Prof. Johannes P. Louw for their careful readings of a draft of this paper. Their comments have resulted in several improvements, but it hardly needs to be said that the remaining defects are all my own work.

means identical, and further investigation revealed that neither programme was able to recognise the numerous vocative occurrences of the Greek form *agapētoi* ("beloved"). So an additional search by the time-honoured method of reading the text was also necessary, and since this method is not infallible either, it remains possible that one or two examples of vocatives have escaped unnoticed. However, it is not likely that they would be numerous enough to distort the overall picture that emerges.

Distribution of Vocatives

I began with the naïve assumption that vocatives were distributed more or less evenly through the epistles, and was surprised to find that this was by no means the case. So the first step is to present the distribution in chart form (Figure 11.1 below). For this purpose I shall divide the NT epistles into two groups, Romans to Philemon (13 letters), and Hebrews to Jude (8 letters). This is a rough and ready division, and treats all the letters traditionally ascribed to Paul as by the same author. Since the second group contains letters by at least five different authors, it does not matter a great deal for present purposes if, say, the Pastoral Epistles are actually by someone other than Paul.

The figures in brackets give a maximum count, but we need to recognise a basic distinction between vocatives that show interaction between the writer and his entire readership, and those that do not. Those that do not are of two categories. The first consists of vocatives in OT quotations. These will have to be excluded from the investigation since they are really part of the context from which they are drawn, and so cannot carry information about the interaction between the NT writers and their readers. The totals at the bottoms of the columns exclude OT quotations, and refer only to the figures not bracketed. In addition to direct quotations from the OT (found in Rom 10.16; 11.3; 15.10, 11; 1 Cor 15.55 twice; Gal 4.27 twice; Heb 1.8; 1.10; 10.7; 12.5), the bracketed figures above include the expressions *abba ho patēr* in Rom 8.15 and Gal 4.6, and *marana tha* in 1 Cor 16.22. It can be seen at once that the frequency of vocatives is significantly higher in the non-Pauline letters: 65 vocatives in 735 non-Pauline verses is about one occurrence per 11 verses; 106 vocatives in 2,032 Pauline verses is only about one occurrence per 19 verses. In other words, vocatives are almost twice as frequent in the non-Pauline letters.

Vocatives in the Epistles

Pauline letters	No. of vocatives	Other letters	No. of vocatives
Romans	(19) 14	Hebrews	(9) 5
1 Corinthians	(27) 24	James	21
2 Corinthians	6	1 Peter	7
Galatians	(17) 14	2 Peter	5
Ephesians	6	1 John	20
Philippians	9	2 John	1
Colossians	6	3 John	3
1 Thessalonians	14	Jude	3
2 Thessalonians	7		
1 Timothy	3		
2 Timothy	1		
Titus	-		
Philemon	2		
Totals	106		65

Figure 11.1: Number of Vocatives in the Epistles

Virtual Addressees

The second category involves a phenomenon that has not occurred in the narrative books of the NT, namely vocatives directed to what I will call virtual addressees. These are not the total group to whom the letter is written, but, so to speak, sets of people who may or may not actually exist among the readership. They fall into two sub-sets. The first consists of sub-groups among the readership who definitely do exist, but are addressed as a class rather than as individuals for the purposes of ethical instruction. This sub-set is found in Ephesians and Colossians, in the same order in both cases: *hai gynaikes* (Eph 5.22; Col 3.18), *hoi andres* (Eph 5.25; Col 3.19), *ta tekna* (Eph 6.1; Col 3.20), *hoi pateres* (Eph 6.4; Col 3.21), *hoi douloi* (Eph 6.5; Col 3.22), and *hoi kyrioi* (Eph 6.9; Col 4.1). It is notable that apart from these vocatives to virtual addressees, those two letters contain no other vocatives at all.

A similar sub-set is found in 1 Peter where the vocatives are *hoi oiketai* (2.18), *hai gynaikes* (3.1), *hoi andres* (3.7), *neōteroi* (5.5), and possibly *pantes* (3.8). In this letter the groups named overlap only partially with those in Ephesians and Colossians, and in 1 Peter, moreover, there are other vocatives. In 1 John 2.12–14 there is a somewhat analogous series of vocatives (*teknia, pateres, neaniskoi, paidia, pateres, neaniskoi*) in which sub-groups among the total readership are addressed specifically. In 1 John too, these are not the only vocatives in the letter. All these examples of addressing sub-groups among the readers are naturally in the plural.

The second sub-set consists of hypothetical addressees who "exist" only in the writer's imagination for the purpose of holding an opinion that the writer goes on to reject. The best examples are in Romans. In 2.1 there is *ō anthrōpe pas ho krinōn*; in 2.3 the longer phrase *ō anthrōpe ho krinōn tous ta toiauta prassontes kai poiōn auta*; and in 9.20 just *ō anthrōpe*. In James 2.20 there is *ō anthrōpe kene*. These two examples are interesting in that they both occur in a paragraph that begins with the explicit establishment of a hypothetical opponent in the words *ereis oun moi* (Rom 9.19), and *all'erei tis* (James 2.18). These examples are all in the singular, and thus contrast with those in the first sub-set.

This distinction may help to determine the status of a few other examples which are not as clear as the ones cited so far. In James we also find the following vocative phrases: *moichalides* (4.4), *hamartōloi* and *dipsychoi* (4.8), *hoi legontes...* (4.13), and *hoi plousioi* (5.1). The last two are perhaps disputable as vocatives, but I treat them as such because they are followed by second person rather than third person verbs, a criterion that I have also applied elsewhere. It is not absolutely clear whether James regards all these groups as actually existing among his readership, but since he addresses them in the plural, I am inclined to think he does. In 1 Corinthians, on the other hand, there are some other unclear examples that are in the singular, namely *gynai* and *aner* in 7.16, and *aphrōn* in 15.36. None of these has the vocative particle *ō* as in Rom 2.1, 3; 9.20; James 2.23, but the last is clearly in the category of hypothetical addressees, since it follows immediately after the establishment of a hypothetical opponent by the words *alla erei tis* in 15.35, and is related to an opinion that Paul rejects. In 7.16, Paul is discussing a matter of principle which some of his readers might have regarded as disputable, and so I consider that the singular vocatives can in the light of the singulars in Romans and James, be seen in this context as part of the rhetorical technique of persuasion, and allocated to the sub-set of hypothetical addressees.

There are in total 35 examples (all cited above) of vocatives to virtual addressees, and it seems wise to put these on one side before considering the remaining 136 examples of "normal" vocatives, that is to say, those in which the writer addresses his entire readership as a group. Of these 88 are in the Pauline letters and 48 in the non-Pauline, that is to say about one in every 23 verses in Paul, and about one in every 15 verses in the other letters. If Hebrews is omitted from the count, the frequency in non-Pauline letters goes up to one vocative in every 10 verses.

Density of Vocatives

It is my impressionistic observation as a native user of English that a higher density of vocatives often indicates a closer relationship between the participants in a dialogue or correspondence. (One of the irritating features of junk mail is that it throws in unnecessary vocatives in order to try to create the illusion of a close relationship between the advertisers and the luckless recipients of their propaganda.) It seems worth considering whether this sociolinguistic feature could be a factor in explaining the distribution of vocatives in the epistles, at least in the Pauline epistles. Among these epistles, the ones with the highest density of vocatives are 1 Corinthians, Galatians, Philippians, and 1 and 2 Thessalonians. In the first two cases, Paul had a very intense even if rather strained relationship with the recipients, and in the other cases, a very warm and friendly relationship. By the time Paul wrote 2 Corinthians, there was probably more stress and less warmth in the relationship, and this may account for the decreased density of vocatives. Even so, the density of vocatives in 2 Corinthians is still comparable with that in Romans.

In both Colossians and Ephesians, on the other hand, there are no vocatives except the ones to virtual addressees in the lists of ethical instructions. Colossians 2.1 indicates that Paul was not personally acquainted with the Christian community there, so the absence of vocatives in this letter is hardly surprising. However, Paul had certainly spent a significant amount of time in Ephesus (Acts 19.10), so the lack of vocatives in Ephesians is more puzzling. Perhaps it lends support to the view that this letter was originally a circular letter to several churches, and was not addressed exclusively to Christians in Ephesus. (Compare the textual problems in Eph 1.1 concerning the destination of the letter.)

The infrequency of vocatives in the pastoral letters is rather unexpected, especially as they are of higher than average frequency in the only other letter to an individual, that to Philemon. This issue will be discussed further when we examine the nature of the vocatives used.

In the non-Pauline letters, the notable features are the low density of vocatives in Hebrews, and the high densities in James and 1 John. The former is readily accounted for by the lack of any specification of the addressees. The addressees in James are described in a manner that may at first seem vague ("the twelve tribes in the Dispersion" in RSV), but could well have been a coded way of referring to people well-known to the writer. In 1 John no addressees are stated, but both the density and the nature of the vocatives point towards a close relationship between writer and readers. This will be discussed again when we study the actual vocatives used.

"Normal" Vocatives: Defining Displacement

As noted in the introduction, in the Gospels and Acts the unmarked position of a vocative is at the beginning of its sentence, where it occurs in about 70% of examples. In the letters on the other hand, only 28 examples out of 136 (about 21%) occur indisputably at the beginning of a sentence, a striking difference. Are these figures to be taken at face value, or are there conditioning factors at work? In any case, what are we to make of this situation?

First of all, it is necessary to examine the data and define what constitutes a displaced vocative in the epistolary genre. In the narrative books we recognised the following lexico-syntactic items as automatically displacing a vocative: one-word adverbial phrases, fossilised imperatives, and interjections. In the epistles there are no interjections, so it remains to look at one-word adverbial phrases and fossilised imperatives. The only possible fossilised imperative is *age* in the repeated phrase *age nyn* in James 4.13; 5.1. It is not clear whether this is fossilised, or is a genuine imperative. The fact that the imperative is singular, but is followed both times by a plural vocative strongly suggests that it is fossilised, but as there are more than a dozen examples in James of an imperative accompanying a vocative, it might also be possible to treat it as genuine, especially in the absence of any examples of unquestionably fossilised forms. Here the phrase seems to impart a scolding tone that fits its contexts well, and is certainly compatible with increased social distance.

The category of one-word adverbial phrases is harder to define in the epistles than in the narrative books. The only example of such a phrase which has already occurred in narrative is *nai adelphe* in Philemon 20. Probably *homoiōs hai gynaikes* (1 Pet 3.1) and *homoiōs neōteroi* (1 Pet 5.5) could also be included, but these both occur in the ethical instruction lists and are not among the vocatives currently under investigation. Another candidate for admission to this category is *(to) loipon* (2 Cor 13.11; Phil 3.1; 4.8). It seems reasonable to count the article and the noun as a single unit rather than as two separate words, especially as the noun occurs in this adverbial function both with the article (in Philippians) and without (in 2 Corinthians). The phrase *to loipon* is in these three cases followed by an imperative verb after the vocative. An example where *to loipon* is accompanied by an imperative verb before the vocative is in 2 Thess 3.1. Perhaps this word order gives a greater urgency to the imperative.

How rigorously then should we insist that the adverbial phrase contains only one word? The adverb *nyn* as in James 4.13; 5.1 above also precedes vocatives in 1 Cor 14.6 and 1 John 2.28, but in the first case the full phrase is *nyn de adelphoi*, and in the second *kai nyn teknia*. If it is assumed that particles and conjunctions like *de* and *kai* are functioning at some level higher than that of the sentence, then it becomes permissible to ignore them for the purposes of deciding whether vocatives are displaced within the sentence. (Thus *kai hoi pateres* (Eph 6.4) and *kai hoi kyrioi* (Eph 6.9) can be regarded as initial vocatives, though these again are part of ethical instruction lists and not immediately under investigation.) When an article and a noun are accepted as a single unit, then *to de telos* (1 Pet 3.8) also enters the category of a unitary adverbial phrase. If the same assumption is extended to include *oun*, then the following would also be accounted for as examples of obligatory displacement: *ara oun adelphoi* (Rom 8.12; 2 Thess 2.15), and *loipon oun adelphoi* (1 Thess 4.1).

There are several other examples where *de, kai*, and *oun* occur before a vocative with one other word, such as *kagō* (1 Cor 3.1), *tauta de* (1 Cor 4.6), *hymeis de* (Gal 4.28; 1 Thess 5.4; 2 Thess 3.13; Jude 17, 20), *egō de* (Gal 5.11), *hēmeis de* (1 Thess 2.17), *sy de* (1 Tim 6.11), *sy oun* (2 Tim 2.1), and *hymeis oun* (2 Pet 3.17). These examples all link the particle or conjunction with a pronoun rather than an adverbial phrase. The conclusion from the narrative books was that displacement of the vocative by a pronoun is a genuine displacement indicating increased social distance. In letters, these emphatic pronouns often serve to switch focus from one referent to another. Switching from one addressee to another by means of a vocative also occurred in some of the speeches in Acts (for instance Acts 26.27).

If particles and conjunctions occurring alone before a vocative are excluded from displacing items, then ten vocatives will cease to be regarded as displaced. The first group is those following *dio(per)* in 1 Cor 10.14; Gal 4.31; 2 Pet 3.14 (but not *dio mallon* in 2 Pet 1.10 since this includes an adverb). The second follows *hothen*, with a single instance in Heb 3.1. The largest and most interesting group of examples of this type, however, are those following *hōste* (Rom 7.4; 1 Cor 11.33; 14.39; 15.58; Phil 2.12; 4.1). Most of them occur near the end of a paragraph rather than near the beginning, and this raises the question whether *hōste* with a vocative always introduces a summary or conclusion. If it does, this will affect our understanding of the paragraph breaks with respect to Rom 7.4 and Phil 2.12, as discussed below.

To sum up then, the detailed examination of apparently displaced vocatives suggests that ten examples preceded only by a conjunction are not really displaced after all. This means that the statistics have to be revised to say that 38 examples out of 136 are in initial position, that is about 28%. This is an almost exact reversal of the position in the Gospels and Acts, and requires some explanation.

In many languages, not least in India and South East Asia, the very fact of writing something rather than saying it compels the use of more formal language, and thus increases the social distance between writer and reader(s). I suggest that some similar constraint may have been in operation in New Testament times, and that the higher frequency of displaced vocatives in the epistles may be an indication that geographical distance was linguistically equated with social distance. Thus the displaced vocative may have become the unmarked form in the epistles, so that the challenge in this genre may be to explain the initial vocatives as the marked forms.

Displacing Elements

The next step is to examine the elements that precede vocative forms, and cause their displacement. It is hardly a surprise to see that certain phrases and clauses occur regularly as displacing items. They often involve verbs of cognition or locution. Examples of verbs of cognition are the following:

> Rom 1.13 *ou thelō de hymas agnoein adelphoi*
> Rom 11.25 *ou gar thelō hymas agnoein adelphoi*
> Rom 15.14 *pepeismai de adelphoi*
> 1 Cor 10.1 *ou thelō gar hymas agnoein adelphoi*
> 1 Cor 15.1 *gnōrizō de hymin adelphoi*
> 2 Cor 1.8 *ou gar thelomen hymas agnoein adelphoi*
> 2 Cor 8.1 *gnōrizomen de hymin adelphoi*
> Gal 1.11 *gnōrizō gar hymin adelphoi*
> Phil 1.12 *ginōskein de hymas boulomai adelphoi*
> 1 Thess 4.13 *ou thelomen de hymas agnoein adelphoi*
> Heb 6.9 *pepeismetha de peri hymōn agapētoi*

(At this point one might also include the six examples with *graphō/egrapsa hymin* displacing a vocative in 1 John 2.12–14, though these are outside the immediate range of discussion.) There is one counter-example in 1 Cor 12.1 *peri de tōn pneumatikōn adelphoi ou thelō hymas agnoein*, where the clause with the verb of cognition follows the vocative. This is probably accounted for by the occurrence as a displacing element of the formula *peri de* frequent in 1 Corinthians as a topic-changing marker of a new paragraph or section. A similar example is found in 1 Thess 5.1 *peri de tōn chronōn kai tōn kairōn adelphoi*.

Perhaps second and third person examples should also be included:

Rom 7.1 *ē agnoeite adelphoi*
1 Cor 1.11 *edēlōthē gar moi adelphoi*
1 Cor 1.26 *blepete gar tēn klēsin hymōn adelphoi*
Phil 4.15 *oidate de kai hymeis Philippēsioi*
1 Thess 2.1 *autoi gar oidate adelphoi*
1 Thess 2.9 *mnēmoneuete gar adelphoi*
Heb 3.12 *blepete adelphoi*
2 Pet 3.8 *hen de touto mē lanthanetō hymas adelphoi*

Examples of verbs of locution are:

Rom 12.1 *parakalō oun hymas adelphoi*
Rom 15.30 *parakalō de hymas adelphoi*
Rom 16.17 *parakalō de hymas adelphoi*
1 Cor 1.10 *parakalō de hymas adelphoi*
1 Cor 7.29 *touto de phēmi adelphoi*
1 Cor 15.50 *touto de phēmi adelphoi*
1 Cor 16.15 *parakalō de hymas adelphoi*
Phil 4.3 *nai erōtō kai se gnēsie S/syzyge*
1 Thess 4.10 *parakaloumen de hymas adelphoi*
1 Thess 5.12 *erōtōmen de hymas adelphoi*
1 Thess 5.14 *parakaloumen de hymas adelphoi*
2 Thess 2.1 *erōtōmen de hymas adelphoi*
2 Thess 3.6 *parangellomen de hymin adelphoi*
Heb 13.22 *parakalō de hymas adelphoi*
2 John 5 *erōtō se kyria*

It seems perfectly plausible that first person verbs of instruction or request should be softened by displacement of an accompanying vocative. There is however one counter-example where this does not happen, *agapētoi parakalō* in 1 Pet 2.11. It is less obvious why second and third person verbs should also be accompanied by displacement, unless it is a case of pressure of analogy from the more common first person forms.

I have not been able to discern any other lexical trends in displacing elements. It is however notable that there is a significant number of examples of imperatives, for instance in the following places:

1 Cor 1.26 *blepete gar tēn klēsin hymōn adelphoi*
Gal 4.12 *ginesthe hōs egō hoti kagō hōs hymeis adelphoi*
Phil 3.17 *symmimētai mou ginesthe adelphoi*
2 Thess 3.1 *to loipon proseuchesthe adelphoi*
Heb 3.12 *blepete adelphoi*
2 Pet 3.8 *hen de touto mē lanthanetō hymas adelphoi*
1 John 3.13 *kai mē thaumazete adelphoi*

There are no less than nine examples in James, five positive and four negative: does this perhaps indicate a more authoritarian tone in James than in any other letter? The examples are:

James 1.2 *pasan charan hēgēsasthe adelphoi mou*
James 1.16 *mē planasthe adelphoi mou agapētoi*
James 1.19 *iste adelphoi mou agapētoi*
James 2.5 *akousate adelphoi mou agapētoi*
James 3.1 *mē polloi didaskaloi ginesthe adelphoi mou*
James 4.11 *mē katalaleite allēlōn adelphoi*
James 5.7 *makrothymēsate oun adelphoi*
James 5.9 *mē stenazete adelphoi*
James 5.10 *hypodeigma labete adelphoi*

The Vocative Forms Used

In the 136 "normal" vocatives that we are now studying, by far the most common vocative form is *adelphoi*, which occurs 92 times, 71 of them in the Pauline letters, the two occurrences in Philemon having the singular form *adelphe*. Of the remaining 21 occurrences, no less than 15 are in James. In 70 of the 92 instances *adelphoi* occurs on its own. In 14 cases it is lengthened to *adelphoi mou*, and in 5 to *adelphoi mou agapētoi*. In Heb 3.1, there is the unique *adelphoi hagioi*. It is plausible to suggest that the longer *adelphoi* formulae, especially *adelphoi mou agapētoi*, show greater warmth than the basic form. In the letters of Paul, *adelphoi mou agapētoi* never occurs more than once per letter. It is found in 1 Cor 15.58, and in Phil 4.1 is expanded even further to the extravagant *adelphoi mou agapētoi kai epipothētoi chara kai stephanos mou*. In 1 Thess 1.4 there is the related but less personal form *adelphoi ēgapēmenoi hypo tou theou*, and in 2 Thess 2.13 the similar *adelphoi ēgapēmenoi hypo kyriou*. The adjectival vocative form *agapētoi* occurs without a noun 24 times, in two of which it is lengthened to *agapētoi mou* (1 Cor 10.14; Phil 2.12). Of these 24 occurrences only five are in the Pauline letters. Nine are in the letters of John, six in the letters of Peter, three in the letter of Jude, and one in Hebrews.

What conclusions can be drawn from these figures? Probably *agapētoi* as a term of endearment represents a closer relationship or greater warmth between writer and readers than *adelphoi*. On the other hand perhaps it just reflects a more extrovert or flamboyant personality on the part of the writer. Paul is much more sparing in his use of this term than John, and perhaps this supports the view that John was an old man when he wrote. Such terminology from an elderly and respected figure is less open to misinterpretation than from a man in his prime. It is also possible however, that epistolary fashions changed with the passage of time, or with geographical location. Fifty years ago, people in England would often end letters with "Yours truly," but one very seldom sees this formula today. Moreover, I have noticed that letters from Indian speakers of English often end with "Yours affectionately," a formula which I cannot recall ever seeing in letters written by native speakers of British English.

The remaining 20 vocatives show considerable diversity in form. There are three examples of Paul addressing his readers by their location (*Korinthioi* in 2 Cor 6.11, *ō anoētoi Galatai* in Gal 3.1, and *Philippēsioi* in Phil 4.15); it is hard to see any particular sociolinguistic significance in this. A personal name is used in two, or more likely three, places (*teknon Timothee* in 1 Tim 1.18, *ō Timothee* in 1 Tim 6.20, and probably *gnēsie Syzyge* in Phil 4.3). I am inclined to regard the last of these as a personal name rather than a description because there is no other example in the NT of an individual being addressed anonymously with a descriptive term. The occurrence of *ō anthrōpe theou* in 1 Tim 6.11 does not constitute such an example since Timothy has already been identified by name in 1 Tim 1.18.

The use of *teknon* in combination with the name Timothy leads on to a consideration of this and related forms on their own. In 2 Tim 2.1 we find Timothy addressed as *teknon mou*, and the Galatians as *tekna mou* in Gal 4.19. All the other examples are in the letters of John, and show the diminutive *teknia* in 1 John 2.28; 3.7, 18; 4.4; 5.21, expanded to *teknia mou* on the first occurrence in 1 John 2.1. John also has the similar and probably more intimate form *paidia* in 1 John 2.18 (compare John 21.5; 1 John 2.14). Just as in the case of Timothy we know that he was much younger than Paul, so in the case of John we may infer that he was much older than his readers, an inference in line with ancient tradition. The other vocative used by John is *kyria*, addressed figuratively to a church in 2 John 5.

The remaining three cases are all participial vocatives, and are all in Galatians: *hoi hypo nomon thelontes einai* in 4.21, *hoitines en nomō dikaiousthe* in 5.4, and *hymeis hoi pneumatikoi* in 6.1. Does not the clustering of such forms in one letter subtly reinforce the exasperation with his readers which the writer undoubtedly felt?

How can we assess the relative interactional significance of the different forms used as vocatives? The most common form *adelphoi* must be regarded as the most neutral form. Where its occurrences are densest, it probably reflects a closer relationship between writer and readers. Where it is lengthened to *adelphoi mou*, and especially *adelphoi mou agapētoi*, it probably conveys additional warmth. The second most common form *agapētoi* should surely be seen as indicating a basically more intimate relationship between writer and readers than *adelphoi*. Where this is lengthened to *agapētoi mou*, it may be even more sociolinguistically significant.

It remains to observe a few other distinctive points. The first is the scarcity of vocatives in the Pastoral Epistles. We know from Acts that Paul had a close relationship with Timothy (compare 1 Cor 4.17; 1 Thess 3.2), so we might have expected that, whether those letters come from Paul himself or from a skilled imitator of Paul, this closeness would be reflected in a higher density of vocatives in the letters to Timothy, but it is not. However (with the possible exception of Phil 4.3), it is only in the letters to Timothy that a personal name is used in a vocative (1 Tim 1.18; 6.20), and this surely indicates a close relationship. Moreover, apart from Gal 4.19 (*tekna mou*), the intimate term *teknon (mou)* occurs as a vocative only in 1 Tim 1.18 and 2 Tim 2.1. It is repeated in the opening greetings in 1 Tim 1.2 and 2 Tim 1.2, where it is linked with *gnēsiō* and *agapētō* respectively. Elsewhere *tekna* is used by Paul of his addressees only descriptively, and only in the letters to Corinth (1 Cor 4.14 *tekna mou agapēta*; 2 Cor 6.13 *hōs teknois legō*), where as we have seen already, his relationships are known to have been close. In the letter to Titus alone of all the NT letters there are no vocatives of any kind. From Acts we may infer that Titus was more like an equal colleague of Paul than a protégé, though it must be noted that he is described as *gnēsiō teknō* in Titus 1.4, just as Timothy is in 1 Tim 1.2.

The second point is the high density of vocatives in James, combined with a high frequency of accompanying imperatives. Though James uses the relatively bland term *adelphoi*, it is softened to *adelphoi mou* eight times, and to *adelphoi mou agapētoi* an additional three times. Would it be too fanciful to say that this combination creates the impression of a benign despot? I am reminded, perhaps a little unfairly (though not at all unkindly), of the principal of the theological college I attended many years ago!

The third point is the preponderance of *agapētoi* over *adelphoi* in the letters of Peter, John, and Jude (18 occurrences as against two). It seems impossible to decide whether this difference arises from the personalities of the writers or from variations in epistolary style in different areas and different times. In the case of 1 John, we must note the occurrence eight times (once in the section 2.12–14 that is outside the present range of interest) of the diminutive form *teknia*, a term found elsewhere in the NT only once (John 13.33). The combination of a term of endearment with a diminutive term for children, does, as noted above, support the traditional view that the writer was an old man.

The Position of Vocatives: Within the Sentence

It remains to discuss the positions of the vocative forms in the epistles, both within the sentence and within the paragraph. In the case of the ethical instruction lists in Ephesians, Colossians and 1 Peter, the vocatives can all be treated as initial within their sentence, and we may safely assume that the purpose of this is to make clear a change of addressee.

There are rather few examples of a vocative occurring at the end of a sentence. According to the punctuation as printed in UBS[4], the clearest examples of this are in 1 Cor 14.26, Gal 6.18, Phlm 7, and James 1.16 and 4.11. It would be tempting to suggest that the punctuation in UBS[4] should be altered so that these vocatives occur at the beginning of the next sentence. This might work in 1 Cor 14.26 and James 1.16, though it brings no obvious advantage, and sounds less natural in both cases. It is however impossible in the other cases. In Gal 6.18, the vocative occurs in the last sentence of the letter, and is followed only by the word *amēn*. In Phlm 7, the next sentence, which is probably the beginning of a new paragraph, begins with *dio*, and as there is no other example of a vocative preceding *dio*, changing the punctuation in this instance would create more problems than it solved. In James 4.11, the sentence with the plural vocative *adelphoi* is very short, and includes an imperative verb, a common combination in James. The following sentence is a generic statement in the singular, so adding a plural vocative to it would create unnecessary complications.

There are a few more possible examples that depend on changing the punctuation of UBS[4]. This is limited to places where a well-formed finite clause is followed by a colon or comma that might be changed to a full stop. The first is in Rom 2.1, but this is one of the instances of a virtual addressee, and can be left aside. Other places include 1 Cor 16.15, Gal 5.13, James 1.19; 2.5, but in none of them is there any advantage in changing the printed punctuation. With so few clear examples of a sentence-final vocative, it is impossible to say what its pragmatic or sociolinguistic effect may be.

In James 4.8 in a passage directed to virtual addressees, there are two more examples of vocatives, each at the end of its clause within a single sentence, and both (*hamartōloi* and *dipsychoi*) unique in the NT as vocatives. In these cases, the vocatives are covert predicates, to use the term used in my earlier articles.

Of the 136 vocatives that are addressed to the readers as a whole, we have already observed that 38 can be considered as occupying the initial position within the sentence. Of these 10 follow a conjunction as described above, and our attention will now be focussed on the other 28. Does the occurrence of a vocative at the beginning of a sentence carry any pragmatic or sociolinguistic implications? Again the distribution of sentence-initial vocatives is very uneven. Of the nine examples in Paul's letters, four are in Galatians (Gal 3.1, 15; 4.19; 6.1), and no other letter has more than one (Rom 10.1; 1 Cor 14.20; Phil 3.13; 1 Thess 5.25; 1 Tim 6.20). Of the other 19 examples, 14 are in the letters of John (1 John 2.1, 7, 18; 3.2, 7, 18, 21; 4.1, 7, 11; 5.21; 3 John 2, 5, 11), two each in James (2.1; 5.19) and 1 Peter (2.11; 4.12), and one in Jude (v. 3). It is easier to claim that this distribution must have some meaning than to discern what that meaning may be! That almost half of the Pauline examples are in one relatively short letter, and that letter the very one in which Paul is at his most agitated strongly suggests that sentence-initial vocatives convey something about the emotional state of the writer. (See especially in Gal 3.1 and 4.19.) It is hard, however, to transfer this conclusion to 1 John despite its 11 examples of initial vocatives. Perhaps there the density of initial vocatives somehow reflects the writer's personality rather than his emotional state. The only other notable correlation is that sentence-initial vocatives co-occur with imperatives and hortatives in 11 cases, but since non-initial vocatives also co-occur with imperatives frequently, it is hard to see any special significance in this.

The Position of Vocatives: Within the Paragraph

This is a very complex topic. I have started with the paragraph divisions of UBS[4], though experience has taught me to look at these with a very sceptical eye. I have compared them with the paragraph breaks in NA[27] and in the RSV, and have in some cases made my own recommendations which do not correspond with any of these. Ideally, this discussion would be set in the context of an analysis of all paragraph divisions in the epistles, but that is unfortunately beyond the scope of the present essay. Such an analysis would surely offer enough material for a book!

Of the 136 vocatives classified above as "normal" vocatives, almost two thirds occur in the first sentence of a paragraph, and this is clearly the commonest place for a vocative to occur. I refrain from giving exact numbers, because what counts as the first sentence of a paragraph depends on where one reckons the paragraph to begin, and since the occurrence of a vocative is one of the possible factors in making this decision, the argument could in some cases become circular. In the majority of cases, however, the decision would find general agreement. Many of these examples occur following the common displacing elements listed earlier, involving verbs of cognition or locution. Since a vocative near the beginning of a paragraph is, so to speak, the default option, I shall not discuss these examples any further. Interest lies rather in the residual examples where the vocative occurs in some other position. These fall into three groups.

The first group comprises those cases where a vocative occurs very near the end of a letter. In these instances, the question of whether such vocatives are at the beginning of a paragraph or not is of marginal interest, because the endings of letters often consist of several short sentences with little evidence of paragraph structure to link them. The seven members of this group are found in Gal 6.18 (*adelphoi*); 1 Thess 5.25 (*adelphoi*); 1 Tim 6.20 (*ō Timothee*);

Heb 13.22 (*adelphoi*); James 5.19 (*adelphoi mou*); 2 Pet 3.17 (*agapētoi*); and 1 John 5.21 (*teknia*).

The second group comprises those cases where a vocative occurs near the end of a paragraph. We have already noted that in several of these, the sentence in which the vocative occurs is introduced by *hōste*. This raised the question of whether the occurrence of *hōste* with a vocative is in itself a marker of the conclusion of a paragraph. In four places (1 Cor 11.33; 14.39; 15.58; Phil 4.1) there is no real doubt, but if *hōste* means that paragraphs end at the end of the sentences with the vocatives in Rom 7.4 and Phil 2.12, then we should mark new paragraphs at the beginning of Rom 7.5 and Phil 2.14. I cannot see any obvious reason why this should not be done.

There are several more cases where a vocative occurs in the vicinity of some other item that may serve to indicate that a paragraph is coming to a conclusion. The following are examples. In 2 Cor 7.1 *oun* occurs in the same sentence with the vocative. This verse is widely recognised as the conclusion of a paragraph. The combination *ara oun* co-occurs with vocatives in Rom 8.12 and 2 Thess 2.15, and although both these verses are marked as the beginning of a paragraph in UBS⁴ and NA²⁷, I can see no reason why they should not be analysed as the conclusion of the previous paragraph. RSV does indeed begin a new paragraph at 2 Thess 2.16 (rather than 2.15). RSV also has a dash at the end of Romans 8.12, which again suggests that it sees some sort of disjunction between vv. 12 and 13. In Gal 5.11, the vocative occurs in a short interrogative sentence, and the next sentence begins with *ara*; although the two are not here in the same sentence, the combination in close proximity may still serve to mark a conclusion. Indeed a paragraph break at the end of 5.12 is widely recognised.

A tricky question lies in the paragraph division around Gal 4.31–5.1. The vocative *adelphoi* occurs in 4.31, and is followed by *oun* in 5.1. I am inclined to think this combination supports a paragraph break after 5.1 (as UBS⁴ and RSV) rather than before it (as NA²⁷). The conjunction *dio* also occurs in 4.31, and although this seems to mark the beginning of a new paragraph in such places as Eph 2.11; 4.25; Phlm 8; 2 Pet 3.14, there is no obvious reason why it should always do so. If it is part of a cluster of indicators of a conclusion in Gal 4.31, then may not *dioper* also have a similar function in 1 Cor 10.14.? Despite the fact that UBS⁴, NA²⁷ and RSV all begin a new paragraph there, the content of 10.14 relates more readily to the previous paragraph than to the following one.

There are a few examples where a sentence with a vocative occurs near the end of a paragraph, and lacks any supporting indicator of a conclusion, but the next sentence begins with what is clearly an opening marker. Such a case is in 1 Cor 7.24, where the following verse begins with the formula *peri de* that unquestionably marks the beginnings of several major divisions in this letter. Another possible case is in 1 Cor 7.29a, where the vocative *adelphoi* is preceded by *touto de phēmi*. The second half of the verse begins with *to loipon*, a phrase that is an opening marker in several places such as Phil 3.1; 4.8; 1 Thess 4.1; 2 Thess 3.1. So perhaps 1 Cor 7.29a should be seen as closing the previous paragraph, and 7.29b as beginning a new one, though the question is not very clear. The formula *touto de phēmi* occurs again in 1 Cor 15.50, and since the following verse begins with *idou*, which is a likely opening marker, 15.50 is probably better analysed as belonging to the end of the previous paragraph with RSV than taken to begin a new paragraph, with UBS[4] and NA[27].

The third group comprises those cases where a vocative occurs in the middle of a paragraph. Examples are found in for instance Rom 10.1; 12.19; 1 Thess 2.14; 3.7; James 5.9. There does not seem to be sufficient evidence to enable generalisations to be made about this group. Indeed, its apparent existence may call into question the paragraph divisions in printed editions of the Greek text, and a lot more study is needed before a reliable system of paragraph divisions can be regarded as firmly established.

Implications for Translators

The use of vocatives in the epistles shows surprising variation, not only between different writers, but also between different letters from the same writer. Our understanding of the significance of these variations is far from complete. Before translators can decide how to handle these variations, they will need to investigate how vocatives are used in epistolary discourse in the receptor language. Such information is almost never already available, and discovering it presents a serious challenge. Yet the ability to mirror not the superficial form, but the interpersonal and socio-linguistic impact of the nature, frequency, and distribution of the vocatives in the NT letters will surely play a significant part in achieving a natural translation. Much work remains to be done!

12

STRUCTURAL SIMILARITIES IN 1 AND 2 THESSALONIANS: COMPARATIVE DISCOURSE ANATOMY

Introduction

On the whole it is not difficult to discern where the discourse breaks occur in Paul's two letters to the Christians in Thessalonica. The structural outlines given in the Translator's Handbook can be accepted as a useful starting point, though some adjustments will be proposed. It is, however, considerably harder to perceive hierarchical relationships between the paragraphs that are produced by recognising the discourse breaks.

The purposes of this article are to examine the structural parallels between the two letters, and to arrive at some tentative conclusions about the hierarchical relationships of the divisions in the letters.

Comparison of the Two Letters

Both letters begin with an opening greeting formula such as characterises most of the NT letters (1 Thess 1.1 and 2 Thess 2.1–2), and both end with the analogous closing greeting formula (1 Thess 5.28 and 2 Thess 3.18). In both letters these closing greetings are preceded by some words written in the author's own hand. These "autograph" units use the first person singular form of the verb rather than the first person plural that is normal in the rest of each letter for reference to the author and his associates. The first person plural is used in 1 Thess 2.18 and 3.1 even when Paul is speaking about himself alone, and the first person singular occurs outside the autograph units only in 1 Thess 3.5 and 2 Thess 2.5. The formulaic greetings and autograph material stand outside the main body of the letter and will not be further discussed in this article. Whether the closing greeting was also written by the same hand as the autograph cannot be determined with certainty, but it seems very probable.[1]

The main discourse feature that commands general agreement is that the principal division in 1 Thess comes at 4.1, and the principal division in 2 Thess comes at 3.1. In both letters the new unit follows a prayer that has a parallel at the end of the second section (1 Thess 3.11–13 parallel with 1 Thess 5.23–24, and 2 Thess 2.16–17, parallel with 2 Thess 3.16). The beginnings of the new units are marked by the phrases Λοιπὸν οὖν in the first letter, and Τὸ λοιπόν in the second. In both cases, RSV, TEV and most other English versions translate as "Finally," but since in neither letter does this phrase indicate that the end of the letter is imminent, something like "Next," "Furthermore," or "Now" (as in The Translator's New Testament) would be more appropriate in English.[2] In both letters the phrase is followed by the vocative ἀδελφοί ("brothers"), which in the epistles generally is associated more often than not with the beginning of a new discourse unit. In 2 Thess 3.1, this is further reinforced by the occurrence before the vocative of the imperative verb προσεύχεσθε ("pray"); an imperative is also quite common at or near the beginning of the unit. In each letter, the first section deals more with personal and doctrinal issues and the second more with pastoral and ethical issues. In the first letter, the second section is about three quarters of the length of the first, and in the second letter about half.

The other very noticeable feature of these letters is that they contain a greater frequency of vocatives than any other of Paul's letters (14 in 1 Thess and 7 in 2 Thess). This high frequency is very probably an indication of the

---

[1] See Jeffrey A.D. Weima, *Neglected Endings: The Significance of the Pauline Letter Closings* (T&T Clark, 1994), 122.

[2] This would correspond with meaning 89.98 in Louw and Nida (L-N). However in a personal communication, Prof. Johannes Louw expressed the opinion that in 2 Thess 3.1 Τὸ λοιπόν really does carry the meaning "finally" (meaning 61.14 in L-N). Even if this is the case, however, the fact that the same Greek word is used in both letters in the first sentence following a prayer still supports the view that a major structural unit begins at this point. In Philippians, it seems likely that both meanings of Τὸ λοιπόν occur, "furthermore" in 3.1, and "finally" in 4.8.

warmth of the apostle's relationship with this particular church, but from a discourse point of view, the interesting feature is the distribution of the vocatives rather than their frequency. In an earlier article[3] I have reported that about two thirds of all vocatives in all the epistles occur in the opening sentence of a paragraph. This means that in a majority of cases the occurrence of a vocative, if not a diagnostic indicator of a new paragraph, is at least supporting evidence for such an analysis. This certainly seems to be a helpful approach in the letters to the Thessalonians, where most of the vocatives can either confidently or at least plausibly be taken as occurring in the first sentence of a discourse unit or sub-unit. Figure 12.1 displays both the major parallels of discourse features between the two letters, and also a tentative set of discourse unit divisions and subdivisions obtained when each vocative is understood to belong to a different (sub)-unit.

1 THESS	2 THESS
1.1 Greeting	1.1–2 Greeting
=============================	=============================
1.2–10 1.2–5a εὐχαριστοῦμεν τῷ θεῷ πάντοτε… ἔμπροσθεν τοῦ θεοῦ καὶ πατρὸς ἡμῶν… ἀδελφοὶ ἠγαπημένοι ὑπὸ [τοῦ] θεοῦ,… 1.5b–10 καθὼς οἴδατε οἷοι ἐγενήθημεν [ἐν] ὑμῖν δι' ὑμᾶς/,/ 6 καὶ ὑμεῖς μιμηταὶ ἡμῶν ἐγενήθητε…	1.3–12 εὐχαριστεῖν ὀφείλομεν τῷ θεῷ πάντοτε… ἀδελφοί,… ἀπὸ προσώπου τοῦ κυρίου…
2.1–16 2.1–8 αὐτοὶ γὰρ οἴδατε, ἀδελφοί,… 2.9–12 μνημονεύετε γάρ, ἀδελφοί,… 2.13 καὶ διὰ τοῦτο καὶ ἡμεῖς εὐχαριστοῦμεν τῷ θεῷ… 2.14–16 ὑμεῖς γὰρ μιμηταὶ ἐγενήθητε, ἀδελφοί,…	2.1–12 2.1–4 ἐρωτῶμεν δὲ ὑμᾶς, ἀδελφοί,… 2.5–10 οὐ μνημονεύετε… 2.11–12 καὶ διὰ τοῦτο…

---

[3] "Vocatives in the Epistles," ch. 11 of this volume, previously published in *BT* 57, no. 3 (2006): 109–115.

2.17–3.13 2.17–3.5 ἡμεῖς δέ, ἀδελφοί,... ἔμπροσθεν τοῦ κυρίου ἡμῶν Ἰησοῦ... 3.6–10 ἄρτι δὲ ἐλθόντος Τιμοθέου... διὰ τοῦτο παρεκλήθημεν, ἀδελφοί,... ἔμπροσθεν τοῦ θεοῦ καὶ πατρὸς ἡμῶν... 3.11–13 αὐτὸς δὲ ὁ θεὸς καὶ πατὴρ ἡμῶν καὶ ὁ κύριος ἡμῶν Ἰησοῦς...	2.13–17 2.13–14 ἡμεῖς δὲ ὀφείλομεν εὐχαριστεῖν τῷ θεῷ πάντοτε... ἀδελφοὶ ἠγαπημένοι ὑπὸ κυρίου,... 2.15 ἄρα οὖν, ἀδελφοί,... 2.16–17 αὐτὸς δὲ ὁ κύριος ἡμῶν Ἰησοῦς Χριστὸς καὶ [ὁ] θεὸς ὁ πατὴρ ἡμῶν...
============================	============================
4.1–8 λοιπὸν οὖν, ἀδελφοί, ἐρωτῶμεν ὑμᾶς καὶ παρακαλοῦμεν...	3.1–5 τὸ λοιπὸν προσεύχεσθε, ἀδελφοί,...
4.9–12 περὶ δὲ τῆς φιλαδελφίας... παρακαλοῦμεν δὲ ὑμᾶς, ἀδελφοί,...	3.6–12 παραγγέλλομεν δὲ ὑμῖν, ἀδελφοί,... παραγγέλλομεν καὶ παρακαλοῦμεν...
4.13–18 οὐ θέλομεν δὲ ὑμᾶς ἀγνοεῖν, ἀδελφοί, περὶ τῶν κοιμωμένων... ὥστε παρακαλεῖτε ἀλλήλους...	
5.1–11 5.1–3 περὶ δὲ τῶν χρόνων καὶ τῶν καιρῶν, ἀδελφοί,... 5.4–11 ὑμεῖς δέ, ἀδελφοί,... ἄρα οὖν... διὸ παρακαλεῖτε ἀλλήλους...	3.13–15 ὑμεῖς δέ, ἀδελφοί,...
5.12–22 5.12–13 ἐρωτῶμεν δὲ ὑμᾶς, ἀδελφοί,... 5.14–22 παρακαλοῦμεν δὲ ὑμᾶς, ἀδελφοί,...	
5.23–24 αὐτὸς δὲ ὁ θεὸς τῆς εἰρήνης ἁγιάσαι...	3.16 αὐτὸς δὲ ὁ κύριος τῆς εἰρήνης δῴη...
============================	============================
5.25–27 Autograph ἀδελφοί, προσεύχεσθε...	3.17 Autograph
5.28 Greeting	3.18 Greeting

Figure 12.1: Comparsion of 1 and 2 Thessalonians

The blank squares in the right hand column indicate where there are units in 1 Thess that have no structural equivalent in 2 Thess.

Features in Common

Both letters begin with the use of the verb εὐχαριστεῖν ("to thank," 1 Thess 1.2; 2 Thess 1.3), in the indicative in the first letter and in the infinitive with an auxiliary verb in the second. In both letters this verb is accompanied by the phrase τῷ θεῷ πάντοτε ("[thank] God always") and the verb is used again apparently with some cohesive value later in the letter. In 1 Thess it recurs in 2.13 and seems to form an inclusio with 1.2, indicating closure at some level of unit. In this occurrence, the additional phrase is τῷ θεῷ ἀδιαλείπτως ("[thank] God unceasingly"), with an adverb that accompanied a different verb in 1.2. It seems to have a roughly parallel function in 2 Thess 2.13 (again with τῷ θεῷ πάντοτε), coming at the beginning of the last unit of the first section of the letter. In 1 Thess the picture is complicated by the fact that καὶ ὑμεῖς μιμηταὶ ἡμῶν ἐγενήθητε ("you became imitators of us") in 1.6 is also echoed by ὑμεῖς γὰρ μιμηταὶ ἐγενήθητε ("you became imitators") in 2.14, apparently forming what may be loosely called an inclusio that overlaps the first one.

There are further parallel features in the first sections of the two letters. First μνημονεύετε ("you remember") in 1 Thess 2.9 corresponds with οὐ μνημονεύετε ("do you not remember?") in 2 Thess 2.5, and then καὶ διὰ τοῦτο ("and because of this") in 1 Thess 2.13 is repeated exactly in καὶ διὰ τοῦτο in 2 Thess 2.11. The difference in capitalisation in UBS⁴/NA²⁷ is a modern editorial decision and does not reflect ancient manuscripts. In 1 Thess the phrase is also echoed in διὰ τοῦτο in 3.7. The next parallel is between ἡμεῖς δέ ("but we") in 1 Thess 2.17 and the identical words in 2 Thess 2.13. Then the prayers in 1 Thess 3.11–13 and 2 Thess 2.16–17 open in a similar way, though with the elements reversed (αὐτὸς δὲ ὁ θεὸς καὶ πατὴρ ἡμῶν καὶ ὁ κύριος ἡμῶν Ἰησοῦς "[May] our God and Father himself and our Lord Jesus" in 1 Thess 3.11, and αὐτὸς δὲ ὁ κύριος ἡμῶν Ἰησοῦς Χριστὸς καὶ [ὁ] θεὸς ὁ πατὴρ ἡμῶν "[May] our Lord Jesus Christ and God our Father" in 2 Thess 2.16), and both use infinitive verbs in the main clause. In 1 Thess there is another repetition that has a cohesive effect, namely the repetition of ἔμπροσθεν τοῦ θεοῦ καὶ πατρὸς ἡμῶν ("before our God and Father") from 1.3 in 3.13. This phrase has further echoes in ἔμπροσθεν τοῦ θεοῦ ἡμῶν ("before our God") in 3.9 and ἔμπροσθεν τοῦ κυρίου ἡμῶν Ἰησοῦ ("before our Lord Jesus") in 2.19. A final resemblance between the first sections of the two letters may be suggested in that the ἔμπροσθεν phrase in 1 Thess 1.3 has a kind of converse in ἀπὸ προσώπου τοῦ κυρίου ("separated from the presence of the Lord") in 2 Thess 1.9.

To sum up then, there are no less than seven points in common (not including vocatives) in the first sections of the two letters, and six of them are in the same order in both letters, surely a remarkable similarity. We may also note that all the vocatives except one in each letter consist of the simple form ἀδελφοί ("brethren"). In each letter there is one lengthened vocative: in 1 Thess it comes in the first unit of the first section (ἀδελφοὶ ἠγαπημένοι ὑπὸ [τοῦ] θεοῦ ["brethren beloved by God"] in 1.4), and in 2 Thess in the last unit of the first section (ἀδελφοὶ ἠγαπημένοι ὑπὸ κυρίου ["brethren beloved by the Lord"] in 2.13). Neither phrase occurs in any other NT letter, so their similarity in these two letters is striking, even though they do not amount to a close parallel.

Abstracted from Figure 12.1 above, the parallels may be presented as follows in Figure 12.2, with the item out of order shown in brackets.

1 THESS	2 THESS
1.2 εὐχαριστοῦμεν	1.3 εὐχαριστεῖν ὀφείλομεν
1.3 ἔμπροσθεν τοῦ θεοῦ καὶ πατρὸς ἡμῶν	1.9 ἀπὸ προσώπου τοῦ κυρίου
2.9 μνημονεύετε	2.5 οὐ μνημονεύετε
2.13 καὶ διὰ τοῦτο	2.11 καὶ διὰ τοῦτο
(2.13 εὐχαριστοῦμεν)	(2.13 ὀφείλομεν εὐχαριστεῖν)
2.17 ἡμεῖς δὲ	2.13 ἡμεῖς δὲ
3.11 αὐτὸς δὲ ὁ θεὸς καὶ πατὴρ ἡμῶν καὶ ὁ κύριος ἡμῶν Ἰησοῦς	2.16 αὐτὸς δὲ ὁ κύριος ἡμῶν Ἰησοῦς Χριστὸς καὶ [ὁ] θεὸς ὁ πατὴρ ἡμῶν

Figure 12.2: Parallels from Chart 1 Simplified

The second sections of the two letters also show some significant parallels, though in this case 1 Thess has a more complex structure. As noted above the second section in each letter is marked by the occurrence in the first letter of λοιπὸν οὖν, and in the second Τὸ λοιπὸν (compare Phil 3.1; 4.8 for other occurrences of this phrase as a discourse marker). In 1 Thess, this is followed by the verb pair ἐρωτῶμεν ὑμᾶς καὶ παρακαλοῦμεν ("we ask and encourage you") which helps to form the discourse framework for the second section. Both verbs are repeated in the hortatory part of the section (5.12–22), ἐρωτῶμεν in 5.12 and παρακαλοῦμεν in 5.14. Moreover παρακαλοῦμεν is repeated also in 4.10, and in this occurrence it has a parallel in 2 Thess 3.12. In 1 Thess 4.9–5.11 there is the threefold occurrence of περὶ ("concerning") as a marker of change of topic, and to this there is no parallel in 2 Thess, though it does occur in this function in 1 Cor 7.1, 25; 8.1; 12.1; 16.1, 12. Within this part of 1

Thess, the verb παρακαλεῖν ("to urge") comes near the beginning of the first of the three units marked by περί (4.10) and at the ends of the second and third units (4.18 and 5.11) in the imperative form παρακαλεῖτε ἀλλήλους ("encourage one another").

There are two further parallels between the second sections of the two letters. In 1 Thess 5.4 the contrastive ὑμεῖς δέ ("but you") is matched by ὑμεῖς δέ in 2 Thess 3.13, and in the final prayers of the two letters, αὐτὸς δὲ ὁ θεὸς τῆς εἰρήνης ("[May] the God of peace himself") in 1 Thess 5.23 is paralleled by αὐτὸς δὲ ὁ κύριος τῆς εἰρήνης ("[May] the Lord of peace himself") in 2 Thess 3.16.[4] As in section 1, the four parallels occur in the same order in both letters. These parallels can be set out as follows in Figure 12.3.

1 THESS	2 THESS
4.1 λοιπὸν οὖν	3.1 τὸ λοιπὸν (προσεύχεσθε)
4.10 παρακαλοῦμεν	3.12 παρακαλοῦμεν
5.4 ὑμεῖς δέ	3.13 ὑμεῖς δέ
5.23 αὐτὸς δὲ ὁ θεὸς τῆς εἰρήνης	3.16 αὐτὸς δὲ ὁ κύριος τῆς εἰρήνης
(5.25 προσεύχεσθε)	
Figure 12.3: Parallels in the Second Sections of 1 and 2 Thessalonians	

We may note one more resemblance that may not unfairly be termed a pseudo-parallel. This is that the request in the autograph in 1 Thess 5.25 (προσεύχεσθε ["pray"]) is repeated in the body of the letter in 2 Thess 3.1. Since the autograph units are outside the main focus of this study, this resemblance is shown in brackets in Figure 12.3 above. In total then there are no less than eleven parallels between the two letters, and ten of these are in the same order in both letters. It remains to note that there are also a couple of parallels between the second half of 1 Thess and the first half of 2 Thess. The verb ἐρωτῶμεν ("we ask") in 1 Thess 4.1 and 5.12 is echoed in 2 Thess 2.1, and the formula ἄρα οὖν ("so then") that introduces a conclusion occurs in both 1 Thess 5.6 and 2 Thess 2.15.

Can any inferences be drawn from the above observations? The parallel features noted are of a structural nature, and since structure in letters is

---

[4] It seems curious that Weima prefers to include 1 Thess 5.23–24 (*Neglected Endings*, 174–175) and 2 Thess 3.16 (ibid., 187) in one unit with the autograph despite the fact that he argues that they are not part of the autograph (ibid., 121). Structurally the change of writer together with the parallel prayers at the end of the first section of each letter surely demand that the prayers be treated as the end of the body of the letter rather than the beginning of its closing.

normally at a subconscious level in the mind of a letter-writer, the similarities between the two letters would seem to offer support for the traditional view that they have a common author, namely the apostle Paul. From the point of view of translators, it is good to be aware of structural similarities between letters, so that as far as possible they may be maintained in a translation. This will not necessarily be achieved by reproducing identical words in the two letters where the Greek texts have identical words, but rather by recognising the structural significance of the terminology and reflecting that significance by whatever means are appropriate in the receptor language. These may indeed include identical vocabulary, but may also involve a sensitive use of such linguistic features as particles, adverbs, and/or verbal affixes.

Discourse Units in 1 Thessalonians: Section 1

In this discussion, we shall explore the results of assuming that although vocatives are not the only indicators of new units, every vocative indicates the presence of a new unit or sub-unit.[5] This assumption means that the first unit is 1.2–10, as the Translator's Handbook suggests. There is a vocative in this unit; however, untypically it does not occur in the opening main clause of the sentence but in the subordinate clause in 1.4. At this point we should notice the unusual frequency in the letter of the verb οἶδα ("I know") which occurs twice in this unit. The first occurrence is in a participial form εἰδότες ("knowing" in 1.4, also in 4.5) and the second in a second person plural form οἴδατε ("you know" in 1.5, also in 2.1, 2, 5, 11; 3.3, 4; 4.2; 5.2). Note also the infinitive form εἰδέναι in 1 Thess 4.4 and 5.12. Most of these occurrences are near the beginning of a unit or sub-unit, and with a slight change of the punctuation in UBS⁴/NA²⁷, that could be true here also. I would suggest putting a full stop instead of a comma after καὶ [ἐν] πληροφορίᾳ πολλῇ ("with full conviction") in 1.5, and linking καθὼς οἴδατε οἷοι ἐγενήθημεν [ἐν] ὑμῖν δι' ὑμᾶς ("just as you know what we were like among you for your sakes") with what follows rather than what precedes ("just as you know... you also became imitators..."). This would entail changing the full stop at the end of 1.5 to a comma. The last clause of 1.5 seems to be more relevant to 1.6 than to the earlier part

---

[5] This does not mean that the vocative has to occur at the very beginning of the new unit, though it often does. The assumption is that each time a vocative occurs, it indicates that a new unit or sub-unit has begun since the last vocative occurred. This guideline seems to work quite well in these two letters where vocatives are unusually frequent, but is not proposed as a general rule.

of 1.5, and it is noteworthy that translations like RSV, TEV, NIV, and REB that do not adopt this analysis end up by omitting καθώς ("just as"). If this suggestion is accepted, then 1.2–10 could be divided into two sub-units, 1.2–5a and 1.5b–10. This analysis remains compatible with the Translator's Handbook, but makes a slightly more detailed division.

The next unit begins in 2.1 with both a vocative and the verb οἴδατε ("you know"), which is reinforced by repetition in the next verse. This unit covers 2.1–8, with perhaps a division into sub-units 2.1–4 and 2.5–8 if the third occurrence of οἴδατε in 2.5 is taken as a (presumably lower level) unit marker. In 2.9 there is a further vocative together with the verb μνημονεύετε ("you remember"), indicating another new (sub-)unit. The extent of this (sub-)unit is not entirely certain. The next vocative does not occur until 2.14, but 2.13 is introduced by καὶ διὰ τοῦτο ("and because of this"). This is a fairly significant marker and also has a parallel in 2 Thess 2.11, so I am inclined to treat 2.13 as a separate short sub-unit on its own. As already noted, the recurrence of the verbal phrase εὐχαριστοῦμεν τῷ θεῷ ἀδιαλείπτως ("we thank God unceasingly") in 2.13 forms an important link back to 1.2. The next (sub-)unit will then be 2.14–16, which offers another cohesive link with the very first unit in the repetition of μιμηταὶ ἐγενήθητε. This analysis is again a little more detailed than that in the Translator's Handbook, which links 2.13–16 in a single unit.

The next unit begins at 2.17 with the change of focus from the addressees to the writer, and according to the Translator's Handbook, extends right through to 3.13. This analysis is basically sound, and means in effect that the traditional chapter break is in the wrong place: the third chapter would better begin at 2.17. The vocative in 2.17 is followed by a further vocative in 3.7. This is in the main clause, though it is not at the beginning of the sentence, but rather follows a long genitive absolute construction that accounts for the whole of 3.6. This "delayed" occurrence of the vocative may suggest a lower level unit division beginning at 3.6. A further lower level division may be proposed at 3.11 covering 3.11–13. This is in fact a prayer with the main verbs in the infinitive, and brings the first section to an appropriate climax. It is paralleled by a similar prayer with infinitive main verbs in 2 Thess 2.16–17 in an identical structural position. So to be once again more detailed than the Translator's Handbook, we could propose dividing 2.17–3.13 into three sub-units, 2.17–3.5; 3.6–10; and 3.11–13. The first of these sub-units has an internal inclusio with the words μηκέτι στέγοντες... ἐπέμψαμεν ("when we could bear it no longer... we sent") in 3.1–2 and μηκέτι στέγων ἔπεμψα ("when I could bear it no longer, I sent") in 3.5. It would also be possible to regard the prayer in

3.11–13 as a separate unit rather than as a sub-unit on the grounds that it is parallel with the prayer in 1 Thess 5.23–24 at the end of the second section, which seems better regarded as a separate unit.

Discourse Units in 1 Thessalonians: Section 2

The first unit in this section is 4.1–8. The division in the Translator's Handbook into 4.1–2 and 4.3–8 seems unnecessary, as the introduction leads seamlessly into the discussion of sex ethics. The verbs in 4.1 ἐρωτῶμεν ("we ask") and παρακαλοῦμεν ("we encourage") are repeated in 5.12–22 and each dominates one half of that unit.

In 4.9 comes the first of the three occurrences of περί ("concerning"), each introducing a topic that in all probability Timothy had reported as causing some difficulty to the Thessalonian Christians. In all three cases (4.10, 13; 5.1) περί is accompanied by a vocative so we treat 4.9–12; 4.13–18; and 5.1–11 as units that are roughly parallel with each other. This is in agreement with the division in the Translator's Handbook.[6] There is no reason to subdivide 4.9–12 or 4.13–18, though we should notice that 4.18 and 5.11, the final sentences of their sections, both contain the words παρακαλεῖτε ἀλλήλους ("encourage one another"). In 5.1–11, the vocative in 5.4 suggests that the passage could be divided into two sub-units 5.1–3 and 5.4–11. This division corresponds with the move from theoretical to practical questions in the subject matter.

The next unit is 5.12–22, as also recognised in the Translator's Handbook. It can be regarded as a single unit because it echoes two key verbs ἐρωτῶμεν and παρακαλοῦμεν from 4.1. But in this unit the two verbs are separated and each is accompanied by a vocative (5.12 and 5.14), so there is reason to divide this unit into two sub-units, 5.12–13 and 5.14–22. Once again this is compatible with the Translator's Handbook, but a little more detailed. The second of these sub-units consists almost entirely of terse imperative verbs. In the first five clauses (5.14–15), the imperative is the first word of its clause, and in the remaining eight (5.16–22), it is the last word of its clause.

The final unit under consideration is 5.23–24. This takes the form of a prayer with the main verb in the infinitive, as in 3.11–13. Thus the two sections both end in a parallel fashion. The Translator's Handbook surprisingly

---

[6] In the 1975 edition of the Translator's Handbook, the unit is given as 4.13–17, but this is clearly a typographical error since 4.18 is not allotted to any other unit in the introduction on page ix, and is treated with 4.13–17 on page 103. This error may have been corrected in later printings which I do not have.

takes 5.23–28 as a single unit, despite recognising the beginning of the autograph in 5.25. The more detailed division proposed here seems more realistic in discourse terms.

Discourse Units in 2 Thessalonians: Section 1

Using the same presuppositions as in 1 Thess, after the opening greeting (1.1–2) the first unit in the body of 2 Thess is 1.3–12. Though this is longer than most units in 1 Thess, there is no strong structural reason for subdividing it, so the Translator's Handbook seems in this instance more detailed than is necessary. If any subdivision is justified, it would begin at 2.11, which partially echoes 2.3. The next unit is 2.1–12, another long unit. Reasons for subdividing it are not overwhelming, but in the light of the parallels with 1 Thess noted above, we may consider subdivisions starting at 2.5 and 2.11. The first subdivision (beginning with οὐ μνημονεύετε in 2.5, parallel with μνημονεύετε in 1 Thess 2.9) gains some support from the presence in 2.6 of the verb οἴδατε, which we have noted as occurring frequently near the beginning of a (sub-)unit in 1 Thess. The second depends wholly on the parallel of καὶ διὰ τοῦτο in 2.11 with the same phrase in 1 Thess 2.13, and this may not be a sufficiently convincing reason. At any rate, we can find no structural support for the division in the Translator's Handbook into 2.1–2 and 2.3–12.

The situation in the next unit, 2.13–17 is the reverse, where structural considerations support the Handbook subdivision at 2.16. Apart from the parallel of ἡμεῖς δέ between 2.13 and 1 Thess 2.17, the repetition of ὀφείλομεν εὐχαριστεῖν τῷ θεῷ πάντοτε forms an anaphoric link with 1.3. However, if we take each vocative to indicate a new (sub-)unit, then we need to recognise an extra sub-unit marked by a vocative and consisting just of 2.15. This verse also shows the inference marker ἄρα οὖν ("so then") that occurred in 1 Thess 5.6, though this cannot be considered a strong parallel. Moreover 2.16–17 forms a prayer with the main verbs in the infinitive that closes the first section of the letter, and is parallel with the prayer in 1 Thess 3.11–13. It would also be possible to regard the prayer in 2.16–17 as a separate unit rather than as a sub-unit on the grounds that it is parallel with the prayer in 2 Thess 3.16 at the end of the second section, which seems better regarded as a separate unit.

Discourse Units in 2 Thessalonians: Section 2

The first unit is 3.1–5, marked not only by τὸ λοιπὸν plus a vocative, but also echoing the request for prayer that came only in the autograph in 1 Thess. This unit is the same as in the Translator's Handbook. For the following unit, however, the Handbook offers 3.6–15, but if each vocative marks a new (sub-) unit, this needs to be split into two, 3.6–12 and 3.13–15. The first of these has some parallel with 1 Thess 4.10 in the verb παρακαλοῦμεν ("we encourage") in 3.12, but this is not strong because here the verb παραγγέλλομεν ("we command") is more prominent, occurring in both 3.6 and 3.12, and giving an element of inclusio to the unit. The final unit is the single verse, 3.16, a prayer whose opening words are closely parallel with the prayer in 1 Thess 5.23. The difference is that whereas the verb in 1 Thess 5.23 is in the infinitive, here it is in the subjunctive.

Summary and Comparison with the Translator's Handbook

This essay is rather experimental in that it has tried to provide a preliminary discourse analysis of two letters simultaneously, using both internal criteria in each letter and comparative criteria common to both. Not all the internal recursions within each letter have been mentioned, only those that seem the most significant for structural purposes. Obviously the comparative method can be used only when there is good reason to suppose a close link between the texts compared. In the present case there is by traditional consent common authorship, a common audience, common topics, and only a brief time interval between the two letters. Whether such a method could be usefully employed with any other pair of NT letters remains to be seen.

We close with a summary of the units proposed in this article set in parallel columns with those in the Translator's Handbook (Figure 12.4). The degree of indentation corresponds to the perceived degree of structural subordination. It must be stressed, however, that no powerful structural criteria have been discovered for deciding whether to treat a given piece of text as a unit or a sub-unit, and in this respect, the analysis remains somewhat impressionistic. Nevertheless the discussion in this article should help translators analyse the structural evidence more closely and hopefully come to more firmly founded decisions about paragraph breaks and about distinguishing between major and minor sections of the text.

Structural Similarities in 1 and 2 Thessalonians

This Essay	Handbook
1 Thess	1 Thess
1.1	1.1
1.2–10	1.2–10
1.2–5a	
1.5b–10	
2.1–16	2.1–12
2.1–8	
2.9–12	
2.13	
2.14–16	
	2.13–16
2.17–3.13	2.17–3.13
2.17–3.5	
3.6–10	
3.11–13	
===============	===============
4.1–8	4.1–2
	4.3–8
4.9–12	4.9–12
4.13–18	4.13–18
5.1–11	5.1–11
5.1–3	
5.4–11	
5.12–22	5.12–22
5.12–13	
5.14–22	
5.23–24	5.23–28
5.25–27	
5.28	

This Essay	Handbook
2 Thess	2 Thess
1.1–2	1.1–2
1.3–12	1.3–12
	1.3–4
	1.5–10
	1.11–12
2.1–12	2.1–12
2.1–4	2.1–2
2.5–10	2.3–12
2.11–12	
2.13–17	2.13–17
2.13–14	2.13–15
2.15	2.16–17
2.16–17	
==============	==============
3.1–5	3.1–5
3.6–12	3.6–15
3.13–15	
3.16	3.16–18
3.17	
3.18	

Figure 12.4: Essay Analysis Compared with Translator's Handbook

13

DISCOURSE STRUCTURE IN EPHESIANS, WITH SOME IMPLICATIONS FOR TRANSLATORS

Introduction

Discourse analysis is broadly the attempt to see how language uses patterns in units larger than the sentence. In this article we shall try to use two approaches that are complementary:
1. A structural analysis will look at the text from a formal point of view, to try to see how the paragraphs are structured and how they fit together (or why they don't).
2. To this analysis observations are added in terms of rhetorical categories that were recognized in the ancient world itself.[1]

Not only does the letter draw on the OT, but its argumentation and semantic structure are based on classical patterns of rhetoric: we find an *exordium*, a *narratio*, a *digressio*, an *exhortatio*, and a *peroratio* (these terms are explained where they are first used in the text below). On the other hand, quotations, mostly but not all (see 5:14) from the OT, form the foundation of

---

[1] For the observations on rhetorical categories and for other helpful comments, I am much indebted to my colleague Dr. Lénart de Regt. We shared the teaching in a translation seminar on Ephesians in Moscow that gave the initial impetus to preparing this essay. Stimulating comments on an earlier draft were also made by Rev. Dr. Paul Ellingworth and Rev. Dr. Ernst Wendland. Credit for such defects as remain is mine alone.

ways of argumentation that are interesting, if at times perhaps surprising to the modern reader.

In looking at the text from different perspectives, we hope to provide arguments and points of view that may not be familiar to translators. It is not our aim to provide a single set of right answers to all questions, but rather to see what sort of problems arise, and why. In the end, translators themselves have to decide how to solve the problems of representing the Greek text as well as possible in terms of their own language and culture. We shall not discuss questions of authorship, interesting though they are, but for the sake of simplicity we shall refer to the author of Ephesians as Paul. This, at any rate, is how the letter is presented.

Discourse Analysis: Aims and Methods

What do we do in preparing an analysis of the discourse structure of a text? Primarily we observe the details of how the text is put together.

1. The analysis must be done on the text in the language in which it was originally written, in this case Greek.
2. We look not just at the general meaning of the text, but at how paragraphs are constructed, how they are linked or not linked, where repetition of words occurs, unusual word order, changes of verb mood and so on.
3. We shall always view with great caution the punctuation in the printed Greek text because this is not found in the oldest manuscripts, and is the result of editorial decisions by modern scholars. They have not usually studied the discourse structure, so different editions (even UBS[4] and NA[27]) have different punctuation and different paragraph breaks, some of which are very hard to understand.
4. When the main breaks in the text are established, the relationships of the different topics will stand out, and the focus in the intention of the writer will be clearer and sharper. This should lead to more intelligible and meaningful translation, provided that translators are familiar with the correct usage of the corresponding discourse-marking and rhetorical techniques of their own language.

Overview of Ephesians

Both structurally and rhetorically this letter breaks easily into two halves more or less equal in size but quite different in structure. These are chapters 1–3 and 4–6. Even a quick look at the outline below shows that the first half consists of a relatively small number of relatively long sections, whereas the second half consists of a relatively large number of relatively short sections. The analysis that follows is in English, but the detailed outline is based on the Greek. English glosses are taken from the RSV whenever possible, but when something more literal is needed to show the Greek structure, I have provided my own.

Principal Divisions of Ephesians

Part 1: 1.1–3.21 – Mainly Theological Content

1.1–14	1.1–2 Opening greetings
	1.3–14 Doxology (anacoluthon with no explicit main verb)
1.15–2.10	1.15–23 Thanksgiving and prayer (indicative main verb 1.16)
	2.1–10 Theological reflection (indicative main verbs 2.5, 6)
2.11–22	2.11–12 Exhortation (imperative main verb 2.11)
	2.13–18 Further theological reflection (indicative main verbs 2.13, 14, 17)
	2.19–22 Theological conclusion
3.1–19	3.2–13 Digression (indicative verbs 3.2, 8, 13)
	3.1, 14–19 Prayer (indicative main verb 3.14)
3.20–21	Doxology (no main verb)

Part 2 4.1–6.24 – Mainly Ethical Content

4.1–16	General instructions to believers how to behave (indicative verb with imperatival infinitive 4.1) NB περιπατῆσαι 4.1 (walk)
4.17–24	General instructions to believers how not to behave (indicative verb with imperatival infinitive 4.17) NB περιπατεῖν 4.17 (walk)
4.25–32	Specific instructions how not to behave (imperative verbs 2nd person 4.25, 26, 30, 32, 3rd person 4.26, 27, 28, 31)

5.1–6	General instructions how to behave (imperative verbs 2nd person 5.1, 2, 5, 3rd person 5.3, 4) NB περιπατεῖτε 5.2 (walk)
5.7–14	General instructions both how not to behave and how to behave (imperative verbs 3rd person 5.6, 2nd person 5.7, 8, 11) NB περιπατεῖτε 5.8 (walk)

5.15–6.9	General instructions both how not to behave and how to behave (imperative verbs 2nd person 5.15, 17, 18, 25; 6.1, 2, 4, 5, 9, 3rd person 5.33)
	NB περιπατεῖτε 5.15 (walk)
	    5.15–21 All believers
	    5.22–24 Wives
	    5.25–33 Husbands
	    6.1–3 Children
	    6.4 Parents
	    6.5–8 Slaves
	    6.9 Masters

6.10–22	Final instructions to all believers (imperative verbs 2nd person 6.10, 11, 13, 14, 17)
6.23–24	Closing greetings

Ephesians 1.1–14

This section consists of the formal opening of the letter (1.1–2), followed by a long and complex doxology (1.3–14).

1.1–2

The opening greetings are fairly typical of ancient letters; this opening is in ancient rhetorical terms referred to as the *inscriptio*. No main verb is expressed, but the sense is a wish for grace and peace to be experienced by the readers. In translation the wish is normally expressed either by the verb used, or by an optative form.

1.3–14

In UBS⁴/NA[27] this paragraph is printed with full stops at the ends of 1.6, 1.10 and 1.12, but there is no secure reason for doing so, and some editions such as Souter and BFBS print this as a single sentence. If taken this way, it is the longest single sentence in the NT. If the paragraph is broken up, the units beginning in 1.7, 11 and 13 are relative clauses, and not fully formed sentences. From a translator's point of view it may be helpful to have the paragraph broken up, but from the point of view of discourse analysis, it really is syntactically a single sentence. In view of its length, it is all the more remarkable that formally it does not contain a finite main verb! One has to understand the adjective Εὐλογητός in 1.3 as a wish: "May God be blessed." In translation, this is usually expressed by a full verb. In 1.3 there is also the first occurrence of the phrase ἐν τοῖς ἐπουρανίοις, which recurs in 1.20; 2.6; 3.10; and 6.12. There is no observable pattern in these recurrences.

The rest of the sentence is a string of relative clauses, which in translation are usually expressed as main verbs. The first one extends from ὁ εὐλογήσας ("who has blessed") in 1.3 down to the end of 1.6, and describes the activity of God the Father in blessing his people. There are three principal actions mentioned. The first is carried by the participle ὁ εὐλογήσας, the second by the indicative verb καθὼς ἐξελέξατο ("even as he chose") in 1.4, and the third by the participle προορίσας ("destined") in 1.5. The second action seems to be syntactically subordinated to the first by the conjunction καθὼς ("even as").

This part of the sentence concludes in 1.6 with a reference to Christ as the agent through whom God shows grace to people. The rest of the paragraph (1.7–14) is an expanded description of how people are blessed through Christ. It is in three sections each introduced by ἐν ᾧ ("in him" in RSV in 1.7, 11, 13: literally "in whom"). A second occurrence of the phrase ἐν ᾧ in 1.13 seems to be a resumption of the first occurrence rather than a new aspect of the description.

In all, this paragraph is syntactically complicated, but not brilliantly structured. It would not have got high marks from the classical Greek stylists: Paul's fervent faith gets the better of his syntactic sensibility! However, it is a powerful and eloquent ascription of praise to God for the work of Christ. As such, this paragraph functions as the *exordium*, that is, the introductory part of the letter, before the main topic is set out more systematically and reflectively. It illustrates the fact that the ability to write in a convincing and moving way does not depend solely on the ability to control syntax in a strict manner. We shall see this again in ch. 3.

Ephesians 1.15–2.10

This section falls into two parts, 1.15–23 and 2.1–10, the first initiated by the phrase διὰ τοῦτο ("For this reason") in 1.15, and the second marked by the inclusio of περιεπατήσατε/περιπατήσωμεν ("you once walked/we should walk") in 2.2 and 2.10. Although in rhetorical terms there is a transition from the *exordium* to the *narratio* at 2.1, nevertheless in formal terms, there is no closure marker at the end of 1.15–23, and no major opening marker at the beginning of 2.1, so 1.15–2.10 is regarded formally as a single unit. This is the main point in Ephesians where formal and rhetorical criteria pull in opposite directions.

1.15–23

As with 1.3–14, different printed editions of the Greek text vary in their punctuation. UBS⁴ and NA²⁷ place a full stop after 1.19, but other editions such as Souter and BFBS treat 1.15–23 as a single sentence. Syntactically this is more convincing, as the whole of 1.20–21 is a relative clause. It would be syntactically possible to begin a new sentence at 1.22, but the available editions do not do that. Nevertheless since it is not syntactically clear in Greek how 1.22–23 would relate to 1.15–21 if they were all one sentence, it is better in translation to treat them as a separate sentence.

The opening words of 1.15 διὰ τοῦτο ("For this reason") relate back to the whole of 1.3–14, and give the reason why Paul prays as he does in the following verses. In other words, the *exordium* of 1.3–14 still continues in 1.15–23, but the positive reference to the addressees serves to gain the sympathy of the readers, and thus functions as what ancient rhetoricians called a *captio benevolentiae*. The main verbs that dominate the structure of the paragraph are found in 1.16, οὐ παύομαι εὐχαριστῶν ὑπὲρ ὑμῶν μνείαν ποιούμενος ἐπὶ τῶν προσευχῶν μου ("I do not cease to give thanks for you, remembering you in my prayers"). The rest of 1.17–21 (at least) is the content of Paul's prayer. In terms of the syntax, there is actually only one prayer request, represented by the verb δώῃ ("may give") in 1.17. The whole of 1.18–21 is subordinate to this. As in 1.3–14, Paul's passion overrides his syntax, and so it is not clear just how 1.22–23 relate to 1.15–21. Semantically they seem to be part of the prayer, and form its theological climax. If this is so, a participle ὑποτάξας ("having put under"), parallel to καθίσας ("having seated") in 1.20 would have been smoother than the finite verb ὑπέταξεν ("he has put... under"). The finite verb is perhaps found here because this clause is a citation of Ps 8.7 in the Septuagint, and a finite verb occurs there. Syntactically this has the effect of making these verses a separate sentence.

There is in this paragraph one other oddity that should be noted. In 1.17, the Greek for "you" is in the dative case, whereas the next reference to "you" at the beginning of 1.18 is in a different case. If one includes [ὑμῶν], as printed in UBS[4] at v. 18, then it is in the genitive, and if not, then it is in the accusative in the participle πεφωτισμένους ("being enlightened"). This is a relatively small stylistic infelicity and does not obscure the meaning.

2.1–10

After the long introduction, the theological reflection of Part 1 of the letter actually begins here in 2.1. This is where the speech of praise has stopped and the *narratio* (2.1–3.21) begins. This term does not mean 'narrative,' but is used in the rhetorical sense of "setting out the issue," namely the redemption of mankind through Christ into a single body.

The paragraph 2.1–10 is again rambling and not well polished syntactically. 2.1–7 forms one sentence, 2.8–9 another, and 2.10 a third. Souter prints 2.1–9 as a single sentence, but BFBS, UBS[4] and NA[27] are on firmer ground in taking 2.8–9 as separate. Certainly these two verses contain a finite verb and constitute a well-formed sentence. There is no doubt that 2.10 is a separate sentence.

The basic structure of 2.1–7 is simple: ὑμᾶς ὄντας νεκρούς... ("you being dead" in 2.1) συνεζωοποίησεν τῷ Χριστῷ... ("[God] made us alive together with Christ" in 2.5) καὶ συνήγειρεν καὶ συνεκάθισεν... ([God] raised us up with him, and made us sit with him" in 2.6). The last two verbs take up the statements applied to Christ in 1.20, ἐγείρας αὐτὸν ἐκ νεκρῶν καὶ καθίσας... ("having raised him from the dead and made him sit") and apply them to the believers. Thus the main verbs in this paragraph have a close link with the central part of the previous paragraph. This is one reason for taking these two paragraphs together as one section.

The basic structure is complicated by two factors. The first is the repetition of ὑμᾶς ὄντας νεκροὺς τοῖς παραπτώμασιν... ("you being dead through trespasses") in 2.1 as καὶ ὄντας ἡμᾶς νεκροὺς τοῖς παραπτώμασιν ("we being dead through trespasses") in 2.5. The change of pronoun from second person plural to first person plural makes it seem that the writer has lost track of his original train of thought. This change in the outward form is probably triggered by the phrase ἠγάπησεν ἡμᾶς ("he loved us") at the end of 2.4, but semantically it seems most likely that it resumes the opening phrase of 2.1. Theologically the statement remains true whether Paul is addressing the Ephesian believers solely or including himself with them.

The second complicating factor is the intrusive clause χάριτί ἐστε σεσῳσμένοι ("by grace you have been saved") in 2.5. This statement anticipates the fuller development of this theme in 2.8–9, but does not fit at all into the syntax in 2.5. Printed editions place these words between dashes (BFBS, UBS[4] and NA[27]) or in brackets (Souter) to indicate their awkwardness. Once again Paul's enthusiasm overcomes his sense of style, and one feels that the words are tumbling out of his mouth faster than the scribe could put them on paper. In translation it will probably be necessary to put these words in brackets, possibly running 2.5–6 together and putting the bracketed material at the end.

As already noted, the occurrence of περιπατήσωμεν ("we should walk") in 2.10, repeating the same root περιεπατήσατε ("you once walked") in 2.2 serves to round off the paragraph.

Ephesians 2.11–22

The opening conjunction Διὸ ("Therefore") seems to provide a rather general link with the whole of 2.1–10 rather than a specific link with 2.10. UBS[4] and NA[27] place full stops at the ends of vv. 12, 13, 16, 18 and 22. Souter and BFBS are similar except that they do not have a full stop at the end of 2.16. UBS[4] begins a new paragraph at 2.14 and NA[27] a new subparagraph at 2.14. From a discourse perspective this is doubtful. The main verb μνημονεύετε ("remember") in 2.11 is imperative, but the main verb ἐγενήθητε ("you have become") in 2.13 is indicative, as are the main verbs in 2.14–22. The change of verb mood suggests that a new paragraph may begin at 2.13 rather than 2.14, a view that can be supported by the contrast between ποτὲ ("at one time") in 2.11 and νυνὶ δὲ ("But now") in 2.13. The statements in 2.14–18 are introduced by γάρ ("For") which links them closely with 2.13.

The break in NA[27] between 2.18 and 2.19 on the other hand does find support from a discourse perspective. 2.19–22 begins with ἄρα οὖν ("So then"), a form frequently used to introduce the conclusion or summing up of an argument. It can therefore be inferred that these verses do stand slightly apart from those that precede.

The discourse structure of this section may therefore be set out as:

2.11–12 Exhortation to consider the past
2.13–18 Reflection on the present
2.19–22 Theological conclusion

We may note a structural similarity between 2.17 and 1.22. In both places an indicative main verb introduced by καί ("and") occurs after a series of participles, and in both places the syntactic relationship between that verb and what has preceded is not entirely clear. It is interesting to observe that none of the available Greek texts begin a new sentence at 1.22, but UBS[4] and NA[27] do begin a new sentence at 2.17, a good example of lack of consistency in making punctuation decisions.

Ephesians 3.1–19

This section provides another example of rough style, probably induced by strong emotion. The section begins with the phrase τούτου χάριν ("because of this") linking it with the theological conclusion at the end of ch. 2. This is intended to be the basis for a further prayer, but instead of expressing his prayer Paul embarks on a long digression covering 3.2–13. In classical rhetorical terms, this *digressio* of 3.2–13 interrupts the *narratio*. This is not to say, however, that the *digressio* is not relevant to the rest of Part 1 and serves no purpose. On the contrary, when Paul speaks of himself in this *digressio*, his witness as apostle to the Gentiles is bound up with the uniting of Jews and Gentiles in the same body (in the rest of Part 1, but particularly in ch. 2).

3.1–7 is in fact an anacoluthon with no finite main verb. Paul then repeats τούτου χάριν ("because of this") at the beginning of 3.14, and comes at last to his real prayer in 3.14–19. In translation, because the gap between the beginning of the prayer in 3.1 and its continuation in 3.14 is so large, it will usually be best to insert into 3.1 some verb of prayer, such as "I pray" (compare TEV). 3.14 will best begin a new paragraph as in TEV.

3.1–13

3.1–7 shows a high degree of syntactic subordination, but also a marked theological depth. These two features go together elsewhere, for instance in the letter to Titus. It is almost as if Paul slips his most important insights into his text as asides. They are there for the careful and perceptive reader (or hearer), but in such a way that they do not distract the more naïve reader/hearer from the simpler thoughts.

In 3.8–13, all the available printed Greek texts begin new sentences at 3.8 and 3.13. There is no conjunction at the beginning of 3.8, so that the connection with the preceding verses is not fully explicit. It seems to depend on a verbal link rather than a logical link. The mention in 3.7 of τῆς χάριτος τοῦ θεοῦ τῆς δοθείσης μοι ("the grace of God given to me"), taking up the topic of 3.2, seems to lead Paul to expand on this theme. Again in 3.8–12 there is a long sentence with deep syntactic subordination matched by deep theological content.

The final sentence of the paragraph in 3.13 begins with διό ("So"). As in 2.11 this seems to form a general link with 3.1–12 rather than a specific link with any particular part of it. The Greek does not indicate who is the subject of the infinitive verb ἐγκακεῖν ("to lose heart"). Most translations take the subject to be the Ephesian believers, but does this really make the best sense? The theme of 3.8–12 has been God's grace shown to Paul, and there has been no second person reference since 3.4. If Paul intended a change of subject at this point, it would surely require to be marked by a pronoun, and it is not. It therefore seems more likely both syntactically and semantically that Paul is praying for himself at this point, that in the light of God's grace (3.8) and wisdom (3.10), he will not give up his ministry despite the hardships of his situation in prison. This view is represented in the alternative renderings in RSV and NRSV ("that I may not lose heart"), but is very much a minority view. However, it is the view that receives most support from discourse analysis.

3.14–19

This is another single sentence in Greek. It begins by repeating τούτου χάριν ("because of this") from 3.1, but this time Paul really does express his prayer in 3.16–19. It contains three instances of ἵνα ("in order that") followed by a subjunctive verb (vv. 16, 18, and 19). It is possible that these three ἵνα clauses are co-ordinate with each other, but if this were so, one might expect them to be linked with καί ("and"), and they are not. It therefore seems better to regard the second and third clauses as governed by what precedes them, and marking increasingly deep subordination. In many languages such a succession of purpose clauses cannot be included within a single sentence, so translators will need to break this paragraph up into several sentences.

Ephesians 3.20–21

This doxology is a very short unit to be treated as a separate section, and indeed it could be taken as the conclusion to the previous section. It is treated as separate because it does not have particularly close links either syntactically or semantically with 3.1–19. Moreover, if taken as a separate unit, it balances the doxology at the beginning in 1.3–14, and is like that section in that it has no main verb. It forms a fitting close to the first half of the letter, and is marked by the particle "Amen" in v. 21. Thus, the addressees may realize already during this doxology of 3.20–21, and not just after it is over, that the first major part of the letter is drawing to a close. The more narrowly theological part of the letter is complete, and from this point on the focus changes to Christian ethical conduct.

Possible Chiastic Pattern in Ephesians 1–3?

In the first half of the letter it remains only to raise the possibility that there is a chiastic pattern present. It is not as clear or as strongly marked as in other parts of the Bible, but is worth mentioning. Leaving aside the formal opening of the letter in 1.1–2, we have already noticed that there are doxologies in 1.3–14 and 3.20–21. There are also prayers in 1.15–23 and 3.1–19 (or more specifically 3.1, 14–19). Again there is theological reflection in 2.1–10 and 2.13–22. This leaves only 2.11–12 at the centre. This unit is the only one in which an imperative verb occurs. The pattern could be set out as follows:

1.3–14 Doxology (anacoluthon with no main verb)
    1.15–23 Thanksgiving and prayer (indicative main verb 1.16)
        2.1.10 Theological reflection (indicative main verbs 2.5, 6)
            2.11–12 Exhortation (imperative main verb 2.11)
        2.13–22 Further theological reflection (indicative verbs 2.13, 14, 17, 19)
            [3.2–13 Digression (indicative verbs 3.2, 8, 13)]
    3.1, 14–19 Prayer (indicative main verb 3.14)
3.20–21 Doxology (no main verb)

It is interesting to notice that 3.2–13, the passage that is syntactically the most awkward, is also the very passage that fits least well into the chiastic structure. In this unit, Paul went off at a tangent both syntactically and semantically!

The other interesting point here is that often the theme that occurs at the central point of a chiasm is what comes into focus in the next unit. In the present case, the central unit contains the only imperative verb in the first half of the letter. In the second half of the letter where ethical instruction predominates, imperatives become frequent. In terms of rhetorical categories, most of the second half of the letter, 4.1–6.9, is an *exhortatio*, and the same applies to the central unit of the first part, 2.11–12. The first and second halves of the letter are a combination of two classical rhetorical genres: the epideictic and the deliberative genres respectively.[2] That is, the theological reflection of Part 1 is an oration of praise and points to something glorious, while the exhortations of Part 2 persuade the addressees to follow certain recommendations and take a particular course of action.

Overview of Ephesians 4–6

It is hard to discern any detailed large-scale pattern covering the whole of chapters 4–6. There are however some features which help to distinguish units within this half of the letter. In particular the recurrence of οὖν ("therefore" in 4.1, 17; 5.1, 7, 15) marks the beginning of a paragraph. It is accompanied in each case by various forms of the verb περιπατεῖν (literally "to walk") in 4.1, 17; 5.2, 8, 15). In 4.1–24 instructions are veiled, with indicative verbs followed by an imperatival infinitive, but from 4.25 on plain imperatives, both second and third person, occur frequently. From 4.1–5.14 we may see something of a pattern in that of the five units (4.1–16; 4.17–24; 4.25–32; 5.1–6; 5.7–14) all except the centre one (4.25–32) contain general instructions and are identified by both οὖν and the verb περιπατεῖν. The central paragraph has neither of these features, but deals with specific rather than generic instruction. Its beginning is marked by the change to the imperative mood.

Ephesians 4.1–16

In this section the various editions of the Greek text agree in placing full stops at the ends of vv. 6, 7, 8, 10, and 16, plus a question mark at the end of v.

---

[2] A. T. Lincoln, *Ephesians*, WBC 42 (Word, 1990), xli–xlii.

9. Paul begins his instruction section with the polite verb παρακαλῶ ("I beg you [to]") followed by an infinitive. Syntactically 4.4–6 is in apposition to what has preceded, though the connection is a bit loose. Presumably the mention of τὴν ἑνότητα τοῦ πνεύματος ("the unity of the Spirit") leads on to the list of single entities in 4.4–6 already shared by the author and addressees.

In 4.7–16, there is a lexical inclusio in the mention of ἑνὶ δὲ ἑκάστῳ ("to each one") in 4.7 and ἑνὸς ἑκάστου ("of each one") in 4.16. The quotation from Ps 68.18 in 4.8 (introduced by διὸ λέγει: "therefore it says") leads to a discussion of its interpretation in 4.9–10. Then follows its application to the life of the church in 4.11–16. This sentence contains the most complex subordination in the second half of the letter, and is also the passage that gives the profoundest theological undergirding to the ethical instruction.

Ephesians 4.17–24

Whereas 4.1–16 provided general instruction on how believers should behave, 4.17–24 by contrast provides instruction on how they should not behave, or rather how they should no longer behave. It is assumed that in their pre-Christian lives they used to behave in the same way as unbelievers still do. Now they have to lay aside all that and become new people in Christ (4.23–24). The section is not syntactically very complex, and needs little comment. It contains two moderately long sentences (vv. 17–19 and 20–24) but neither has deep subordination. As in the previous section, the instructions are introduced politely, with verbs of speaking λέγω καὶ μαρτύρομαι ("I affirm and testify" in 4.17) followed by an infinitive.

Ephesians 4.25–32

This section begins with διὸ rather than οὖν which occurs more commonly in chs. 4 and 5, though both are translated "therefore" in RSV. Διὸ seems to give a somewhat loose general connection with the whole of 4.1–24 (compare 2.11, 3.13). The syntax is basically very simple, and the paragraph is constructed from a string of imperative verbs (no longer with polite introductions) making eight short sentences. Of the imperatives some are second person and some third, some positive and some negative, but there is no obvious patterning in their occurrence. The emphasis is more on behaviour to avoid than on behaviour to encourage, and the advice is fairly detailed. The move to direct imperatives is matched semantically by a move from general principles towards specific aspects of Christian conduct.

Ephesians 5.1–6

As in 4.1 and 4.17, this section is introduced by οὖν ("therefore"). Again the basic structure is simple, with a string of five imperatives constituting four sentences of fairly general ethical instruction. The paragraph breaks in UBS⁴ and NA²⁷ are different from each other and both are less than helpful for translators. NA²⁷ begins a new paragraph at 5.3 and continues it till the end of 5.14. UBS⁴ has 4.25–5.5 in one paragraph, and 5.6–14 in another. Both of these overlook the fact that the occurrence of the combination of οὖν and περιπατεῖτε ("walk") in 5.1–2 and 5.7–8 indicates the beginning of new paragraphs at 5.1 and 5.7. This is made even clearer by the contrast of γίνεσθε οὖν ("Therefore be...") and μὴ οὖν γίνεσθε ("Therefore do not be...") in these two places. Furthermore, despite the asyndeton at the beginning of 5.6, this verse is clearly a contrast with 5.5 (ἴστε γινώσκοντες: "be sure," against μηδεὶς ὑμᾶς ἀπατάτω: "Let no one deceive you"). For a similar contrast compare 5.17 ("Do not be foolish, but understand...").

Ephesians 5.7–14

As already noted the beginning of a new paragraph is marked by οὖν and περιπατεῖτε in 5.7–8. The content continues to be general ethical instruction. The structure of the paragraph is rather loose and printed editions vary in their punctuation. There is subordination, but it is neither very complex nor very clear. The occurrence of γὰρ ("for") no less than four times (5.8, 9, 12, 14) makes the degree of subordination debatable. It is rendered as "for" in RSV in all four cases, the last one being in 4.13 in the English text. The main verbs are μὴ... γίνεσθε (5.7: "do not be"), περιπατεῖτε (5.8: "walk"), μὴ συγκοινωνεῖτε... μᾶλλον δὲ καὶ ἐλέγχετε (5.11: "Take no part... but instead expose"), and φανεροῦται (5.13: "becomes visible"), and it is suggested that translators should take each of these verbs as the kernel of a sentence. This would lead to starting new sentences at the beginning of 5.7, 5.8c, 5.11 and 5.13. The paragraph is rounded off with another citation introduced by διὸ λέγει ("therefore it says," compare 4.8), but it is not from a single identifiable OT passage. The other feature in this paragraph that should be noted is the recurrence of the ποτε... νῦν δὲ ("once... but now") contrast in 5.8, as in 2.11, 13.

Ephesians 5.15–6.9

This section has the clearest internal subdivisions of any in Ephesians 4–6. Its beginning is also marked by the occurrence of οὖν ("therefore") and περιπατεῖτε ("walk") in 5.15. It then breaks into seven short paragraphs each addressed to a different group of people. In 5.15–21, no addressees are specified, and the instructions are directed to believers in general. Then follow six specific groups, in three pairs, each addressed with a vocative, wives (αἱ γυναῖκες 5.22–24) and husbands (οἱ ἄνδρες 5.25–33), children (τὰ τέκνα 6.1–2) and parents (οἱ πατέρες 6.4), slaves (οἱ δοῦλοι 6.5–8) and masters (οἱ κύριοι 6.9). These are in fact the only vocatives found in Ephesians. Each group except the first is instructed with one or more imperative verbs, and an imperative is clearly implied with the first group. It is in fact found in some manuscripts.

The structure of this section is mainly clear, and the most interesting question is how 5.21 relates to its context. UBS[4] and NA[27] put a full stop at the end of 5.20 and link 5.21 with 5.22ff. BFBS and Souter on the other hand link 5.21 with 5.20, and place a full stop at the end of 5.21. This shows more respect for the syntax of 5.19–21 with its string of four participles before the final participle ὑποτασσόμενοι ("being subject") in 5.21. The difficulty with this punctuation is that the previous four participles all refer to verbal activity (in RSV "addressing one another… singing and making melody… giving thanks…"), whereas ὑποτασσόμενοι does not. Nevertheless this seems the less difficult option. If 5.21 is linked with 5.22–24 then the paragraph 5.22–24 has no main verb. When 5.21 is linked with the instructions that precede, then a repetition of the verb ὑποτασσόμενοι in an imperative form is clearly implied in 5.22, and has obviously given rise to the variant readings. These offer both a third person imperative ὑποτασσεσθωσαν ("let them be subject") and a second person ὑποτασσεσθε ("[you] be subject"). In the light of the second person imperatives in the following five paragraphs (5.25, 6.1, 4, 5, 9) a second person imperative is clearly preferable in 5.22. In translation it will normally be necessary to include it irrespective of the textual variant chosen. In short, translators are recommended to begin a new paragraph at 5.22, not at 5.21. However, it may be convenient to make 5.21 a separate sentence, as RSV has done, but it is better to attach it to the end of the previous paragraph.

It is not necessary to say a lot about the remaining paragraphs of the section. We may note that the first two, dealing with wives and husbands both include comparisons linking the marriage relationship with the person of

Christ. These are presented chiastically (5.24 ὡς... οὕτως...: "As... so..."; compare οὕτως... ὡς..., "Even so... as..." in both 5.28 and 5.33), thus subtly strengthening the link between the two paragraphs. The section dealing with husbands also includes an OT citation from Gen 2.24 in 5.31, and an application of it.

The middle pair of paragraphs dealing with children and parents are both short and simple. The last pair, dealing with slaves and masters both contain a concluding reason introduced by εἰδότες ὅτι... ("knowing that" in 6.8, 9). Except at 5.21, the syntax throughout this section is clear and simple.

Ephesians 6.10–22

This section is marked as a final section by the introductory words Τοῦ λοιποῦ ("Finally") in 6.10. In other words, 6.10–22 form the *peroratio*, that is, the final exhortation and summing up of essential points before the letter is drawn to a close. Although vv. 21–22 are too specific and local to be part of the *peroratio*, they are included in this paragraph because there is no other example in the NT of a new paragraph beginning with a ἵνα clause. The main structure is carried by more imperative verbs in 6.10, 11, 13, 14, and 17. In accordance with this, new sentences begin in 6.10, 11, 13 and 14 in all the available printed editions. There is however considerable difference over the punctuation in 6.16 and 17. UBS[4] and NA[27] have full stops at the end of 6.17, and NA[27] even has a new paragraph beginning at 6.18. Souter begins a new sentence at the beginning of 6.17 and continues it to the end of 6.20, and BFBS has a single sentence running through from the beginning of 6.14 to the end of 6.20. In light of the way that each of the other sentences is structured around the occurrence of an imperative verb, it seems that Souter's punctuation is the most convincing from a discourse perspective. Translators are therefore recommended to begin a new sentence at 6.17. There is very little subordination in this section, and no further comment need be made up to the end of 6.20.

In 6.21 however there is a situation unique in the epistles in that the sentence covering 6.21–22 begins with a purpose clause introduced by Ἵνα ("in order that"). Such clauses much more often come after the main verb to which they are subordinate. 6.21–22 also stand apart from 6.10–20 in that they contain a statement in the indicative rather than commands in the imperative. This could be taken as sufficient reason to detach them from the preceding verses as a separate unit. However, in the few other places where a Ἵνα clause begins a sentence (Matt 9.6 and parallels, Matt 17.17, Acts 24.4), it is heavily dependent on what has preceded, so that seems the more likely analysis here. 6.21–22 have no closer semantic link with 6.23–24 than they have with 6.10–20. One wonders whether they started life as an afterthought, inserted after 6.23–24 had been written.

Ephesians 6.23–24

These closing greetings are similar to those in other letters. The two verses form separate sentences. Neither has a finite verb, but as in the opening greeting, the sense is that of a wish.

14

A DISCOURSE MARKER IN JOHN: ἀμὴν ἀμὴν λέγω ὑμῖν/σοι

Introduction

In chapter nine I examined the occurrences of the formula ἀμὴν λέγω ὑμῖν/σοι ("truly I say to you") in the Synoptic Gospels with a view to assessing its function(s) as a discourse marker.[1] The present article follows up by examining the 25 occurrences of the similar formula ἀμὴν ἀμὴν λέγω ὑμῖν/σοι ("truly, truly I say to you"), which is unique to the Gospel of John. As before, it is assumed that it makes no difference to any discourse function whether the indirect object "to you" is plural (ὑμῖν) or singular (σοι). In John all the examples except four (3.3, 5, 11; 21.18) are in the plural.

In the Synoptics, 48 of the 49 occurrences of ἀμὴν λέγω ὑμῖν/σοι could be accounted for in terms of four categories:

(1) those cases where the formula was clearly linked with the end of a unit or sub-unit in the speech;

(2) those cases where the formula occurred in the only full sentence of a speech and was associated with the end of a unit larger than just the speech in which it occurred;

(3) those cases where the formula was clearly linked with the beginning of a unit;

(4) those cases where the formula occurred in the only sentence of a

---

[1] Previously published in *BT* 55, no. 3 (2004): 318–328.

speech and was apparently linked with the beginning of a unit rather than the end.

In categories (3) and (4) there was a high degree of association with surprise and/or reversal of expectation. A further category (5) consisted of cases that required more detailed discussion before reallocation into another group. Almost all were eventually assigned to one of the other four groups, and in the end there remained only one anomalous case. This was Luke 12.37, where the formula occurred in the middle of a speech. It too was associated with reversal of expectation.

The Distribution of ἀμὴν ἀμὴν λέγω ὑμῖν/σοι in John

The same kind of categories that were used in the analysis of the Synoptics also prove to be useful in an initial analysis of John. In group (1) we find two examples (8.51 and 13.20) and in group (2) also two (1.51 and 8.58). In group (3) there are seven examples (3.5; 5.19; 6.26, 32, 53; 8.34; and 10.7) and in group (4) two (3.3 and 13.21). In group (5) there are twelve examples (3.11; 5.24, 25; 6.47; 10.1; 12.24; 13.16; 13.38; 14.12; 16.20, 23; and 21.18). We shall now examine the examples individually.

Ἀμὴν ἀμὴν λέγω ὑμῖν in the Final Sentence of a Unit

There is no uncertainty about the two examples in group (1), 8.51 and 13.20. They both occur in the final sentence of a multi-sentence speech, and can be linked only with the closure of the speech. Of the two examples in group (2), the first (1.51) occurs in the final utterance of Jesus' conversation with Nathaniel. Its function as marking the conclusion of that episode seems to be underlined by the use of a new quotative formula at the beginning of v. 51 despite the fact that there is no change of speaker from v. 50 (compare Mark 9.1). In 8.58 the formula introduces Jesus' astonishing and mysterious claim to have existed before Abraham, and thus brings to a conclusion the whole conversation about relationship with Abraham that has dominated the exchanges from v. 52 onwards. In groups (1) and (2) all the examples above happen to have the indirect object in the plural.

Ἀμὴν ἀμὴν λέγω ὑμῖν/σοι in the Opening Sentence of a Unit

Group (3) is much the largest group in John's gospel. In 3.5 the formula (in the singular) is used at the beginning of a longer, but still enigmatic, explanation of the cryptic remark already made by Jesus in 3.3. Compare the comments on 3.3 below. In 5.19 the formula introduces a long speech (5.19b–47) and can only be an opening marker. There may be an element of surprise in the following comment, but if so it seems less prominent than elsewhere.

In 6.26 the formula introduces a short speech (6.26b–27). This is a response to a question from the crowd in 6.25, but is certainly not an answer to that question. Perhaps the formula is used to reinforce the change of subject, which would presumably have been surprising and puzzling to the questioners. In 6.32 the formula opens another speech which is also short (6.32b–33), but which introduces a double contrast with the ideas of the crowd: they were thinking of Moses as the source of earthly bread, whereas Jesus focuses on God as the source of true bread. There is therefore a strong reversal of expectation here. In 6.53 Jesus again uses the formula to open a remark that emphasizes the contrast between his thinking and that of the Jews, and so reinforces the bafflement of his audience.

In 8.34, the formula introduces a remark that flatly contradicts the position expressed by the speakers in the previous verse, so again there is a strong element of reversal of expectation. In 10.7 the formula opens a longer speech (10.7b–18), though one that continues the sheep metaphor from the preceding verses. If there is surprise here, it probably lies in the change of application of the metaphor. In 10.1–5 Jesus seems to imply that he is the shepherd, but in 10.7 there is an abrupt change, and he presents himself as the door for the sheep.

Turning to group (4), in 3.3 the formula (in the singular) is used to change the subject from Nicodemus' opening remark in a surprising and deliberately provocative manner. In this way it sets the tone for the whole conversation that follows. In 13.21, which has parallels in Matt 26.21 and Mark 14.18, the formula is used to introduce a new and surprising subject, Jesus' betrayal. Again it sets the scene for the episode that follows.

Doubtful Cases

In 3.11, the formula (in the singular) occurs in the second sentence of the speech, following a rhetorical question in the first sentence. In the Synoptics, there are examples where their equivalent formula follows a rhetorical question (Matt 24.2; Mark 8.12), but this verse is unlike them in that here a longer speech follows. It seems, therefore, that this verse should be reassigned to group (3). The next two cases, 5.24 and 5.25, need to be taken together. There is no example in the Synoptics where their equivalent formula occurs twice in successive verses. NA[27] prints its text with a new paragraph beginning at 5.24. UBS[4] does not begin a new paragraph, but does begin 5.24 (but not 5.25) with a capital letter, implying a new sub-unit of some kind. Souter prints neither verse with an initial capital. In terms of what has been observed elsewhere, the most likely hypothesis is that the formula in v. 24 marks the end of the (sub-)unit beginning in 5.19b, while that in v. 25 marks the beginning of a new (sub-)unit. This would be the only case where our formula both begins (5.19) and ends (5.24) the same unit, though even one such case gives support to the view that the same formula can be used both as an opening marker and a closing marker. The content of v. 24 is certainly compatible with such an analysis: the participial clause in v. 24 provides a neat antithetical balance to that in v. 23, whereas there is no such link with v. 25. We therefore propose to reallocate 5.24 to group (1) and 5.25 to group (3). This analysis fits with the only other place in John where our formula occurs in successive verses (13.20–21). There, a new quotative introduction at the beginning of v. 21 makes it clear that the formula in v. 20 ends one unit while that in v. 21 begins another.

In 6.47, UBS[4] and NA[27] show the formula in the middle of a long paragraph (6.41–51). Jesus' actual speech begins in 6.43, and it would be clearer to begin a new paragraph there. The flow of thought through the speech in 6.43b–51 is not self-evident. The key terms of v. 47, πιστεύων ("believing") and ζωὴν αἰώιον ("eternal life"), occur neither in the preceding verses nor in the following ones. However, there is a change of focus from predominantly generic third person statements in vv. 44–46 to predominantly first person and third person specific statements in vv. 48–51. Verse 47 contains a generic third person statement, and thus seems to be linked structurally more with what precedes than with what follows. We therefore treat the formula as marking the end of a sub-unit rather than the beginning of a new one, and reassign it to group (1).

Although 10.1 begins a new chapter in the traditional numbering, it is not the beginning of Jesus' speech, which actually starts in the previous verse at 9.41b, and opens by answering a question posed in 9.40. That the break between chs. 9 and 10 is badly placed is indicated by the closing comment in 10.6, which surely refers back to 9.41. There is a comparable place in Matthew (17.20) where a question is answered before the formula occurs. There the formula introduced a single-sentence utterance, but here the speech is much longer (9.41b–10.5), so it is reasonable to assume that the formula is linked with the opening of a (sub-)unit within the speech. So it can be confidently reassigned to group (3). In 12.24 the situation is somewhat similar. The formula introduces the second sentence of a speech (12.23b–28a), following a programmatic statement (compare Matt 5.18). It is thus linked with the beginning of a (sub-)unit rather than the end, and is also reassigned to group (3).

In 13.16 the formula occurs both in the middle of the speech that extends from 13.12b–20 and again in the last sentence in v. 20. The occurrence in v. 16 could be analyzed as ending one sub-unit or beginning another. The fact that the end of this speech is definitely marked by the formula in v. 20 suggests that the earlier occurrence also functions as a closure marker (compare the three occurrences in one speech in Matt 10.15, 23, 42). The content of v. 16 is certainly related to what precedes rather than what follows. We therefore reallocate 13.16 to group (1). If this analysis is accepted then the next sub-unit should begin in 13.17 rather than 13.18 as in NA[27].

In 13.38 as in 3.11 the formula is in the second sentence of an utterance after a rhetorical question. Here the speech covers 13.38b–14.4, a fact often obscured by the chapter division, and in UBS[4] by an unfortunate page break at the end of 13.38. It seems, therefore, that as in 3.11, the formula here should be taken as introducing a new sub-unit that probably extends to the end of 14.4. Thus 14.1–4 should be understood in light of 13.38. We therefore reassign 13.38 to group (3). The formula in 13.38 has parallels in Matt 26.34 and Mark 14.30.

In 14.12 we find the formula in the middle of a speech extending from 14.9b–21. Verses 9b–11 arise in response to a request by Philip in 14.8, and vv. 9b–10a are in the second person singular. Jesus reverts to the plural in vv. 10b–11, but the content of those verses is clearly linked with what has preceded, namely the relationship of Jesus with the Father. Verse 12 introduces a new topic and thus is analyzed as opening a new sub-unit, and reassigned to group (3). NA[27] is therefore right to begin a new paragraph with this verse.

We take 16.20 and 16.23 together. They are both part of a speech that extends from 16.19b–28. The formula in v. 20 is preceded only by a rhetorical question, as in 3.11 and 13.38, and here as in those places it opens the main body of the speech. It is therefore to be reallocated to group (3). In 16.23 the formula begins a new sentence in the middle of a verse according to the traditional numbering. Nevertheless it seems perfectly plausible to analyze it as the beginning of a new sub-unit. We may note that the verb ἐρωτήσετε, usually translated "ask" in v. 23a, has the primary meaning of "ask a question"; and so it fits very well with the preceding material in vv. 19b–22, which arises from a question the disciples were asking. In vv. 23b–24 there occurs three times in different forms (αἰτήσητε, ᾐτήσατε, αἰτεῖτε) another word also usually translated "ask," meaning "to ask for, to make a request." Thus there is a sharper break in the Greek in the middle of v. 23 than may appear from the English in versions like RSV, GNT, NIV, and CEV. It therefore seems likely that the occurrence of our formula in 16.23b marks the beginning of a new sub-unit. The new paragraph at the beginning of 16.23 in NA[27] would therefore be better placed in the middle of the verse. The second word for "ask (in the sense of request)" recurs in v. 26, and so provides a cohesive link beyond vv. 23b–24. This suggests that the new paragraph at 16.25 in both UBS[4] and NA[27] would be better removed. Probably the unit that begins in v. 23b with our formula continues to the end of the speech in v. 28. Anyway, we can reassign 16.23 to group (3).

In 21.18, the formula (in the singular) introduces the only sentence of a speech after a command (compare Mark 11.23). The command is the last of three parallel commands in 21.15–17, and the formula introduces a statement that forms a climax to the whole unit 21.15–19. Thus the formula probably has a closing function within the unit as a whole, so is to be reassigned to group (2).

Summary and Implications for Translators

When all the doubtful cases are reassigned, we end with group (1) having five members (5.24; 6.47; 8.51; 13.16, 20), and group (2) three (1.51; 8.58; 21.18). In group (3) there are fifteen members (3.5, 11; 5.19, 25; 6.26, 32, 53; 8.34; 10.1, 7; 12.24; 13.38; 14.12; 16.20, 23) and in group (4) still only two (3.3; 13.21). All the doubtful cases have been resolved, so group (5) is no longer required. In the first two groups, in which the formula is associated with the closing of a unit, there is a total of eight members, whereas in the other two groups, in which the formula is associated with the beginning of a unit, there are seventeen. That is to say in John's gospel just over two thirds of the occurrences of ἀμὴν ἀμὴν λέγω ὑμῖν/σοι are associated with the beginnings of units, and only one third with the ends. This is an almost exact reversal of the distribution in the Synoptics where two thirds of the examples were linked with the ends of units. But as in the Synoptics, when the formula is used at the beginning of a unit, it is normally associated with surprise or reversal of expectation.

For translators, there are some interesting consequences to this study.

The first is that since in Greek the formula in John is slightly different from the parallel formula in the Synoptics, so it is desirable in the receptor language to maintain a slight difference if at all possible. This is because the formula is used with a somewhat different focus in John, marking the beginning of units twice as often as their closure. In English, many versions ignore the distinction, but several maintain it. For instance, REB has "In truth I tell you" in the Synoptics, and "In very truth I tell you" in John. NKJV has "Assuredly, I say to you" in the Synoptics and "Most assuredly, I say to you" in John. Perhaps the most effective and natural is NJB, which has "In truth I tell you" in the Synoptics, and "In all truth I tell you" in John.

The second consequence is that it may be desirable not to use an identical expression every time the formula occurs in John. In a receptor language there may be particles, verb tenses, or some other devices that help to indicate the beginning or end of a unit. If so, they should be used appropriately in adjusting the formula according to the above analysis. For instance, particles indicating surprise or reversal of expectation may often be appropriate as part of the formula in an opening function, but not in a closing function.

The third consequence is that a recognition of the function of the formula may sometimes have a wider impact in deciding where to put paragraph breaks and even section headings. The printed Greek texts most commonly used by translators, UBS[4] and NA[27], do not agree with each other on this important matter; and neither is based on any clear principles of discourse analysis. Although there is still a long way to go in preparing discourse analyses of all the books of the NT, and complete unanimity about their structures is unlikely ever to be attained, every piece of information is useful and should be taken into account by translators. Hopefully the study of these two formulae in the gospels will help to fit another piece of the jigsaw into place.

ACKNOWLEDGEMENTS

All of the following essays have been republished in this volume by permission with our grateful acknowledgement.

"Our Father in Heaven," *BT* 30, no. 2 (1979): 210–213.
"After Three Days," *BT* 30, no. 3 (1979): 340–343.
"Discourse Structure in Matthew's Gospel," *Scriptura Special Issue* S1 (1982): 1–97.
"Vocative Displacement in the Gospels: Lexico-Syntactic and Sociolinguistic Influences," *BT* 47, no. 3 (1996): 313–321.
"The Sermon on the Plain: Structure and Theme in Luke 6.20–49," *BT* 47, no. 4 (1996): 428–434.
"Vocative Displacement in Acts and Revelation," *BT* 50, no. 1 (1999): 101–110.
"Discourse Structure in Titus," *BT* 53, no. 1 (2002): 101–117.
"Discourse Structure in Jude," *BT* 55, no. 1 (2004): 125–137.
"A Discourse Marker in the Synoptic Gospels: ἀμὴν λέγω ὑμῖν/σοι," *BT* 55, no. 3 (2004): 318–328.
"Discourse Structure in 3 John," *BT* 57, no. 3 (2006): 109–115.
"Vocatives in the Epistles," *BT* 57.1 (2006): 32–44.
"Structural Similarities in 1 and 2 Thessalonians: Comparative Discourse Anatomy," in *The Intertextuality of the Epistles: Explorations of Theory and Practice*, New Testament Monographs 16, eds. Thomas L. Brodie, Dennis R. MacDonald and Stanley E. Porter (Sheffield: Sheffield Phoenix Press, 2006), 196–207.
"Discourse Structure in Ephesians, with Some Implications for Translators," *BT* 58, no. 1 (2007): 41–53.
"A Discourse Marker in John: ἀμὴν ἀμὴν λέγω ὑμῖν/σοι," *BT* 58, no. 3 (2007): 123–128.

www.ingramcontent.com/pod-product-compliance
Lightning Source LLC
Chambersburg PA
CBHW052053110526
44591CB00013B/2191